HEALING YOUNG BRAINS

Also by Hill and Castro

*Getting Rid of Ritalin: How Neurofeedback
Can Successfully Treat Attention Deficit
Disorder without Drugs*

ROBERT W. HILL, PHD, AND EDUARDO CASTRO, MD

HEALING YOUNG BRAINS

DRUG-FREE TREATMENT FOR CHILDHOOD DISORDERS— INCLUDING AUTISM, ADHD, DEPRESSION, AND ANXIETY

for the evolving human spirit

HAMPTON ROADS
PUBLISHING COMPANY, INC.

Cover design by Steve Amarillo
Cover art © iStockphoto.com/Brent Holland

Hampton Roads Publishing Company, Inc.
1125 Stoney Ridge Road
Charlottesville, VA 22902

434-296-2772
fax: 434-296-5096
e-mail: hrpc@hrpub.com
www.hrpub.com

If you are unable to order this book from your local
bookseller, you may order directly from the publisher.
Call 1-800-766-8009, toll-free.

Library of Congress Cataloging-in-Publication Data
Hill, Robert W. (Robert Walter), 1941-
 Healing young brains : the neurofeedback solution / Robert W. Hill and
Eduardo Castro.
    p. ; cm.
Includes bibliographical references and index.
 Summary: "Examines the benefits of and the techniques for using neurofeedback
to combat many childhood disorders, such as autism, ADHD, depression, and
aggression"--Provided by publisher.
 ISBN 978-1-57174-603-0 (alk. paper)
1. Behavior disorders in children--Alternative treatment. 2. Biofeedback
training. 3. Electroencephalography. I. Castro, Eduardo, 1946- II. Title.
 [DNLM: 1. Mental Disorders--therapy. 2. Biofeedback
(Psychology)--methods. 3. Child. 4. Treatment Outcome. WS 350.2 H647h
2009]
 RJ506.B44H55 2009
 618.92'89--dc22
                                    2009005029

ISBN 978-1-57174-603-0

10 9 8 7 6 5 4 3 2 1
Printed on 100% recycled, acid-free paper in Canada

Whenever a new discovery is reported to the scientific world, they say first, "It is probably not true."

Thereafter, when the truth of the new proposition has been demonstrated beyond question, they say, "Yes, it may be true, but it is not important."

Finally, when sufficient time has elapsed to fully evidence its importance, they say, "Yes, surely it is important, but it is no longer new."
—*Michel de Montaigne (1533–1592)*

Contents

Introduction: The Neurofeedback Solution   ix

1. Autism   I

2. Learning Disabilities   23

3. The Labyrinth of Attention-Deficit/
   Hyperactivity Disorder (ADHD)   41

4. You Don't Just Outgrow ADHD   61

5. The Source of the Problem   75

6. Checklists for Assessing Difficulties
   and Following Progress   91

7. Other Disorders and Checklists   101

     Epilepsy 101
     Depression 103
     Bipolar Disorder 109
     Anxiety and Panic Attacks 110
     Diaphragmatic Breathing 117
     Self-Esteem 120
     Attachment Disorder 126
     Sleep Disorders 130
     Immaturity 136
     Tic Disorder/Tourette's Syndrome 139

8. Headaches   143

9. Temperature Training   151

10. Closed Head Injury   155

11. Addictions   161

12. Obesity   165

13. Peak Performance   167

14. Medications   171

15. The Healing Power of Neurofeedback   181

16. How Neurofeedback Works   191

17. A Typical Neurofeedback Session   205

18. Nutrition: The Good, the Bad, and the Ugly   217

19. Toxicity   241

20. The Box in the Room: How Television May
Play a Role in Unwanted Behavior   263

21. More about Aggression and Dysregulation   275

Afterword: The Neurofeedback Solution . . .
Getting Started   293

Appendix A: Finding a Provider in Your Area   299

Appendix B: Hidden Sources of MSG   305

Appendix C: The Feingold Association of the
United States List of Food Additives   307

Appendix D: Laboratory Testing for Heavy Metals   309

Appendix E: Nutritional Recommendations   311

Appendix F: Glycemic Index   315

Appendix G: qEEG and Continuous Performance Tests   317

Endnotes   321

Glossary   335

Index   339

The Neurofeedback Solution

This book is about rescuing children from pervasive and devastating disorders that affect millions of young people. Problems like autism, attention-deficit/hyperactivity disorder (ADHD), and even depression can have lifetime consequences. The simple truth is that when we rescue the child, we save the adult. We have seen countless adults who have bemoaned the fact that they did not get the needed help when they were younger; as a consequence, their adult lives have been in some way handicapped by what are now very treatable disorders. When we wrote *Getting Rid of Ritalin,* we were excited to tell the story of how children all over the world were being helped by a nonpharmaceutical brainwave training program (neurofeedback). Neurofeedback, or brainwave biofeedback, offered hope for millions of children and adults with ADHD. We knew that brainwave training would meet with skepticism from some medical practitioners, so we wanted to get the message out to families everywhere. Since that time, neurofeedback has grown by leaps and bounds. Practitioners all over the world have been trained to help individuals with a number of problems. Psychologists, psychiatrists, neurologists, social workers, and counselors in many countries have added neurofeedback to their treatment regimens.

Since we wrote the first book, exciting things have happened in the field. There have been new studies on autism, ADHD, learning disabilities, dyslexia, depression, anxiety, and other disorders. We are now able to treat Tourette's syndrome and a wider variety of behavioral problems. People with sleep disorders and premenstrual syndrome (PMS) are seen in neurofeedback clinics on a daily basis, as are people seeking performance enhancement programs.

Early in the development of neurofeedback, several practitioners proposed the idea of global dysregulation. The idea behind this theory is that if brainwaves are dysregulated, there is a strong likelihood of a cluster of symptoms rather than just a single problem. This made sense because seldom will you find anyone with just one symptom related to any disorder. For example, a child with ADHD is likely to have sleep problems, low self-esteem, depression, and perhaps angry outbursts. Another child with the same diagnosis may show generalized irritability, defiance toward authority, and perhaps a tic disorder, and so there is usually a cluster of symptoms, not just a single problem. Practitioners observed that when they started to regulate the ADHD brain, other symptoms began to disappear. For example, not only did the child become more focused, but sleep also improved, tics disappeared, and the child became much easier to work with. In addition, therapists noticed that self-esteem improved, attitude brightened, and depression dissolved. We observed that symptoms in the cluster improved in practically every disorder we treated with neurofeedback. This reinforced the idea of global dysregulation and that various symptoms cluster with other problems; when you regulate one symptom, the others improve.

Allopathic medicine generally focuses on the primary complaint and tries to ameliorate the single problem with a treatment modality such as medication. Medications, however successful, generally carry unwanted side effects. Often a patient will have one drug to treat a single problem and two other drugs to treat the side effects of the first drug. Neurofeedback, on the other hand, seldom, if ever, has unwanted side effects. In fact, the effects of neurofeedback are generally the amelioration of additional symptoms in the cluster. If the training session does cause an unwanted side effect such as a headache or a sleepless night, it can be remedied in a single neurofeedback session. Many physicians we work with complain that their patients come in with a laundry list of problems; how do you treat five or ten problems at once? In neurofeedback, we expect multiple symptoms with every problem and so this is not a concern. We target the primary problem while charting the other problems in the cluster, knowing that we are addressing more than a single symptom. We recognize that symptoms cluster rather than come in one nice little package with one single complaint.

Now we have a really exciting story to tell you. It's a story of heartbreak and hope, of people devastated by a multitude of disorders finding happiness and success, a story of brave and dedicated professionals swimming against the tide of conventional wisdom.

In this book, we address the basics of neurofeedback and approach a wide variety of disorders being treated with this non-pharmaceutical training program. Autism, ADHD, learning disabilities, and emotional disorders are discussed in many different contexts. Practically everyone in America has heard of most of these childhood disorders and they are often the topic of conversation among concerned moms and dads. What most people know about these disorders, however, they learned from ninety-second TV reports and hearsay. There are even professionals who know only a minimal amount of scientific information about many of these disorders. It is not that they are disinterested or uncaring, but there is a whole different body of literature to each disorder, and with everything else they have to know, it gets overwhelming. For many very busy physicians, the "simple" solution is to place the child on a medication that is reported to help. For example, Ritalin stimulates the disinterested, lethargic child, and through what appears to be a paradoxical process, slows down the hyperactive child. So, the problem is solved and everyone is happy. It is just not that easy. Drugs have side effects and they generally focus on only one symptom.

Autism is not only a problem of social engagement, just as ADHD is not only a problem of inattention in the classroom. Depression is not only a problem of feeling a little down, just as sleep disturbance is not only a nighttime problem. These are all problems that fall in clusters of problems that can only be described as serious, and they may well be the first manifestation of lifelong problems. Children who have autism may have lifelong problems of disengagement with the world around them and children with ADHD have a higher probability of developing aggressive, violent, and antisocial behavior. ADHD children are more likely to use drugs and alcohol when compared to children without ADHD. In all the disorders we cover in this book, the children affected have a higher likelihood of exhibiting poor school performance, thereby ending up with less education than nonaffected children. In dealing with childhood disorders, we can now project the consequences in later life. When these disorders are carried into adulthood, we see more failed marriages, less job success, more auto accidents, rockier personal relationships, and trouble with the legal system. We know scientifically that most of our medications do not "fix" these childhood disorders.

Inappropriate brainwave activity is at the core of most of these problems. In ADHD, for example, the dominant brainwave is a slow-frequency brainwave. Ritalin is a stimulant medication that speeds up the brain. It is, however, only a temporary treatment. Remove the stimulant and the brain slows down again. Not only does Ritalin not fix the problem, it also has side effects, and we do not know the consequences of long-term use. The same is true of most medications prescribed for these childhood disorders. As long as the patient is on the medication, some improvement is noticed; but if the medication is discontinued, there is a high probability of a return to the former state.

There is, however, a different kind of hope for children with these pervasive and destructive disorders. It is neurofeedback. Neurofeedback is a sophisticated form of biofeedback that actually trains the brain to normalize the brainwaves and make them flexible and adaptable to situational needs. It can do on a more permanent basis what most medications can only do for a few hours, and there are no lasting negative side effects as there are with medications.

Neurofeedback is a quick, noninvasive, cost-effective treatment for a wide variety of disorders that affect not only children, but also adults. So without years of medical treatment, taking pills, or managing difficult diets, without months or even years of traditional therapy or behavior modification, we can successfully treat disorders like autism, ADHD, learning disabilities, and emotional/behavioral problems. In this book, we give you a number of case studies on a variety of disorders, but here are two cases from our practice that show neurofeedback in action.

Seth, nine years old, was failing every third-grade subject and had no friends. His mother gave him a birthday party and only two children showed up. Seth had been on Ritalin for several months. Not only did the medication not seem to make any difference, every afternoon he would become more difficult and irritable (Ritalin rebound). We started neurofeedback treatment in the late spring and continued it through the summer. Although Seth had to repeat the third grade, his grades jumped to the B range and he cultivated "lots of friends." Eight years after treatment, his parents report he is doing very well academically and socially.

Carolyn was a quiet, shy, sad-looking child. She was failing the sixth grade, was mildly oppositional and "stubborn" at home, and she had only one close friend. She was not diagnosed with ADHD but should have been. She also suffered from a chronic low-grade depression. In this case, we could not distinguish which came first, the depression or the inability to attend. We saw both symptoms as well as others as part of a cluster of problems. In just twelve weeks of neurofeedback, Carolyn's sad personality began to brighten, her grades improved, she stopped writing gloomy poetry, and she started developing new friends. It took a lot more training, but the palpable sadness began to lift after a few sessions.

These are just two cases out of hundreds we have treated. There were no medications, no major dietary changes, no endless behavior modification or psychotherapy—just neurofeedback. Neurofeedback is a simple treatment that generally involves two sessions a week. The patient is connected to a specialized EEG (electroencephalogram) computer system. By watching a monitor, the patient can see what his or her brainwaves are doing and through training can learn to change dysregulated brainwaves to more functional and flexible brainwave frequencies. The feedback is presented in the form of a sophisticated brainwave-oriented game. The treatment is easy, quick, and not costly. It involves no pain or discomfort—just playing a computer game with your brain.

Autism and ADHD are certainly the disorders of public note in the last decade. Because these two disorders are so often talked about in the media, everyone acts as though they are expert in the field. Children who are quiet and socially unattached are at risk for being diagnosed with autism or Asperger's disorder. A child who misbehaves, is rambunctious, acts bored, or underachieves in school is now at risk of being diagnosed with ADHD. The vast majority of these children are quickly placed on medications by well-meaning clinicians. These two disorders are very real and must be treated. Our concern is that professionals—rather than family, friends, or teachers—need to make these diagnoses. If these children are not treated, we end up with adults who procrastinate, are disorganized, or who have problems that interfere with living a normal, productive life. Countless adults have come to our clinics, self-diagnosed with a disorder, wanting medications. In many cases, they are correct about the diagnosis. Rather than offering them medications, however, we offer neurofeedback as well as help with emotional problems.

Attentional and behavioral disruptions as well as emotional disorders are usually the outward signs of deeper problems. The problem is frequently brain dysregulation, which makes so many children and adults unable to access and utilize their inherent abilities and talents. In the case of ADHD, we are not just dealing with inattention and hyperactivity; we must deal with the frustration and anguish of academic underachievement, the lack of concern for the rights and welfare of others, and the disregard of and contempt for order and authority. Once the brain begins to regulate, however, the cluster of symptoms begins to ameliorate.

An estimated four million children in the United States are prescribed Ritalin. What are the short-term results and the long-term consequences? Are we better off continuing this type of intervention? Is the problem substantially diminishing or increasing as a result of relying on stimulant medications? This book addresses these questions and many more. We look at neurofeedback as a treatment for autism, depression, anxiety, attachment disorder, and other disorders that affect the youth of our country. We also cover nutrition, problems with toxic substances, the effects of television, violence and aggression in society, and a number of other problems. It is our hope that this book will help you in your quest for the best and highest functioning possible for your child or you.

The time is overdue for a serious look at our current treatment regimens and for a realistic approach to the problems that cluster under the large umbrellas of autism, ADHD, and numerous emotional/behavioral disorders. There is a pressing need to discuss the new treatments that go largely ignored in the mainstream. For more than two decades, neurofeedback has demonstrated a successful record in treating a wide variety of problems by regulating brainwave function. It is time to bring it into the mainstream and give it the recognition it deserves.

To achieve a clear understanding of the causes of these disorders, and to intelligently apply the best treatment methods available, we must begin by systematically looking at each disorder and examining the rationale for using neurofeedback. These disorders are generally the result of brainwave dysregulation. The dysregulation, in our opinion, is usually caused by some type of injury. Sometimes the injury is obvious and sometimes extremely subtle. The injury can range from trauma to a genetic injury, but the result is the same: The brain is unable to self-regulate in a normal way. Usually, the injury results in an excess of low-frequency brainwaves. In other words, the brain is too slowed down or too fast for adequate functioning. A slowing of the brain tends to produce a wide variety of symptoms. In the case of ADHD, the allopathic approach is to use a simple "solution" to "fix" the problem: Speed up the brain with stimulants. Unfortunately, this does nothing to correct the problem and often creates other problems. If the brainwaves are too fast, tranquilizers are often prescribed. Tranquilizers, like stimulants, do not fix the problem.

In the 1930s, when the evidence pointed directly to brain injury, ADHD was called minimal brain dysfunction (MBD). In the 1960s, with nothing useful to offer patients, the diagnosis was changed to a descriptive term, "hyperkinetic syndrome," and later it was changed to attention-deficit disorder (ADD), then to ADHD. By changing the term "minimal brain dysfunction" to ADHD, it became easier to forget that anything that compromises proper brain functioning can produce a variety of emotional, behavioral, and neurological symptoms. We moved away from evidence-based diagnostic terms like MBD, perhaps in an effort to satisfy the complaints that MBD sounded worse than ADHD. Modern medicine tends to break the human being down into the smallest particle, rather than looking at the person as a whole, an entire functioning system. Neurofeedback treats the system, rather than a part of the system.

Such factors as birth trauma, poor nutrition, toxic metals, physical injury, allergies, and genetics can play a role in how efficiently the brain functions. There is no doubt that diagnosticians did not wish to stigmatize children with a derogatory label like "minimal brain dysfunction," but the ability to keep a clear understanding of the problem was lost when we changed the diagnostic label. Now we describe the observable behaviors rather than the causative factor. Treatment should always focus on the cause rather than a symptom.

The recognized experts in the fields of autism, ADHD, and emotional/behavioral problems have become precise at describing the syndromes, but few are looking at the role of brain dysregulation. They are very good at describing and labeling the problem, but beyond prescribing medications, psychotherapy, and support groups, they have little to offer in terms of treating the causes of many of these disorders. In contrast with this norm, neurofeedback therapists are not reluctant to address the brain-injury component of autism, ADHD, and other disorders in the cluster. There is not a huge number of neurofeedback providers at this time, but the number is growing rapidly. All over the world, practitioners are adding neurofeedback to their list of treatment modalities because neurofeedback addresses the primary component of most of these disorders: brain dysregulation. When you regulate the brainwaves, symptoms in the entire cluster begin to disappear.

As you will see in later chapters, neurofeedback in the treatment of ADHD is effective in 70 to 80 percent of those who complete the treatment. Not only does attention improve, but the associated behaviors usually resolve as well. Children typically sleep better, have less anxiety and depression, experience diminished learning difficulties, and are less aggressive. With neurofeedback, interactions with others improve, patients generally act more appropriately in social situations, and self-esteem grows. If safety and efficacy are to be used to determine treatment, neurofeedback should be the treatment of choice for the disorders we discuss in this book.

Neurofeedback is a natural, self-regulating approach that helps restore the brain's ability to function in the manner in which it was designed to function. Restoring the brain to its proper functioning restores its intrinsic capacities. Brains are exquisitely designed to be able to interact socially, pay attention, and comprehend information; to achieve full human potential; to focus, think, reason, dream, and create. Brains should thrive on interaction, stimulation, and information and grow in ability and proficiency. Neurofeedback provides that opportunity. Neurofeedback also helps restore the injured brain's inherent abilities. Intelligent and widespread use of neurofeedback by clinicians and educators has the potential to heal some of the deepest and most devastating wounds of our children and our society.

Opponents of neurofeedback, who are entrenched in old medical paradigms or beholden to pharmaceutical firms for their research funding, state that the wide-ranging benefits we claim are anecdotal or temporary. This is not true, but it is their argument. This thinking is typical of those who are wedded to the use of drugs for the relief of symptoms. There is no drug that "cures" these disorders. In the case of ADHD, take away the stimulant medications and the symptoms are as predominant as ever.

While some physicians were putting children on a variety of medications, other health professionals were refusing to settle for the notion that medications were the solution. For more than thirty years, practitioners of early biofeedback technologies have demonstrated that if you feed back appropriate information to the brain, the human being can change the functioning of any organ or system. Biofeedback is a treatment in which a person learns to reliably influence biological responses that are not ordinarily under voluntary control.

For example, a person attaches a thermometer to a fingertip, and by observing closely the temperature changes can learn mental techniques for voluntarily raising and lowering the temperature of the fingertips and hands. In my (Robert Hill) practice, I have had eleven- and twelve-year-old boys who could consistently raise the temperature of a single finger to 103 to 104 degrees Fahrenheit, even though normal skin temperature tends to be around 92 degrees. We have taught people with Raynaud's disease how to warm their cold hands with just the mind. We have taught patients with borderline hypertension to lower their blood pressure, thereby reducing the need for medications. We have taught people to use biofeedback to calm their anxiety or to relax or strengthen any muscle in the body. So why not retrain the brain? Autism, ADHD, and a variety of behavioral/emotional disorders are a problem related to brain function, so the best way to treat these disorders is to retrain the brain, restoring it to proper balance and flexibility. This is done with neurofeedback, or brainwave, training.

A wonderful concept in complementary medicine relates to the idea of human potential. What are human beings ultimately capable of? Why can't humans learn to cure themselves by learning to unlock the secret of what is going on inside the body? Biofeedback is a tool that can help this to happen. When the brain can comprehend what is going on inside the skin, it can begin making changes in events in the body. The thinking brain can learn to give subtle instructions to change these internal activities. Clinicians have been using biofeedback for years in conventional medicine, but we have taken it a step further by going to the central processing unit (the brain).

The notion is simple. Just as your brain can learn to move your fingers with ease across piano keys or a computer keyboard, it can also learn to slow your pulse rate, lower your blood pressure, or have your immune system release more T cells. We just have to let the thinking brain know how our internal organs or systems are responding to our subtle commands. This is not magic; it is a learning process. Biofeedback provides the brain with the information necessary to attain those skills.

Epilepsy was the key to understanding this feedback system. There are countless patients with epilepsy who are unresponsive to medication. They may have twenty, fifty, or even a hundred seizures a day, with medication offering no relief. For years, neurofeedback therapists and researchers have been able to successfully treat these uncontrollable cases of epilepsy. The therapist learned that by giving biofeedback information on a patient's electroencephalogram (EEG: a map of brainwaves) back to the patient, the patient could actually change his or her brainwaves, thus reducing seizures.

Professor Joe Kamiya of the University of California at Berkeley got this approach started in the 1960s with his pioneering research in alpha brainwaves. Then in the 1970s, Dr. Barry Sterman of the Sepulveda, California, Veterans Administration Medical Center did much of the early work on epilepsy. If you can change the brainwaves of a patient with epilepsy, then why not change the brainwaves of a person with autism, ADHD, depression, anxiety, and a host of other problems? This was the basic question asked by Dr. Joel Lubar, professor of psychology at the University of Tennessee. After all, there are similarities among the brainwave patterns in people with epilepsy and ADHD. While Dr. Sterman worked tirelessly to help patients train their brains to be more resistant to seizures, in the mid-1970s, Dr. Lubar and his wife, Judith, dedicated their work to helping children train their brains to be more resistant to attentional lapses and hyperactive outbursts.

So much credit is due to pioneers like Joe Kamiya, Barry Sterman, and Joel and Judith Lubar. They had to stand up to tidal waves of professional neglect and peer doubts. Yet it is their work and courage that have inspired thousands of professionals to use neurofeedback in the treatment of many disorders. Because of these pioneers, we are truly at a breakthrough point in human potential.

Human beings have far more potential than our ancestors dared to consider.

Neurofeedback is perhaps the biggest breakthrough in noninvasive medicine in the last fifty years. It is a self-regulating process that offers patients some control over their own recovery. Although patients are usually helped by such treatments as nutritional strategies, elimination of toxins, allergy treatments, homeopathy, and behavior modification, neurofeedback can stand alone as a safe and effective treatment for so many emotional, behavioral, addictive, and neurological disorders Once brainwave patterns begin to normalize, all the symptoms in the cluster of problems begin to improve. For example, we treated one young man (Tommy, age fifteen) for ADHD. Not only did his attention and concentration improve, but his nightmares also ceased, his tics resolved, and he stopped fighting at school.

Neurofeedback is the logical replacement for drugs typically used to treat these disorders because it is safer and addresses the core problem rather than treating single symptoms.

Throughout this book, we have elected to use the term neurofeedback, but in the field of biofeedback, neurofeedback is used interchangeably with terms like EEG biofeedback, neurotherapy, and brainwave feedback.

We hope this book will acquaint you with the power and possibility of this exciting new treatment. We have also included other information that will help parents help their children to maximize their functioning and improve the quality of their lives. We have included chapters on nutrition, the effects of toxic substances, and the influence of television and video games on the brain. We also wanted to cover the strong relationship of brainwave dysregulation to aggression and violence. At the end of the book, you will find out how to locate a provider and how to evaluate the credentials of these providers.

This book arises from our clinical experience in treating hundreds of children and adults with a variety of difficult disorders and the symptoms that clustered around these disorders. We hope our years of clinical findings help you to find answers to difficult problems. Neurofeedback may be just the answer you are looking for. Even the most ardent critics have stopped saying it doesn't work. Now they say that the results we are getting are temporary, accidental, or anecdotal. The results we are getting are very real and there are scientific data to prove it. Welcome to the exciting new world of neurofeedback.

1

Autism

Shawna doesn't keep up with the debate about vaccinations causing autism. She doesn't know whether the vaccinations her children, Sean and Sierra, got had mercury in them. She isn't certain what they mean by a gluten-free diet; what would it matter anyway? She is just so tired. She hasn't slept more than two hours in a row in a year, since Sierra was fifteen months old. She just wishes she could wake up from this nightmare.

It was hard with Sean, but she managed. His pediatrician told her he had Asperger's, a form of autism. Her smart beautiful boy is just so detached. He is like a little professor, a grouchy one. She wishes he would look at her and smile just once. She wishes he would talk to her about anything but Mars. How could an eight-year-old know so much about a planet? Why isn't he doing better in school? She wishes he had friends.

Those first fifteen months with Sierra were heaven. She was so affectionate, so loving, just a delightful chatterbox. Now, it is just over four months since Sierra has said a single word. She just moans, and rocks, and rubs her forehead with her palms. At night, she wakes up every few hours screaming, and is inconsolable. She almost never eats anything but dry puffed rice and peanut butter on a spoon. She won't let her mother hold her. If Shawna tries, Sierra digs her fingers into her and screams.

Autism: It is one of those words that strikes fear in the hearts of parents. It was a rare diagnosis years ago, and now is a seeming epidemic. Medical researchers say no, not an outbreak, just better at diagnosing.[1] This is typical of controversies that surround autism. The whole topic is filled with controversy, disagreement, and debate.

We begin this book with autism because it is so prevalent, so devastating, and, to parents who have not yet been guided to the very real treatment options for autism, so terrifying and hopeless. If there is hope with autism, there is hope for anything. We state with conviction: There is more than hope.

In this chapter, we discuss major topics: what autism is, what it is not, how neurofeedback can play a central role in its treatment, and other terrific treatment options.

Autism is a developmental disorder that can disrupt communication, relationships, behavior, and physiology. It strikes seemingly normal infants and toddlers, usually by age three. It causes lifelong struggles that range from mild to severe. The effects on the lives of the children stricken and on their families range from difficult and sad to catastrophic and heartbreaking.

Diagnosis

Conventional medicine considers autism a psychosocial disorder, and one that has a strong genetic component. It is not thought to be curable, so approved treatments include drugs and various therapies designed to improve functioning, such as speech therapy and/or behavior modification.

The diagnosis is based on the criteria in the *Diagnostic and Statistical Manual of Mental Disorders, Fourth Edition (DSM-IV),* published by the American Psychiatric Association.[2] The criteria include various combinations of impairments in social interaction, communication, and behavior. Autism is considered one of five disorders listed under Pervasive Developmental Disorders (PDD). Because of similarities of symptoms in the five PDDs, this group is called the Autistic Spectrum Disorders. When we discuss autism, we include associated disorders such as Asperger's and Rett's.

The DSM-IV criteria for autism are a bit like a restaurant menu where you take two items from column A, one from column B, and one from column C, as follows:

Autistic Disorder

A. A total of six, or more items from 1, 2, and 3 with at least two from 1, and one each from 2 and 3:

1. Qualitative impairment in social interaction, as manifested by at least two of the following:

   A. Marked impairment in the use of multiple nonverbal behaviors such as eye-to-eye gaze, facial expression, body postures, and gestures to regulate social interaction

   B. Failure to develop peer relationships appropriate to developmental level

   C. A lack of spontaneous seeking to share enjoyment, interests, or achievements with other people (e.g., by a lack of showing, bringing, or pointing out objects of interest)

   D. Lack of social or emotional reciprocity

2. Qualitative impairments in communication as manifested by at least one of the following:

   A. Delay in, or total lack of, the development of spoken language

   B. In individuals with adequate speech, marked impairment in the ability to initiate or sustain a conversation with others

   C. Stereotyped and repetitive use of language or idiosyncratic language

   D. Lack of varied, spontaneous make-believe play or social imitative play appropriate to developmental level

3. Restricted repetitive and stereotyped patterns of behavior, interests, and activities, as manifested by at least one of the following:

   A. Encompassing preoccupation with one or more stereotyped and restricted patterns of interest that is abnormal either in intensity or focus

   B. Apparently inflexible adherence to specific, nonfunctional routines or rituals

    C. Stereotyped and repetitive motor manners (e.g., hand or finger flapping or twisting, or complex whole-body movements)

    D. Persistent preoccupation with parts of objects

B. Delays or abnormal functioning in at least one of the following areas, with onset prior to age three years:

    1. Social interaction,

    2. Language as used in social communication, or

    3. Symbolic or imaginative play.

Conventional medicine focuses on the genetic component in autism, and this is documented in twin studies.[3] Medicine also uses sophisticated brain scans to study autism, and has found several common abnormalities that are present in a significant number of children with autism.[4]

In brief, the conventional medical understanding of autism is:

- Autism is a psychosocial disorder, largely determined by genetics.

- Autism has been generally present in the population for some time, though it is now better recognized, largely due to changes in the diagnostic criteria.

- Treatment should focus on reducing the severity of symptoms and troublesome behaviors.

Sierra's pediatrician reassured Shawna that she had not done anything wrong, that she unfortunately carried the genes that cause autism, and that was why both of her children were on the autistic spectrum. He also told her not to worry about the vaccinations; it was just a coincidence, for this is the age range that the children with the gene begin deteriorating. He prescribed the antipsychotic drug Haldol for Sierra to reduce her outbursts, and the tranquilizer Klonopin to help her sleep. Her sleep did not change, but her muscles became very tight and painful and she started back-arching. Her pediatrician eventually changed the Haldol to Risperdal, which she appeared to tolerate better. It reduced her outbursts somewhat, but now she spent more time lying on her side with a blank stare. Her face looked as empty and hopeless as Shawna felt.

An Old Disorder or a New Epidemic?

Has autism been around a long time in steady numbers or have its numbers exploded?[5-6] The answer is important because it will determine our approach to treatment. If conventional medicine is right and the increased number of children in the autistic spectrum is due to better diagnosing, there should be high fives all around for getting good, real good, at identifying so many of those children who had been missed. And attention will continue to focus on genetic research, brain imaging, and the development of new drugs.

If the answer is that the autism we see today is a new and frightening outbreak, it is a very different matter because it will direct our full attention to identifying the recent changes that are causing it. This answer will indicate that the genetic component is a built-in vulnerability and not a life sentence, and also that the abnormal brain imaging is documenting disease processes, not evidence of defectively designed brains.

For more than thirty years, we have worked in the field that diagnoses and treats autism. We find it hard to understand how we could have missed seeing so many children whose lives and whose families' lives were so colossally disrupted by the bewildering array of symptoms and behaviors that we routinely see in today's autistic children. And it is not just the numbers that are different. The autistic child of yesteryear, that sad, rare case we saw every few years, bears little resemblance to today's child. We are seeing not just more in numbers, but also a more severe form.

Young Brains under Assault— Autism Is a Biological Disorder

We also disagree with the conventional medical assertion that autism is a psychosocial disorder primarily determined by genetics. It simply does not fit the clinical experience of those who do not accept the conventional view. Informed parents and clinicians who have attacked autism as a medical illness tell a very different story. Parents who have worked tirelessly to optimize their children's nutrition and systematically eliminate potentially harmful substances tell about the important progress their children have made. In clinics that treat these children with methods such as neurofeedback and detoxification, the progress is often remarkable. It is clear that the severe psychological problems are the result of treatable physiological disruptions. In some cases, there is complete cure.

The DSM-IV criteria are useful in organizing our thinking about diagnosing autism, but they do not cover the physiological disturbances commonly seen that reveal autism to be a medical disorder. These may be deficits in speech and sensory, motor, cognitive, and autonomic nervous system functioning. As a physician, I cannot explain how a psychosocial disorder could produce, for instance, deficits such as abnormal reflexes, poor visual skills, and poor coordination.

We believe it is clear that autism is the result of injury due to toxicity.[7] The brain, when subjected to repeated insults, can experience destabilization of its fine-tuning and sophisticated regulatory mechanisms. Young brains are even more vulnerable since their regulatory mechanisms are in a state of development. Genetics certainly plays a role in determining vulnerability to toxic insults, but playing a role is very different from cause and effect.

The idea that toxicity is the major factor in autism matches the clinical experience well. Toxic conditions damage brains, but toxins can be removed and behaviors changed. Virtually any rational efforts at supporting the brain, gastrointestinal tract, and liver with nutrition and/or detoxifying treatments almost always result in unambiguous clinical improvements in a significant number of children.[8] With the addition of neurofeedback, even greater improvements are realized. We see these same improvements in most of the children who have a stronger genetic vulnerability. The degree of improvement varies. Some have a noticeable decrease in the severity of symptoms or behaviors. Others show new and more appropriate behavior and begin to use words again, sleep at night, and/or show affection. Some are cured.

I t was easy to decide how to proceed with Sierra; we did what she would allow. She wouldn't let us touch her head, so neurofeedback was initially out of the question. Shawna reported that Sierra had experienced several ear infections treated with antibiotics. The infections started at seven months of age, so Dr. Castro prescribed antifungal medication. Shawna was able to disguise the antifungal powder in peanut butter, and administered suppositories to her. When Sierra would allow it, she rubbed essential fatty acids, thiamine tetrahydrofurfuryl disulfide (TTFD), and glutathione into her skin, and she added Epsom salts to her bath. Changes were slow at first, and occurred primarily in eating. She started accepting different foods, and Shawna began to work the nutritional supplements we had discussed into Sierra's diet. Her screaming fits decreased over the first month, then disappeared in the fifth week of treatment. Then she abruptly began saying words, sleeping five to seven hours at a time, and playing with toys, though she still went stiff if Shawna tried to cuddle her.

Certain toxins are implicated in autism, including microbial toxins, metals, synthetic chemicals, and electromagnetic fields. These have been around for some time, so why has the number of children with autism erupted in the past decade? There is credible evidence that we live in an increasingly toxic world—atmosphere, oceans, rivers, soils, and food supply. We are straining the limits of tolerability. Recent serious efforts to clean up our planet are just getting under way but are lagging at this point.

As many have said, children with autism are the canaries in the coal mine, the unmistakable signal that for those who are most vulnerable, the environment is becoming unsafe. Other conditions on the rise are sounding the same alarm. How else can we explain the rise of so many degenerative and immune-compromised diseases in numbers that were not seen a few decades ago? There is the frightening rise in Alzheimer's, the legions with chronic fatigue, sick building syndrome, and previously unheard of chronic pain syndromes like fibromyalgia. In addition, there is an alarming rise in the number of cases of ultra intolerances such as multiple chemical sensitivities, marked allergic hypersensitivities, and easily triggered severe asthma. All fit the toxicity model.

In many ways, autism is the condition that most epitomizes a dysregulation disorder. Varying toxic loads affect different regulatory mechanisms in the brain differently. Children with autism may share any of a number of symptoms, but there is no disorder in the DSM-IV that has such an array of differences. Even in identical twins with autism, it is not unusual for them to have different behaviors and neurological deficits. Both have toxic burdens, but the toxic substances may differ and their tissue uptake in the brain may differ.

Children in the autistic spectrum are more likely to have certain other dysregulation disorders, such as seizures. Seizure is the first disorder that the developer of neurofeedback, Dr. Barry Sterman, treated. He started treating the brain's regulatory centers with neurofeedback more than forty years ago, and his work has been replicated over and over with the same high level of success.

Risk factors for a child developing autism include problems surrounding labor and delivery, such as a breech position or a preterm delivery. These problems also increase the risk of other dysregulation disorders, including ADHD and learning disability.

The disruptions present in the brains of autistic children are in the regulatory centers. Neuropsychologist Rob Coben has studied the brainwave activity of autistic children extensively. Dr. Coben's research findings reveal that the brains of children with autism have areas that have too much electrical connectivity and other areas that are too loosely connected.[9] Too much leads to decreased resilience and reduced ability to reorganize itself, and too little decreases the communication necessary to organize by reducing the numbers and intricacies of the interfaces.

What is important about Dr. Coben's work is that it does not only identify how the brains of autistic children differ from other children's, it also helps us form strategies for how to improve their brains.

After treatment, some of our patients have told us that the experience of their condition was one of bewildering, unbearable overstimulation. In many children, this is no doubt what produces the avoidance of touch, unresponsiveness, "irrational" fears or inability to exhibit fear, or the need for sameness and marked difficulty with any changes. In such a state of overwhelming and intolerable stimulation, the behaviors these children exhibit make perfect sense.

Some children are able to focus intensively on a single thing to help reduce stimulation. This likely is a reason some children will spin or rock for long periods of time. Parents and clinicians call this type of repetitive behavior *stimming,* for self-stimulation, but the repetitive behaviors may be more for overall stimulation reduction.

This ability to focus to the exclusion of all else may be productive and can result in remarkable degrees of knowledge or skills in the area or subject of focus. It appears that when parts of the brain are not functioning, other areas are more likely to develop beyond usual limits. Children with such skills may be highly artistic or musically or mathematically gifted, or have prodigious memories in a specific subject, such as trains, seashells, or, like Sean, Mars. They tend to do or think about little else aside from their subject of interest. When these children are treated, the artistic, musical, and mathematically skilled continue to develop their talents while becoming increasingly well rounded in their lives. In the children with a singular interest, the encyclopedic knowledge tends to fade as they develop other interests and make friends.

Early Intervention

Parents should be aware of the early signs of autism.[10] Often when autism occurs in infancy, there is an unfolding of behaviors over time. The child:

- May not appear to enjoy being cooed to or sung to.

- May not babble.

- May not enjoy being lifted or swung.

- May not make eye contact or play peek-a-boo.

- May not climb and explore.

- May not ask or show interest by pointing.

- May not use words.

- May not show interest in others.

- May not pretend or imitate.

- May not play with toys as toys; for example, rolling a car or stacking blocks and not just holding or mouthing it.

- May begin highly repetitive behaviors, such as repeating a word or phrase continuously, or repeating a body movement.

- May exhibit exaggerated reactions to sound, light, odors, or textures.

- May engage in rituals in behavior and react with great distress or tantrums if interrupted.

- May harm him- or herself by biting, scratching, head banging, or squeezing.

The presence of some of these at times does not mean a child is autistic. Children are different. But patterns of these behaviors may mean a child's brain is being overwhelmed and is preventing him or her from being able to function and to respond.

When autism strikes a perfectly normal, healthy, loving toddler, it is painfully evident. When that bright little boy who played dress-up, proudly wielded swords, and pretended to be different movie characters regresses into a nonverbal, easily frightened child who becomes sedentary and reclusive, there is no question that disruptive events are taking place in that child's brain. These deteriorations often follow an illness, and, of course, many parents report dramatic problems arising in their children after routine vaccinations.

We ask parents to fill out the Diagnostic Checklist Form E-2 from the Autism Research Institute, which can be accessed at www .autism.com/autism/first/e2.pdf. Using this checklist as a point of discussion with parents helps us understand what our young patients are experiencing. The checklist is not so much for diagnosis as to help develop a treatment strategy and identify which neuro-feedback protocols are likely to be most effective.

Causes and Triggers—A Manmade Illness

Autism has multiple causes. The level of exposure to a toxic condition, combinations of toxic conditions, the ability of the immune system and the liver to respond, the functioning of the gastrointestinal tract, and individual genetic variability may all play a role. The usual suspects for causing or triggering autism either damage tissues, suppress immune function, interfere with detoxification, or cause allergic reactions. Some toxins, like mercury, do all four.

We shall discuss this more fully in the toxicity chapter. Following is a summary of the toxicities that are linked with autism:

Metals[11–15]

- Include mercury, lead, arsenic, nickel, aluminum, and cadmium

- Are neurotoxic and immunotoxic

Vaccinations[16–19]

- Introduce neurotoxins (mercury or aluminum and formaldehyde)

- Suppress immune function for more than a month

Microbes That Produce Neurotoxins[20]

- Yeast-related illness from repeated courses of antibiotics or from immune suppression, allowing an overgrowth of yeast and other fungi in the bowel

- The more virulent form of *Borrelia burgdorferi,* the bacteria that causes Lyme disease; can be transmitted by insects other than deer ticks and by human-to-human contact

Diet and Foods

- Nutritional deficiencies

- Genetically modified foods (produce toxins and allergens)

• Aspartame, monosodium glutamate, artificial colors, artificial flavors, artificial sugars, artificial preservatives (can be neruotoxic)

• Casein and gluten in susceptible individuals

Environment[21-23]

• Synthetic chemicals

• Electromagnetic fields

The two most recent offenders added to the list are the Lyme disease bacteria and electromagnetic fields (EMFs). The more virulent, easily transmissible form of Lyme is not yet recognized by conventional medicine, so diagnosing it and treating it is very controversial.

While evidence is accumulating linking certain EMF exposures with autism and other brain disorders including brain tumors, it is advisable to take immediate precautions. Due to the thinness of children's skulls, the most important precautions are to not allow a child to use a cell phone (unless with speaker phone or the use of an air tube headset, discussed in the chapter on toxicity) and to unplug the wireless phone system in the home. We understand that, for many people, the use of landline phones is very inconvenient, but we believe it is worth the trouble until safer devices are designed. Brain tumors are now the leading cause of cancer deaths among children. Let's not let them be guinea pigs while science investigates the issue.

Genetics—A Whole New Ballgame

A word about genetics is in order because of its importance in health and disease, and also because of general unawareness of how it functions. Genetics clearly plays a role in the development of the autistic spectrum disorders, but not in the way that most people think it does. In fact, genetics is nothing that we expected it to be. Although this has not yet seeped into accepted thought, genetic theory has been turned on its head, a 180-degree turn. Do you remember when the Human Genome Project was under way? The promise was that once the genetic code was sequenced, we would hold the keys to the kingdom—health, medical cures, longevity. Have you noticed how little we have heard about it since the sequencing was completed? Guess what? Genes don't behave the way we thought they did. The theory that a gene determined a specific outcome is long gone, a laughable notion to genetic researchers. At first, it was evident that a gene may not be expressed, that is, it may be idle. But before long, it became evident that genes were not turned on or off, but that a single gene could express itself in *thousands* of ways.

So what determines how a gene expresses itself? The chemical and electromagnetic environment of the gene and even beliefs affect gene expression. So a gene subjected to toxicity is not a broken gene, just one that is expressing itself in one way. Remove the toxic substances and provide a different environment for the gene with diet and nutrition, and it expresses itself in another way.

What is exciting about the developing understanding of genetic control, the field of epigenetics,[24] is how much gene activity can be shaped. Some well-designed studies with mice showed that mutant mice with major gene defects could function normally if provided with precisely timed nutritional support, and normal mice could have their gene expression altered to abnormality by the introduction of toxic substances during their development. So with changes in intake and toxic exposure, the genetically defective mice looked normal and the normal mice looked defective. Despair turned to hope.

A child with a genetic predisposition to autism has just that—a predisposition and nothing more. The introduction of neurofeedback and nutritional support and the removal of toxic substances can alter destiny. We already know, for example, that in a serious genetic disorder like Down syndrome, the highly predictable defects can be reduced and functioning can be improved with nothing more than focused and aggressive nutritional supplementation. In autism, the genetic component is almost always only a fraction of influence. With nutritional support, dietary management, antifungal medications, hyperbaric oxygen, magnetic fields, and neurofeedback, there is the hope that a child can live an unencumbered life, free of limitations from physiological imbalances, free of a predetermined nightmarish existence.

Waking Your Child from the Nightmare

Just as there are usually multiple causes of autism, the most successful treatment regimens have multiple approaches. On some occasions, a child is cured with one type of treatment, but most children benefit more widely from combinations of treatments.

Priceless information about how effective or ineffective numerous treatments have been for autism is available from the Autism Research Institute. They have compiled information about the benefits and the adverse effects of a range of biomedical treatments and post the current data on their website at www.autism.com/treatable/form34qr.htm. This information constitutes medical evidence; it is not anecdotal information. A word of explanation about medical evidence may be useful before discussing the data. Please note that it is not necessary to know the research terms (in italics) in the next paragraph in order to understand the importance of the institute's data.

Evidence-based medicine, endorsed by most physicians, is a name used since 1990 for a system of classifying the scientific soundness of various forms of clinical evidence,[25] for the purpose of improving medical treatment. It ranks the different types of evidence. At the top of the list are *well-controlled, randomized* studies, the type of study that drugs must be subjected to before they are approved because of the inherent dangers of introducing synthetic chemicals into the body. *Unrandomized studies* are next in the ranking, then *case control analytic* studies, then *case series* studies. The data accumulated by the Autism Research Institute constitute case series evidence, as they track patients who have received treatments for autism and use parent ratings to determine the relative benefits and adverse effects. It is worthwhile noting that the category of evidence that ranks below a case series is *expert opinion*.

The Autism Research Institute lists treatments, including drugs, nutritional supplementation, hyperbaric oxygen treatment, allergy treatment, removal of heavy metals (chelation), and dietary changes. Parents used a six-point scale in three categories to rate whether their child got better, exhibited no change, or got worse, and the number of cases per treatment is provided. The data are eye-opening and encouraging. There is also calculation of the benefit to adverse effect ratios. The best ratios are from treatments that reduce toxicity, like chelation and antifungal medications, or that reduce the effects of brain injury, like hyperbaric oxygen. Other winners are nutrients, like digestive enzymes, essential fatty acids, and the B vitamins. Dietary changes as a group had the highest ratings for benefit and the lowest adverse effects.

The drugs that are used to decrease symptoms, such as antidepressants and stimulants, generally had more adverse effects than benefits, with the exception of Risperdal. This is an antipsychotic drug, often used in desperation, to suppress the most severe behaviors.

Every parent with an autistic child should study this Autism Research Institute treatment list (www.autism.com/treatable/form34qr.htm).

You will note that neurofeedback is *not* on the list of treatments. This is one of the major reasons we wrote this book, to inform parents and clinicians about this powerful treatment for every child on the autistic spectrum.[26-30]

The Mother of Dysregulation Disorders Meets the Mother of Regulation Training

Our brains are exquisitely designed. They organize an incalculable amount of internal and external stimuli, process it instantaneously, and encode it for communication to our bodies and brains. Our brains, like life itself, are electromagnetic in nature. Certainly a brain is made up of chemicals, but those are not its essence. A brain functions and regulates itself through vibratory patterns, through timed rhythmic firing of clusters of cells. The presence of this neurotransmitter or that one does not determine the rhythms; it is the other way around. The rhythmic patterns determine the activity of the chemicals.

Certainly, chemical intervention has usefulness, but if we are to address the fundamental nature of a brain's regulation, we look at its electromagnetic functioning. Brainwave training with neurofeedback addresses central regulation so well that we see significant improvements in autistic symptoms and behaviors even while the brain is still subject to dysregulating toxicities. During neurofeedback, the various regulatory centers in the brain must communicate with each other to respond to the challenges that neurofeedback presents it, challenges to produce specific brainwave patterns. This communication results in a fine-tuning of the regulatory network. The more finely tuned a brain is, the better it functions and the more resilient it is to disruptive influences, whether stress, mercury, or fungal toxins.

The fine-tuning impacts all the brain's regulatory centers. An emotionally distraught child who is socially withdrawn, or irritable and aggressive, or who tantrums, can regain normal behavior. If there are motor disturbances, such as clumsiness and incoordination, they typically improve significantly. Just think about it for a moment: Motor behavior is improved by sitting still with a few electrodes on your scalp and watching a monitor; it only makes sense if neurofeedback is improving the function of the brain. Physiological disruptions, such as severe sleep problems, often normalize nicely. Abnormal sensory processing, such as marked sensitivity to sound, texture, or light, also improves with neurofeedback. And, as we shall discuss in the chapter on learning disabilities, after a course of neurofeedback treatment, IQ increases. Unfortunately, most clinicians of every stripe still consider neurofeedback to be nothing more than relaxation training.

A t the six-week point in treatment, Sierra allowed us to place electrodes on her head and ears. We began neurofeedback the way we usually do with a child under four or five years, with Mommy providing the feedback. Usually the child sits in Mom's lap, but Sierra still stiffened too much when we tried this. She did allow Shawna to hold her hand. Shawna watched the monitor and lovingly praised Sierra every time her brainwaves were in the desired pattern. After the third session, Sierra spontaneously went over and laid her *head on Shawna's lap and hugged her leg. Seeing the look on Shawna's face was one of those moments in life that is profoundly moving.*

Neurofeedback treatment for the autistic spectrum almost always provides recognizable benefits at whatever point in treatment it is used. It is best done at the beginning of treatment, however, with any other treatments implemented, as the improvements from neurofeedback are often a godsend. A child who sleeps, eats, speaks, interacts, can be held, or is not as rigid about routine—a much more manageable child—not only opens up the ability to do other treatments, but also signals that the nightmare is ending, which energizes parent efforts. Many parents have been encouraged to redouble their efforts with dietary changes and nutritional supplementation when their child begins to show a softening of inflexibilities.

Like Sierra, however, it is common for an autistic child to not allow the electrodes to be placed. The other common difficulty with autistic children is constant movement. A child needs to sit reasonably still to do neurofeedback.

Getting a child to sit still during neurofeedback is not nearly as hard as one might think. Often it just takes a bit of patience. When many fidgety children begin getting feedback that promotes a more desirable brainwave state, they suddenly slump into the chair and gaze at the monitor. It is as though they are in an unfamiliar state of contentment, and they don't dare move a muscle. We see this frequently in ADHD as well as autism. A favorite quote of ours from a parent, told to us by Sue Othmer, an eminent clinician in Los Angeles, was that upon entering the room where her wildly hyperactive son was finishing his session, slumped in his chair and staring at the monitor, his mother said, "Oh my goodness, he's been deboned." A perfect description of something we had seen so many times with children but had never thought to put in those terms.

At other times, a child simply needs to begin detoxifying treatment, dietary changes, and nutritional support, like Sierra did, and then retry neurofeedback when progress suggests it is possible.

We are privileged in that we have had the opportunity to see how neurofeedback alone works with autism, how other treatments work, and how various combinations work. Although we have at times seen surprisingly good outcomes with a single type of treatment, implementing several treatment modalities usually produces the best results, especially neurofeedback or antifungal medication. It is our opinion that, overall, neurofeedback is the most effective treatment in restoring a child to a level of well-being that is meaningful.

Another of our observations has to do with the way neurofeedback is conducted. There are two basic neurofeedback approaches. One uses a computer-analyzed or quantitative EEG (qEEG) to determine how to go about training the brain, whereas the other is guided by observing clinical changes that are occurring. Both approaches have a great deal of success, and exciting developments continue. Currently, the use of infralow frequencies is showing promise for even further effectiveness. Since we are fortunate to be well versed in both neurofeedback techniques, we have seen the occasional child who does much better on one over the other. The take-home message is that if a child is not achieving expected results after an adequate course of treatment, it may be that the other technique is the answer for that child.

A*fter twenty-two neurofeedback treatments, Sierra discontinued her treatments. It was astonishing how far she had come: She cuddles, dances, paints, pretends, and has a vocabulary that, in a three-year-old, defies explanation. But Shawna was be twice blessed, this time with Sean.*

Brandon and Colleen, visiting from Australia for a month, wanted to continue neurofeedback for their eight-year-old son, Kyle, who had ADHD, while they were here in the States. His appointments overlapped with Sierra's, and Brandon and Colleen spent time talking with Shawna during the neurofeedback sessions. On Kyle's last appointment, his parents instructed me to offer a course of treatment for Shawna's boy, Sean, and they would pay the fees.

Sean's progress was fun to watch. First he talked about subjects other than Mars, though still with his professorial style—facts, details, specifics. Then he began to smile. We knew we were home free when

*he began to tell us jokes. Once, when we teased him about what had
happened to his interest in Mars, he surprised us by saying, "My
girlfriend isn't much interested in space. We like music."*

Other Treatment Options

Although a full discussion of the other treatment options for
autism is beyond the scope of this book on neurofeedback, we
shall discuss some of the treatments that should be considered for
any child with autism. A good place to start learning about treatment options is at the Autism Research Institute website (www
.autism.com). An excellent book, and there are many, is *Autism:
Effective Biomedical Treatments* by Jon Pangborn, PhD, and Sidney
Baker, MD—two heroes in the treatment of autism, even if they
have not yet realized the importance of neurofeedback for children
in the autistic spectrum.

In our experience, the parents who learn about treatments
clearly have a better sense of purpose and determination. Changing a child's diet, for example, is more than daunting, but if parents
have some basic understanding about the reasons to remove gluten and casein, they find they are more patient and steadfast, and
often excited that they are doing something to help their child.

We discuss the following in the chapters on learning disabilities, toxicity, and nutrition:

- Diet

- Nutritional supplementation

- Detoxification

- Optimizing gastrointestinal functioning

- Antifungal treatment

- Lyme disease treatment

- Interactive Metronome

- Vision therapy

- Irlen lenses

- Sound therapy

Another treatment available for children with autism, and also for cerebral palsy, intrauterine stroke, near drowning, and other brain injuries, is hyperbaric oxygen treatment (HBOT).[31-32] HBOT produces improvements even years after an injury has occurred. In this treatment, the child is provided with 100 percent oxygen in a pressurized chamber. This saturates every cell, tissue, and fluid with high oxygen concentrations. High oxygen tensions in the tissues cause new blood vessels to grow into the damaged areas of the brain. A course of forty treatments is necessary for this to occur. Hundreds of hours can be done if a child is still improving, either consecutively or in courses of forty treatments. The improvements gained are permanent with either schedule. Because of time and financial constraints, many parents arrange courses of forty treatments for their children over the summer break. Two one-hour treatments can be performed safely on a daily basis. The treatments must be separated by at least four hours.

We believe that HBOT and neurofeedback should especially be considered for adolescents and adults with autism who tend not to respond as fully as children do to the previously listed treatments, and also for any children not responding. It is likely that the degree of damage is more severe in their brains, and supporting and detoxifying are not sufficient for a fuller recovery.

Another treatment that results in similar improvements in brain injury and is even less well recognized than HBOT is molecular magnetic energizing (MME). We are quite familiar with this since one of a handful of treatment centers in the country is not far from us, in Mocksville, North Carolina, and run by our friend Larry Pearce, MD.

In MME, a child lies in a powerful magnetic field generated by DC currents—in a sense, a live magnetic field, not one from static magnets. The field is safe and promotes healing to a stunning degree. Just as HBOT requires a course of a minimum of forty treatments, MME requires courses of a hundred hours, and more in some conditions. Children can sleep in the magnetic field at night and get hours in during the day.

MME has different mechanisms of action from HBOT, so can be synergistic. Our opinion is that if a person is going to do both treatments, it makes sense to begin with HBOT and provide the brain with improved circulation to the damaged areas on which MME can then exert its healing effects. With either treatment, every effort should be made to include neurofeedback, which can accelerate treatment response. Imagine if every brain-injured person in the United States had easy access to these three treatments.

The inventor of MME, Dean Bonlie, DDS, has also designed a magnetic mattress. Different from others in that it is a purely negative magnetic field and is two to ten times stronger than existing pads, it appears to enhance other treatments for autism. Amy Yasko, MD, PhD, a nationally recognized pacesetter in the biochemical treatment of autism, has noted its benefits in her patients. Magnetic treatments of various forms are considered conventional treatment in parts of the world.[33]

Another treatment that can provide benefit, in sometimes surprising degrees of improvement, is homeopathy.[34] Not only have many parents reported to us the improvements their children gained with this treatment, we have had the opportunity to review the case histories and outcomes of homeopathic treatment by another friend, Vincent Speckhart, MD, a retired oncologist. Dr. Speckhart successfully treated not only cancer with homeopathy, but also neurological, autoimmune, and psychiatric diseases, and often after conventional medicine had failed.

Homeopathy is an energy-based medical discipline and, for that reason, is not well understood among Western-trained physicians and it is hard for them to believe it can be effective. Its mechanisms are vibrational and its essence is electromagnetic, just like life itself.

In our opinion, this is a technique that requires special skill and experience on the part of the practitioner. There is a subjective component in energy medicine treatments that is very different from Western medicine. In Western medicine, there is uniformity.

If a hundred psychiatrists agree on diagnosis and treatment, that is considered a high degree of scientific practice. In energy medicine, five practitioners are likely to come up with five different approaches. Agreement is not important, outcome is. And any one of those five treatments may well be as good as or better than the one treatment strategy on which the roomful of psychiatrists agreed.

We believe that homeopathy guided by electrodermal screening, as Dr. Speckhart has perfected, or by a practitioner highly skilled in muscle testing, is most likely to provide a child with relief of suffering.

Whatever treatments are instituted, autism, as much or more than any other disorder in children, requires the recognition, appreciation, and attention to the whole child and not just symptoms and behaviors. Betty Jarusiewicz, PhD, epitomizes the sensitivity and instincts found in the best therapists. She weaves an intricate and thoughtful therapeutic experience for her young patients, and they thrive under her care. And Dr. Betty will tell you, in no uncertain terms, that neurofeedback is the thing that smoothes the course of their recovery.

A Final Word

This chapter has two important messages we hope you take home. One is that there is reason for hope when a child is on the autistic spectrum. It is a treatable disorder; it can be reversed. If mentioning so many treatment options seems bewildering, simply know that there are many valuable weapons in the arsenal to beat this illness into submission.

Second, neurofeedback should be widely used as a major treatment intervention to optimize outcomes in the treatment of the autistic spectrum of disorders.

2

Learning Disabilities

A child in school who has a learning problem is like a hiker climbing Mount Everest; it is going to be challenging to succeed. For one child, it might only require using certain strategies to compensate for a learning problem, but for another, the obstacles to reaching a modest goal, like graduating from high school, are practically insurmountable. Like ADHD and autism, there is a wide range of disruption, from very mild to extremely severe, with most somewhere in between.

A person with a learning disability (LD) has a problem processing information due to a deficit in the brain's ability to carry out a specific task, such as reading or listening with accuracy. Or, information may get in accurately, but is not organized or stored well enough to communicate it.

Learning disabilities are far more prevalent than most people outside the school system think. Close to three million students, or one out of every twenty students enrolled in public schools in the United States, has been identified as being learning disabled.[1] Applied to the whole U.S. population, there are in the neighborhood of fifteen million people with LD. Most of these, ten to twelve million, have dyslexia, an impairment in written language. That is a lot of struggling people.

There are also many who have not been diagnosed. Some have a learning disability too subtle to recognize, and in others, the condition is not considered severe enough, yet both groups still have a major obstacle to accomplishment. These children may not get diagnosed, but they are frequently labeled lazy, sloppy, clumsy, low IQ, unmotivated, slow learner, bad attitude. A child with unrecognized LD has a higher risk not only of dropping out of school, but also of going to prison. Recognizing that a learning problem is the reason that a child is not succeeding gives that child a new lease on life.

A parent might be reluctant to have a child diagnosed for fear of what the label might mean. The main reason to proceed is to make sure the child has access to the resources that will help him or her succeed in school and in a chosen profession. Success and learning disability can go hand in hand. Albert Einstein, Thomas Edison, Winston Churchill, and Walt Disney, to name a few, did okay.

One More Time

If you have been reading from the beginning of this book, the following will sound familiar. Learning disability is a neurological disorder, but the diagnostic criteria for it are in psychiatry's *Diagnostic and Statistical Manual of Mental Disorders*.[2] Like ADHD and autism, conventional medicine views it as a condition that cannot be cured. The treatments that may help behaviors associated with LD are in the realm of psychiatry; a child with LD who is impulsive may be prescribed stimulants, another who is withdrawn may be placed on antidepressants, and one with a bad attitude may get behavior therapy.

Watch List

Whether a parent uses standard interventions or goes on to add neurofeedback and some of the other treatments we shall discuss, early recognition and intervention is crucial for the child, as it is with ADHD or autism. Early recognition is more likely when parents and preschool teachers are armed with the knowledge of what to be aware of.[3] So let's start there.

The following speech and motor function difficulties provide the earliest clues since children do not read, write, and count until later:

- Delay in using words; no words by one year of age; no sentences by two to two and a half years

- Difficulty naming objects; misnaming

- Unusual mispronunciations of words

- Difficulty with simple commands; asks "What?" or "Huh?" repeatedly

- Difficulty naming letters

- Difficulty repeating a simple phrase

- Little interest in being read to

- Motor delays—coordination, timing, developing preferred handedness

- Poor control holding or handling objects—stacking blocks, crayon, spoon, small toys

- Primitive coloring or drawing ability for level of maturity

By kindergarten, a child's problems may become more apparent. At this age, discrepancies or inconsistencies may become noticeable. For example, a bright, verbal child has trouble identifying letters, or an early reader is not getting the concept of simple counting. The following are other indicators:

- Small vocabulary for age

- Halting speech; numerous uh's between words

- Mispronounces many words

- Is very slow in learning to read

- Problems matching letters to sounds

- Problems rhyming

- When copying a word or writing name, transposes letters in spelling, reverses letters—b/d, p/q, m/w, n/u; writes letters backward

- Poor handwriting—legibility, use of space, size of letters

- Sloppy work

- Clumsy; physically tentative

In school, it becomes evident that the type of problem or kind of error a child makes follows a consistent pattern. Also, the discrepancies between a child's intelligence and accomplishments in an area (speech, reading, writing, math, or motor skills) are more evident.

Speech problems may occur in an excellent reader, writer, or math student:

- Limited speaking vocabulary for age

- Hesitant speech

- Continues to mispronounce words

- Difficulties with verbal instructions

- Doesn't get peers' jokes

- Poor comprehension of stories read aloud to him or her

- Little interest in hearing stories

- Frequently "doesn't get it" in conversations

- Poor at oral testing, even if very knowledgeable about the material being tested

Reading problems may occur in a verbally mature child:

- Poor reader—speed, comprehension, memory

- Avoidance of reading or frustration with reading may give rise to behavioral problems—not sitting in chair, talking, acting up

- Poor at written testing, even if very knowledgeable about the material being tested

Writing problems may occur in a child with a large vocabulary who reads and tells stories with ease:

- Poor at spelling, even with genuine effort

- Poor sequencing or illogical in written sentences

- Leaves words out or inserts words when writing, even when copying

- Much better at multiple choice than written answer testing

Math problems may occur in a child who speaks, reads, and writes beautifully:

- Struggles with basic addition, subtraction, multiplication, division

- Doesn't seem to get times tables

- Slow in math drills even with considerable practice

Motor problems may occur in a gifted student:

- Poor handwriting—legibility, use of space, size of letters

- Though neat and accurate, very slow at writing

- Avoids writing or drawing

- Avoids using the mouse or keyboard

- Unusual grip—pencil, spoon

- Frequent keyboard or dialing errors

- Laces untied, buttons unbuttoned; prefers Velcro

- Difficulty imitating a movement

- Avoids sports; an ungainly athlete or dancer

- May love music but not able to learn to play an instrument despite genuine effort

Spatial problems are more likely to occur with motor problems:

- Reverses left/right, up/down, over/under, front/back

- Gets "turned around" frequently in going from room to room

At times, a child will appear to be working at grade level but then suddenly hit a wall in learning; look out if there is an abrupt onset of shyness, self-doubt, not wanting to go to school, or acting up. Many of these children turn out to be far brighter than was thought; they found ways to compensate for a difficulty in learning until the tasks became too difficult. We have seen this occur as late as college. Watch for a sudden change in life goals or a new negative attitude in older students toward academics.

Diagnosis

Testing has been how children were identified as learning disabled. A significant discrepancy between IQ and achievement, or put another way, a significant difference between aptitude and academic performance, was required to make a child eligible for a school's special services. For schoolchildren, the IQ-Achievement Discrepancy model is being replaced by the Response to Treatment Intervention (RTI) model in an effort not to miss children who need assistance and to have better success rates in academic improvement.[4] It attempts to move away from a wait-to-fail system.

RTI uses screening to identify children at risk.[5] Using a three-tier system, an at-risk child will be carefully monitored over a period of weeks to see how he or she is responding to the educational curriculum. If a child is not performing adequately, special education services will administer a brief standardized achievement test and then design an additional tailored instruction format to be done in small groups of children with the same type of learning difficulty. If after a specified number of weeks, a child's performance is still not adequate, it is at this point that he or she is formally identified as learning disabled. The child will then receive a comprehensive evaluation and extensive testing to determine more accurately what the specific deficiency is and to help determine what the most beneficial interventions are.

The exciting possibility is that neurofeedback is an intervention that can be used. It is not likely on very many special services' radar as yet. Parents should demand that it be included because there is no better treatment for learning disabilities.

RTI is a good system, but if you have concerns, do not wait for your preschooler to be screened in school. Have a pediatrician rule out medical problems. A child with untreated anemia, diabetes, or hypothyroidism is not going to keep up with the other kids. Have his or her vision and hearing tested. If everything is normal at this point, arrange testing by someone who specializes in educational testing; ask your local school's special services for recommendations of well-trained and experienced professionals.

By the way, the need for careful identification of the problem is for the purpose of understanding how to help the child compensate for the problem while maximizing the child's strengths. This kind of accuracy is not at all necessary for treatment with neurofeedback. It doesn't really matter if a child is struggling in school because of a learning problem, an attention problem, a sleep disorder, an anxiety disorder, depression, or because the letters are dancing on the page due to toxicity. With neurofeedback, we know how to go about enhancing the brain's ability to function as it was designed. Neurofeedback practitioners know how to heal young brains.

Not Just Schooling

Children with LD are often burdened with other difficulties. Some of the problems stem from the LD itself, from the frustration, disappointment, discouragement, uncertainty, or embarrassment.

These increase the risk for all the consequences of low self-esteem: depression, anxiety, oppositional behavior, hostility and aggression, risk taking, and thrill seeking. Any of these can lead not only to worse academic performance, but also to flawed judgment, drug abuse, and impaired relationships. Just as early detection of a learning problem is important, early recognition of the possible emotional effects on a child who has LD is essential. Once detected, strategies should be developed with teachers and therapists to lessen the emotional impact of LD. Early intervention that promotes personal and academic success is the best remedy, which is why neurofeedback is so effective.

An additional challenge may coexist for the child with LD. Many children with LD are also diagnosed with ADHD. This is not unexpected. Both conditions, as well as autism, share the same factors that place a child at greater risk for developing one or more of the disorders. The risk factors include birth trauma, preterm delivery, low birth weight, history of head injury, nutritional deficiencies, or history of infection of the central nervous system. By the way, genetics also often plays a role in LD, but as we expanded upon in the chapter on autism, it is not that a brain is defectively designed, it is that that brain is more vulnerable to injury.

Some children with LD certainly do have ADHD and they may benefit from recognized treatment. But in our experience, too many children diagnosed with both appear to look ADHD as a result of having LD. The five-year-old boy who won't sit still and listen during story time and show-and-tell may just not be comprehending it, and the experience for him is that there is meaningless chatter in the background; why not go over and play with a friend?

In either situation—an emergence of emotional or behavioral problems from LD, or the presence of ADHD behavior—pediatricians or therapists routinely refer their patients for medication evaluation. Drugs can help in many instances. But the solution for a girl who is depressed because she hates school and feels different is not an antidepressant, although if she is also clinically depressed, it can be an important tool. We do not criticize the use of medications. We understand that the pediatrician or therapist is desperate to help, but the problem with conventional medicine is that they have limited tools, mainly drugs. These children need help in several domains, as Dr. John Finnick describes it. Nationally recognized for his work with LD children, Dr. Finnick worked for twenty years as a school psychologist before becoming a clinical psychologist. He talks about how in treating a child with LD, it is not just about the learning problem. He uses a two-stage treatment approach with neurofeedback, first to stabilize the brain, and only after that has been accomplished, to target the areas of the brain that are more specific to the learning problem, which is the skill-building component of therapy. He has seen many a dyslexic child not even need to go to the site-specific training after the overall brain stabilization was achieved; it is that important.

Ta-Da . . . Neurofeedback to the Rescue

Conventional medicine considers learning disability a lifelong condition, a hardwired deficit. You might learn to live with it better as you age, but the inborn deficits will not change. It is the same belief about a person with a low IQ. Low intelligence is also hardwired, and is going to be the same at five, at twenty-five, and at fifty years of age. Accept the reality and get on with doing your best in spite the deficits and limitations.

At times, we agree, some deficits appear to be permanent. But in a surprising number of children with learning disabilities, the deficits can be improved and sometimes eliminated. And by this we mean cured. Many people have heard about a spontaneous cure in a serious condition that had been unchanged for years. That is not what we are talking about. We are talking about treating with neurofeedback children who have learning disabilities and seeing significant improvements in most of them.[6-12]

What do we see when we treat LD with neurofeedback? Typically, we get reports from teachers and parents that the child is performing better at the task that had been so difficult, like reading in a child with dyslexia. Test scores improve, grades improve, and a child may no longer need to continue to use the strategies that had been helpful. For instance, the child may no longer need to have a test read to him or her, but is now able to take a written test like the non-LD students. When there are associated problems like anxiety, ADHD, or defiant behavior, we get reports of significant improvements in those areas as well. Sometimes the improvements are small but steady; sometimes they are dramatic.

W*e chuckled over the way we learned of Cory's improvements. He was a rising third-grader, who had been in special education classes due to his low IQ (88), reading disability, and ADHD. He came in for neurofeedback treatment during the first month of his summer break. Early in September, his mother, Cheri, called in a panic. He had been mainstreamed in school! What should she do? How was he going to cope?*

It turns out he had been retested by his school and found to have an IQ of 107 and no evidence of any learning disabilities or attention problems. The school promptly booted him out of special ed. His parents admitted that they had been swept up in their older daughter's tennis activities during the summer, driving all over the East Coast going to tournaments, and living in motels. No one had been reading to Cory, playing word games with him, or asking him what highway signs said.

What should she do? We reassured her and suggested reading to Cory, checking his homework, and talking to him about what he was learning in school, you know, the usual stuff. How would he cope? Like the other kids, by paying attention in class, doing his homework, you know, the usual stuff. We chuckled, but it did give us pause. How many Cheri's are out there, accepting the notion that their precious child is just slow, just not able, just not like the other kids.

Cory is in high school, and continues to do well.

The thing that is most difficult for the professional community (and we mean everyone—pediatrician, teacher, counselor, psychologist) to believe is that IQ almost always increases after neurofeedback training. Physicians, especially when they hear "biofeedback" and "increased IQ" in the same sentence, are quite certain that we are either naively foolish or charlatans. It would be amusing if it weren't for the fact that, in neurofeedback, we have an uncomplicated, accessible tool that can help heal the wounds and damage that threaten to unravel the fabric of our society—learning problems, depression, drug addiction, and violent behavior.

The various subtests that make up IQ testing basically gauge left-brain and right-brain functioning—the verbal, logical left and the synthesizing, big-picture right. The scores are blended to get a person's IQ. Most dyslexics, because of a problem with written language, do not perform as well on the left-brain testing. Some forms of LD have problems with right-brain tasks. When a dyslexic child's left hemisphere starts working the way it was designed to work, he or she scores much higher on those subtests that measure left-brain functioning. It is not unusual for the increases in IQ after neurofeedback to be significant. Are these kids now smarter? No, they were already smart, but they are now much better able to use their God-given talents.

Some of the teenagers we have treated because of their learning disability became gifted artists or musicians. They typically express fears that they will lose their creativity if the neurofeedback training balances their brains. We let them know that there are high-level musicians, opera singers, dancers, and artists who use neurofeedback to enhance their abilities. What has happened in every instance with these teens is that other areas of their lives improve—things like getting good grades in math or English, being less disorganized, or feeling more at ease in social settings—yet not at the expense of their creativity. Their creativity feels better developed, wider ranging. They often describe being able to access it and maintain it more easily in different settings.

Natalia's Story

Neurofeedback can be especially useful for those children who have been tested for learning disabilities but do not have a severe enough problem to meet the criteria. They will not qualify for their school's special services. Neurofeedback can help a child with a lesser difficulty as much as a child with a major difficulty. It even helps children with no problems learn better.

Let me illustrate with a story of my daughter, Natalia. I first started using neurofeedback in my practice when Natalia was in high school. I had just moved back to Charlottesville, Virginia, and it was going to take a month to get my office set up and opened.

During that month, I eagerly trained myself with my brand-new neurofeedback unit. I also trained my wife, both our daughters, friends who stopped by, and basically anyone who would sit still.

My wife, Sandy, and Natalia moved back to Charlottesville ahead of me so she could start the school year at the beginning. One of her classes was Algebra II. A smart girl and a good hard-working student, over the years she had gotten mostly As on her report cards, but always got Cs in math. A year earlier, curious about that, I had asked a colleague to test her. She did a full battery of testing, and it clearly showed no learning problems of any type. I assumed at that time that she was just one of those kids who is not good at math. For whatever reason, she just did not appear able to think nimbly with math concepts like she did with everything else.

In the grading period after I trained her with neurofeedback, she got an A in Algebra II; she had gotten Cs the first two grading periods and then this A midyear. Her explanation was that the work had gotten easier and the teacher was explaining things more clearly. Perhaps if it had been another subject, it might not have been so obvious to me, but this was algebra. The learning steps in algebra are all about the same size, and each step is built on the previous one. Also, I knew her algebra teacher, an excellent and experienced teacher; she had not changed her teaching style midstream.

When I asked Natalia if she thought that the neurofeedback had helped, she looked surprised; it had not occurred to her. From that point on, through the rest of high school, she continued to get As in math. It would be cute if I could report she went on to be a math major in college, but she did not. Her major did require two years of math, however, and she continued her run of As in college. She even greatly enjoyed her statistics class.

Natalia's story beautifully demonstrates how neurofeedback works. In my opinion, Natalia had a subtle learning disability, not prominent enough to be picked up on testing, and neurofeedback corrected it. Her brain was restored to functioning as it was designed to function. Also, her perception of the change is telling: it just seemed easier to get it; it seemed more obvious; it just made sense.

One more story about my time in Charlottesville and then we will move on to other smart treatment options for children with learning problems. This is to show what an uphill battle it still is to get certain people to take brainwave biofeedback seriously, even after decades of remarkable outcomes in a wide range of illnesses and problems.

My friend, Bob Petchel, was on the football coaching staff at the University of Virginia, the defensive ends coach. We talked about how many players on the team had learning disabilities (not surprising in a brain injury sport). There was an army of special education instructors to provide the various services the players required to help them handle the tough curriculum. I told him about the impressive results I was seeing in the young patients I was treating with neurofeedback, the strides they were making in their academic performances, and how my experience was similar to other neurofeedback providers. He asked me to make a presentation to the coaching staff, including the offensive and defensive coordinators. No one showed up. Bob was perplexed. He then arranged a meeting with the coordinator of the educational services for the team and her staff. No one showed up.

Likely, these folks asked someone they respected at the university what they thought about training brainwaves with neurofeedback. And the higher up the academic hierarchy they went, the more likely they were assured that neurofeedback is nothing of substance.

Aside from the Italian soccer team that won the 2006 World Cup, no other athletes make public their use of neurofeedback as their secret weapon to optimize their performances. Imagine a team of student athletes using neurofeedback to dramatically improve not only their classroom accomplishment, but their on-field performances as well.

More Brain Tools

There are three other treatments that parents with learning disabled children should know about: Interactive Metronome, vision therapy, and sound therapy. They share similarities with neurofeedback in that they improve the brain's regulatory centers. A fourth method, using Irlen filters, improves reading in children who have light sensitivities.

Interactive Metronome (IM) is especially useful for children with nonverbal learning disability, especially those who have a motor deficit or sensory processing difficulties.[13-14] In IM training, the child has a sensor on her hands, and headphones that sound a cowbell every second. The child attempts to clap her hands right with the gong. She will receive a tone in one ear if she is early and in the other ear if she is late. She may also watch a computer monitor to get similar visual feedback. She will proceed through single hand, feet, and hand-foot exercises. As she works on her timing, she is training the entire sensory processing-planning-motor-output loop.

Improvements include sustained concentration and attention, language formulation, balance, and coordination. It is highly useful in ADHD, autism, and LD, even more so when there has been a brain injury. You can get information from the Interactive Metronome site at www.interactivemetronome.com.

There are video games, such as Dance Dance Revolution and Dancing Stage, for which a child stands on a mat with sensors and watches a monitor on which scrolling arrows tell where he is to place his feet. He steps quickly in time to the song's beat, and is immediately informed of the accuracy of the timing of each step. It is actually a lot of fun. It does not replace IM—for one thing, it only trains feet—but it does have some of the benefits.

Vision therapy is not for improving visual acuity; a pair of eyeglasses can do that. A child with 20/20 vision can still have sensorimotor problems that interfere with reading and can cause behavior problems. Vision therapy improves dynamic vision—tracking, eye alignment, binocular control, and focusing/refocusing. This is like a tennis player who hurts her knee and gets physical therapy to help her rehabilitate; after an evaluation, she goes through a progression of stretches and exercises, and may get infrared treatments or electric stimulation, all designed to resolve her problem and return her to full functioning. It is the same with vision. After a comprehensive vision evaluation, a program is designed for the child using specialized optical devices and computer programs to train the child's brain to resolve the vision problem.[15-17]

Sometimes it may be apparent that a child needs an evaluation, for instance, if he or she has lazy eye, diverging eyes, or squints or blinks repeatedly. But also watch out for a child who has headaches or is fatigued after school. Your child may be able to read well, but may only do so for short periods of time, or lose his place frequently while reading aloud.

Your ophthalmologist (an MD) may be lukewarm if you ask about vision therapy for your child, just as your child's pediatrician is likely to scoff at treating autism with detoxification techniques. The American Academy of Ophthalmology states that there is no consistent scientific evidence to support the use of vision therapy. A Medline search is not the way to find out if something works, especially for a treatment that is done mostly by optometrists. Find a clinic that specializes in vision therapy, sit in the waiting room for an hour or two, and ask parents a few questions while their children are training. Your optometrist (an OD) is more likely to approve of the idea but may not have the necessary specialized training and equipment. You can get information at www.visiontherapy.org.

Another technique that can help a group of children to be able to read is Irlen lenses.[18-19] Some children, and adults, have scotopic sensitivity. They will be very light sensitive, especially to any kind of glare. In addition to being halting readers, they are likely to have headaches and complain of fatigue after school. Imagine trying to see clearly or read if you woke from sleep to intense sunlight. Your eyes eventually adjust, but theirs do not. In addition to light hypersensitivity, there is a difficulty with repetitive patterns, which includes words on a page. For a person with scotopic sensitivity, it is as though the words are out of focus with a glare, as though certain patterns or color combinations can cause words on a page to appear to flicker like some optical illusion. For others, the page appears chopped into segments. Still others report that only the word or part of a word in the very center of their vision is in focus.

They are not likely to describe these difficulties until after their problem is corrected and they see the way most of us see.

Helen Irlen found that colored overlays on a page can dramatically reduce the visual disturbances. Some colors clearly work better than others for an individual. When the color that works best for a child is put into eyeglass lenses, reading becomes a whole new ballgame.

The American Academy of Ophthalmology does not find scientific support for the use of Irlen lenses either. The technique requires no training of the child or adult with scotopic sensitivity. Simply place the colored overlays over a page of print and determine if the child can read better. The usual response from an adolescent or adult with scotopic sensitivity when the corrective overlay is placed over a page is "Oh, my gosh!" followed by a huge smile. Not scientific, we admit, but it helps a considerable number of children and adults read and relieves numerous physical complaints.

Many neurofeedback practitioners also have Irlen training and the overlays to evaluate your child. You can also get information at www.irlen.com.

Sound therapy, also called auditory integration training, can help those children who have difficulty understanding the spoken word, whether they have LD, ADHD, autism, or no diagnosis at all.[20-21] Consider this treatment for children who have difficulty learning orally, who are highly sensitive to sounds, who startle and cover their ears at certain sounds that others do not find jarring, or who are easily distracted by background sounds. Sound therapy can also help with a child to whom you have to tell the same thing repeatedly before he or she appears to understand, or one who is not interested in reading or story time.

The two major forms of sound therapy were developed by French otolaryngologists, Drs. Alfred Tomatis and Guy Berard, and have many similarities, since Dr. Berard trained under Dr. Tomatis before developing his method, which he believes is a more efficient variation. After evaluation to determine what kinds of hearing difficulties exist, a child listens to music through headphones with alternating full spectrum and high frequencies embedded.

At times, there is a shifting of sounds from one ear to the other. Depending on the underlying problems, training usually requires at least twenty hours of listening.

The process appears to awaken listening skills by presenting the brain with auditory stimulation that activates parts of the brain that had been inappropriately inactive during listening. When activated, they change the way the middle ear responds to sound. There is a reorganization of the auditory system. Children may not only begin to understand and enjoy spoken language much more, they usually improve their speech and attention.

Dr. Tomatis also used his filtering equipment in a novel manner to treat autistic children who did not respond to their parents. He first provided a child with the sound of his mother's voice as he would have heard it in utero. He then gradually reduced the filtering to produce the sounds of her true voice. There were a few instances of children spontaneously looking at their mothers with a look of recognition, and hugging them for the first time. Possibly, he was linking sounds before and after a child's auditory system was damaged by toxicity.

3

The Labyrinth of Attention-Deficit/Hyperactivity Disorder (ADHD)

ADHD has been one of the most talked about disorders in the general public for the past twenty years. It is like religion and politics—everyone has an opinion. Just ask around; the man that mows the yard, the lady that sells insurance, or the eighth-grade teacher—they can all tell you what it is and which children in the neighborhood have it. It is not uncommon for someone in the general public to cite a laundry list of symptoms and often they are correct. We have frequently had parents come into the office and announce that their child has ADHD. When we inquire who made the diagnosis, they respond by saying, "I read it in an article," "Our minister," or "The teacher."

Unfortunately, these people are unhelpful diagnosticians. They frequently mislabel children and give erroneous advice. They often suggest, even demand inappropriate treatments. Though we have no way of knowing what was actually said, some parents have reported that they were told their child could not come back to school without being on medication. With no disrespect to teachers, ministers, article writers, and talk-show hosts, ADHD is a complex disorder and cannot be diagnosed with casual observation. ADHD is like a Gordian knot; it will not be untied by casual observers. The diagnosis can certainly not be based on how annoying a child is to parents and teachers. Even so, ADHD remains a topic of conversation at the dinner table, the bridge party, and with thousands of parents. You cannot go to a Little League game without it coming up in conversation. ADHD seems to have swept across the country like a virus. We almost expect CNN to show us the ADHD map and tell us the disorder is now sweeping across the Great Plains.

The human brain has always been vulnerable to injury and disorders. It is therefore easy to conclude that disorders like ADHD and autism have been common in the human population. We didn't start trying to label these symptoms until the beginning of the twentieth century, however, and we didn't start talking widely about them until the last couple of decades. Brain disorders are a fact of life in our world and to recognize and treat them is important. Medication is not the only way to deal with them and, in many instances, there are much better alternatives.

This is how it works in today's society: little William is disruptive in class; he does not pay attention, he talks constantly, and he picks on other children. The teacher tells the parents, "He needs to be on medication." Both parents work but they manage to take time off to take William to see Dr. Jones, his pediatrician. Dr. Jones has an office full of sick and injured children. The parents describe William's behavior. They say he is hyperactive, can't pay attention, is hard to discipline, and makes poor grades. Dr. Jones runs through the symptoms in his head, and when the parents say William is ADHD, he agrees. William is placed on a stimulant medication like Ritalin. William's poor behavior changes enough to be noticed. The teacher is happy because William is easier to handle in her overcrowded classroom. The parents are happy and they have acted responsibly by getting their child to the physician from whom he received the medical treatment he needed. The pediatrician has offered William the treatment most often prescribed for the presenting symptoms. Everyone has acted appropriately and in good faith. But has William received the best possible treatment available? We don't think so. There is a noninvasive treatment that does not involve drug therapy. Not only does this treatment have no negative side effects, it also goes directly to the core of the problem.

The ADHD Diagnosis

The actual diagnosis for ADHD is made with the aid of a behavioral checklist. There is no blood test, imaging procedure (MRI or CAT scan), psychological test, or even an EEG (brainwave) test that can conclusively detect the brain dysregulation of ADHD. There are, however, two tests that are extremely helpful in the diagnostic process (see appendix G). Unfortunately, only neurofeedback providers commonly utilize these tests. At this point, most clinicians make the diagnosis based on the checklist and behavioral observation. The neurofeedback practitioner, on the other hand, can actually see the brainwave recordings and test continuous performance.

The layperson can certainly observe behaviors and recommend an evaluation but lacks the expertise to make an actual diagnosis. We must all remember that there are numerous disorders that can mimic ADHD and only a trained professional can differentiate between the potential diagnostic problems. It is often the observations of parents and teachers that assist professionals, not only in diagnosing the problem, but also in determining the effectiveness of treatments. It is, however, only the trained professional who can make the diagnosis and follow the patient through the steps of improvement and recovery.

Often it is the professional who determines whether the observed behaviors are just natural childhood stages of development or signs of a serious condition. For example, it would be easy for a new parent to label as ADHD the manifestation of the "terrible twos" or an adolescent's first acting-out period. There are normal developmental behaviors and many complex disorders that have similar signs and are therefore easily confused. Some of the disorders that are confused with ADHD are mild mental retardation, specific brain disorders, antisocial behavior, learning disorders, depression, and anxiety.

The "bible" of mental disorders is known as the *Diagnostic and Statistical Manual of Mental Disorders, Fourth Edition (DSM-IV)*. This book is ostensibly the last word on what is and is not a mental disorder. It lists ADHD in the category of disruptive disorders and describes the essential features of ADHD as "a persistent pattern of inattention and/or hyperactivity/impulsivity."[1] The criteria include the following:

- Fails to give close attention to details or makes careless errors

- Has difficulty sustaining attention

- Not listening when spoken to

- Not following through on tasks

- Organizational problems

- Avoiding tasks that require sustained attention

- Often loses things

- Easily distracted

- Forgetful

The category of hyperactivity includes the following common behavioral characteristics:

- Often fidgets or squirms

- Often leaves one's seat

- Often runs or climbs excessively

- Often has difficulty playing

- On the go

- Talks excessively

The category of impulsivity includes the following:

- Often blurts out answers

- Has difficulty waiting one's turn

- Often interrupts or intrudes on others

The DSM-IV is critical to the diagnosis of ADHD. It sets the standard measurement that mental health professionals use in diagnosis. It does not, nor could it, however, expand completely on all the manifestations of this complex disorder. ADHD is more than just a list of symptoms from three categories to be checked off. It is a pervasive disorder that can present in dozens of different ways. One case can present so differently from another that you might not recognize them as the same disorder. Take for example the simple distinction of attention-deficit disorder with and without hyperactivity. A twelve-year-old boy with the hyperactive component will behave completely differently from a thirteen-year-old female without hyperactivity. He would likely be moving all over the place while she might be sitting so quietly she is hardly noticed. Yet they both have the same broad diagnosis. So, in an effort to demonstrate the variations even further, we will discuss some of the cases we have seen in our office. Names and certain circumstances have been changed to protect confidentiality.

The Ups and Downs of ADHD

Sporadic performance is very common in ADHD. Reggie would make a 95 on one math test and the following week he would make a 45. His parents knew that he had studied for both tests, so they labeled him lazy or in some way trying to get even with them. The simple truth is that Reggie's brain, like most ADHD patients, went on vacation during a test. His parents refused to accept that he was ADHD because he could sit for hours playing video games. This particular situation even confounds many pediatricians; the common misbelief is that if a child can sit still for an hour, then he cannot be ADHD. Wrong! Reggie was subjected to labels of stupid, lazy, mean, and spiteful. After a lot of neurofeedback training, Reggie became academically successful and was no longer saddled with labels.

Before we go any further, we would like to say a few words about TV and video games. First, video games and much of TV programming present constant motion to the viewer. The games also have a wide variety of booms and bangs. All of the motion and noise keeps the person occupied. What teacher could compete with the frantic pace of a video game? Second, people with ADHD have a quality of perseverance. Once they lock on to the motion of a video game, they have trouble turning themselves loose; these individuals who normally bounce from one thing to another are now unable to shift focus. Have you ever tried to call children to dinner when they are watching cartoons? If so, you know what we mean.

The classroom is quite a different situation. If the teacher is giving a lecture on pronouns, she cannot compete with the high-speed activity of a video showing a car race or firefight in a war zone. Teachers in today's schoolrooms have a much more difficult time than teachers twenty years ago. They have to compete with remarkable technologies that can be stuffed into a shirt pocket and carried from room to room. Pronouns and history dates fade when compared with the jumps, bounces, and bangs of handheld videos. If you add to the mix the fact that many children have ADHD, you compound the problem exponentially. We also might mention that many children who are "addicted" to video games are on their way to becoming ADHD. As a society, we are very successful at building weapons that can destroy human life and technologies that reduce the ability to attend, concentrate, and be creative.

Not all ADHD children are "bouncing off the walls." Some children quietly slip away into daydreaming and seldom cause any trouble at school. They are often a great worry to parents who notice their detachment and aloneness. Such children are seldom diagnosed as ADHD and are never labeled hyperactive. A large percentage of these children are female and they usually get tagged with labels like lazy, depressed, dreamy, or unusual. The fact is, most of these children are ADHD without the hyperactive component.

ADHD children without hyperactivity never seem to make good

contact with what is going on around them. They are very internal, quiet, and seemingly distant. It is just as hard for them to focus as it is for the child in perpetual motion. They often miss social cues and are usually passed over for extra help or any other type of assistance. They fall through the cracks and may only be diagnosed with ADHD when they are brought in for other reasons. Perhaps these are the saddest cases of all because they do not get recognized, diagnosed, or treated as often as the hyperactive children. It is like that old saying, "The world greases the squeaky wheel." We pay attention to the most disruptive children and the quiet non-attenders get forgotten. They simply get negative labels from peers, family, and school officials. Depression is common in these children. In neurofeedback treatment, we usually address the depression before we focus on the attentional component; although with neurofeedback, we are treating a cluster of disorders and both may resolve at about the same rate.

Overstimulation and Overload

A normally functioning brain selects what to pay attention to, and it takes an event of a certain magnitude to get it to change focus. If a non-ADHD person is in a restaurant and a door slams, they may be slightly distracted but do not completely lose their focus. The person with ADHD loses focus with the slightest distraction; the slamming of a door is a call to sit up, look around, and survey the entire restaurant, dropping words mid-sentence. The adult ADHD is easiest to spot in a restaurant; they have extreme difficulty focusing on their food and/or the company they are with because they have to pay attention to everyone and everything else in the environment. Drop a spoon with a slight noise and see if you get some, usually male, heads to turn your way. They may also have difficulty returning their eyes and thoughts to their own table. People with ADHD are often in sensory overload. It is hard to carry on a conversation with them. They continually break eye contact to follow other activity in the area and laugh at something going on clear across the room. When they do rejoin a conversation, it is often inappropriately. They may respond to something that was said by someone several minutes before they were distracted. They are unaware that the conversation has moved on.

Overstimulation is a problem in both childhood and adult ADHD. What happens in the example of an ADHD adult in a restaurant is similar to what happens to ADHD children in the classroom. What is going on across the room is much more interesting than the paper or book on the desk. If you can imagine for a moment, everything going on in the classroom is demanding attention—from the girl fixing her hair, to the bird out the window, to the closing of a book at the back of the room. It is easy to conceptualize that ADHD individuals pay attention to everything and everything is asking for their attention. So it is not that they can't attend; it is that everything needs attention. They are overloaded with demands for their attention. They may have a serious inability to concentrate on anything because they are paying attention to everything.

ADHD has many components, which can vary in degree and intensity. Because of the different manifestations, two different cases may not look like the same disorder. Several years ago, we went back through about ten years of charts, pulled out the symptoms we found in the charts, and grouped them according to categories. You will encounter the checklist for each category at the end of the various sections that follow.

There is one thing that we always remind parents and family. ADHD children are not purposefully difficult to deal with. When children or adults have this type of brain injury/dysfunction, they are usually unable to inhibit inappropriate behaviors. They generally want to do better and often try very hard to conform, but they still talk when they should be quiet, run when they should sit, and cry when they should smile. They are irritable when they should be calm, awake when they should be asleep, and gazing out the window when they should be looking at the teacher. It is very easy to assume that they have more control than they actually do. Take this into consideration when you are working with them. They are generally very sweet and want to please. They don't want to constantly be in trouble, but what they are doing is a result of how their brain works.

Age of Onset

The DSM-IV diagnostic definition of ADHD requires that some attentional or behavioral problems be present before the age of seven. Many of the signs may be dismissed, however, as normal behavior. This is a disorder that can manifest in utero or it may not be recognized until high school or even early college. Children with excessive hyperactivity frequently let their mothers know they are ADHD before they are born: they kick, squirm, and wiggle constantly in the womb. One mother said, "He never let me have a minute's peace from the time I conceived him until today. When he was born, he hit the ground running and hasn't stopped since." Incidentally, she was right. Our office staff was exhausted just trying to keep up with this acrobatic nine-year-old. He ran, tumbled, flipped, jumped, and climbed all over the furniture for the first fifteen or twenty sessions until the brainwave training finally started to kick in.

In contrast to the very young children who are easily identified, we frequently see the beginning college student who "never had any problems until now." John was a nineteen-year-old college freshman who had made average grades in high school. He did okay until the work level exceeded his persistence and dedication. When faced with the greater demands of college work, John fell behind quickly. His self-esteem dropped like a rock and he lost all motivation. Not only did he feel paralyzed to study the new material, he felt he could not even remember the material he had studied. There was a complete loss of focusing ability due to the stress he was feeling.

Like John, countless young people with ADHD do well to a certain point, and then the work becomes overwhelming. A great number of these individuals are very bright but cannot focus and concentrate. They get through simply by overwhelming the material. They rely on extra hard work, mechanical study habits, and incredible persistence. As the material gets harder and harder, their compensation strategies begin to fail them. It is at this point that they come into the office, defeated and lost. Their families are in shock because they are not used to seeing failure. They frequently say things like "He never had any trouble in high school" or "He has always been such a good student." They are good students, but the bulk of the material just became too much to deal with.

There are many people with ADHD who never get identified and there are others who are finally discovered later in life. We have had many older adults come in and report that they always knew there was something wrong but didn't know what. We often see faces light up when we tell them they are ADHD because for so long they have struggled to attend and concentrate and didn't know why it was so hard. When we explain that we can success-fully treat the disorder, their mood begins to improve quickly. One adult recently told us, "Now I realize I was ADD. I thought I wasn't very smart." This person was the parent of a child we were treat-ing and she was greatly relieved that she finally had an answer for her attentional inabilities. We successfully treated both mother and son, although it took much longer for the mother because her symptoms were more entrenched.

ADHD Affects More Boys than Girls

It is generally accepted that there is a much greater incidence of ADHD in boys than in girls. The DSM-IV states that the ratio of males to females ranges from four to one to nine to one. We suspect this is an incorrect assumption because we feel that many girls fall through the cracks. They don't get referred as often because many of the females tend to be less hyperactive than the males.

We definitely agree that males have a higher incidence of hyper-activity, impulsivity, and oppositional and aggressive behavior, but when it comes to attentional problems, the ratio may favor females. They sit quietly gazing out the window while the teacher lectures. A female like this is more likely to get the label of disinterested, stu-pid, or indifferent. She may be seen as a bit odd or flaky rather than as a person with attentional difficulties. She may never get referred for any type of help. You can bet, however, that the children who are disruptive get referred with regularity. Everyone thinks the "wild child" needs help, but the quiet, shy, timid girl in the corner who makes poor grades "is just not as bright," "she is not ADHD."

The hyperactive, disruptive child, usually a male, gets all the attention while the "she" is often ignored. Quiet, hypoactive (slowed down) children don't cause trouble. They just sit there and make poor grades. Everyone notices hyperactive, impulsive children. Perhaps it is time to rethink the idea of ratios. We need to look more closely, and with fresh eyes, at the dull, bored, sleepy, disinterested child. That glazed-over look in her eyes may be as telling as the nonstop hyperactivity of another child.

The Problem Is Arousal, Not Attention

Let us first look at the underlying physiological problem of ADHD. The bulk of the scientific evidence accumulated since the 1940s indicates that the central feature of ADHD is poor regulation of the brain's arousal state.

The most convincing argument to explain the role of arousal (how sleepy or awake the brain is) in hyperkinetic (hyperactive) syndrome came from research in the early 1970s by Satterfield and colleagues.[2-3] They proposed that hyperactive children had low states of arousal, that they constantly sought new stimulation. By the late 1970s and early 1980s, this theory, known as the "low arousal hypothesis," was generally accepted in the medical community and it remains so today. This is why a stimulant such as Ritalin has an effect on hyperactive children. It speeds up their low level of arousal. It seems paradoxical to give a hyperactive child a stimulant. What actually happens, of course, is that the stimulant medication is used to wake up the sleepy brain.

The brain can be either overaroused (speeded up) or underaroused (slowed down). In either case, it does not function the way it should. If our brain is in a state of overarousal, we may be jumpy, hyper, or anxious. We are trying to do too much, paying attention to everything at once, or we are nervous and upset. If, on the other hand, the brain is in a state of underarousal, we are probably sleepy, lethargic, or disinterested. We may not care what is happening or even be aware of what is going on in the environment around us. The hyperactivity can be an unconscious, automatic behavior to wake up the brain. The alert professional looks for ADHD symptoms at both ends of the continuum. All cases do not look alike, but they all have problems with arousal states.

A way of conceptualizing brain arousal is to think of the intensity of a light in a room. If the dimmer switch controls the light level, we have every level of light from complete darkness to brilliant light. The "dimmer switch" of arousal in the brain is located in a part of the brain known as the thalamus. Like a dimmer switch that adjusts light levels in a room, the thalamus automatically adjusts the intensity of arousal for the task at hand.

For a restful sleep, the intensity is turned way down. For reading complicated material, the dimmer switch is turned to a more brilliant level. Most activities fall somewhere between sleep and intense thinking. This is normally done automatically, but in the case of many disorders, particularly ADHD, the intensity typically stays adjusted to dim. The set point for the dimmer switch (as in a thermostat) is set too low and does not automatically make the necessary adjustments. In disorders of low arousal, the individual is often so slowed down, he sits and stares, unable to focus or think clearly. Sometimes, however, he automatically becomes hyper, trying to turn the arousal level up. It is like an automatic defensive mechanism to help the person stay in the world. This is the brain's effort to wake up or compensate for low arousal. As you can see, this can account for both the hyperactive person and the hypoactive (slowed down) person.

The chronic low-arousal state in ADHD is like someone trying to work in a dimly lit room. It is hard to concentrate, stay on task, and complete most jobs. It is easy to become discouraged, frustrated, bored, and even depressed. The chronically underaroused brain will frequently seek stimulation. Stimulation seekers are often the hyperactive: There is a lot of purposeless movement and out-of-control behavior. This is why you frequently see risk-taking behavior with little awareness of consequences. The phrase that many parents use is "he knows no fear." ADHD children cannot see consequences; this is why they are in trouble a lot. Everything looks fun and nothing looks dangerous. Drugs and alcohol may play a major role in the life of the ADHD risk-taker. By the time many of these individuals come to the attention of professionals, they have a basketful of problems.

ADHD and its cluster problems usually present a challenge for any treating professional. We frequently see ADHD children who are kicked out of school, in trouble with the law, angry, depressed, and using drugs and alcohol. As you might guess, a single pill a day hardly puts a dent in all the symptoms. Fortunately, brainwave training can deal with all of these cluster problems with remarkable speed and success because all of these problems usually relate to arousal levels in the brain.

To offer a glimpse of what it is like to have ADHD, we will lay out two scenarios. First, imagine someone walks into your room in the middle of the night, wakes you from a sound sleep, and asks you to balance your checkbook. It is not that you do not have the intellect to do the task; you have the wrong level of arousal. You might express several different emotions or behavioral responses in a situation like that; you could be irritable, unfocused, disinterested, or stubbornly defiant. This is exactly how some people with ADHD feel when a task requires a higher state of brain arousal.

The second scenario might go something like this: You are on a whirlwind through your own life. Everything is moving faster than you can keep up with. It seems like everyone is talking to you at once and all deadlines and requests are immediate. You are left spinning, feeling out of control, and knowing that there is no way you can meet the demands of everyone around you.

To make this more concrete, think about driving a long distance at night while fighting off sleep. Look at what we do: We become hyperactive. We turn the radio up loud, sing, tap out the rhythm of the music on the radio on the dash or steering wheel, talk to ourselves, bounce around, open the window, and even do that wavy thing in the wind with our hand just to stay awake. This is exactly what the hyperactive individual does on a chronic basis. They are in a constant battle with low arousal. They are in a constant state of trying to stay in the world; they, too, want to be awake. There is nothing that wakes up the brain like risk taking. This turns out to be a good hypothesis for explaining some criminal behavior.

Committing a crime or being physically aggressive arouses the level of brain activity. Excitement wakes us all up; it lets us know we are alive. If we constantly feel slowed down, we might crave excitement. This is one of the reasons for the high demand for violent movies and TV programs and fast-paced video games.

The Relationship between Arousal and Attention

Arousal and attention have a unique relationship. They are not the same, but they are dependent on each other. Arousal is the level of intensity, how bright or dim the light is. Attention, on the other hand, is how focused the light is. Compare an ordinary hundred-watt bulb to a hundred-watt spotlight. The ordinary light bulb illuminates the entire field around it, whereas the spotlight illuminates a specific spot in the field.

We can be very aroused but not focused on anything specific. Anxiety patients are a classic example, and so is the overaroused ADHD patient. They are in a constant state of overstimulation, not focused on any one thing. Everything captures their attention and nothing holds their concentration. They move from one thing to another, then back again, as often as possible. The anxiety patient is hypervigilant, but, of course, it involves concern or fear. So even with high levels of arousal, they cannot clearly attend or learn or have a sense of control; it takes concentration for that.

Focus or concentration is the "spotlight" that allows us the ability to pick out one object, task, or thought and work on it to the exclusion of other things. Individuals with ADHD not only lack an adequate level of arousal, but they also cannot usually focus on any one task for any extended time. The students with ADHD who are successful must be so disciplined that they focus, lose the focus, and then redirect themselves back to focus. We have seen young men and women who made it all the way through graduate school or medical school through the sheer strength of willing themselves back into focus, but this is surely an exhausting way to get through school. Study is hard enough without having to fight to be awake.

It is not just the classroom that gives the ADHD child problems. They have problems in any situation that requires discipline. Take homework, for example. They will bounce from topic to topic, look at everything in the area, and find any excuse not to settle down to the task at hand. For the most part, sitting still, focusing, and concentrating is painful. As a matter of fact, it is not just painful; it is exhausting. Give it a try. Turn on the TV, radio, and CD player and then have every member of your family talk to you at the same time; you will get a feel for what the brain of the person with ADHD is going through. You end up paying attention to everything and nothing at the same time. In stimulus overload, you cannot focus on any one thing long enough to deal with it.

For many of these children, it is not that they cannot pay attention; they are paying a little attention to everything at once. Therefore nothing gets done, nothing gets absorbed, and nothing gets learned in a meaningful way. You end up with a lot of motion and no purpose. In order to learn, the level of arousal must be high enough to allow the brain to focus in one direction while screening out the distractions. If the brain is incapable of screening, then attention and concentration are inadequate.

Arousal is the basic problem with ADHD, but attention plays a major role in the person's ability to function appropriately in the world. If a child or an adult cannot attend and concentrate, then they become tired and subsequently bored; boredom is always a result of inattention. An individual with good attentional skills can spend a long time examining a single leaf, whereas someone with poor attentional skills may not even notice the leaf.

In our high-tech world of videos, TV, handheld games, and text messaging, children are bombarded with stimuli. Yet the video games, TV shows, and other technologies drive the brain to deeper levels of low arousal. Once the brain learns how to accommodate or deal with the video game or TV, learning stops and the brain shifts into relax or "coast" mode. In a sense, it goes into neutral, requiring only a very small part of the brain to be used on the game or show. Manual skills and physical agility may improve through video game practice, but the brain is lulled into inactivity.

Different Faces of ADHD Behavior

You can quickly see that ADHD presents in many different ways even though the primary problem is inadequate arousal level. Because ADHD looks so different from one person to another, some people do not believe it is a real disorder. Others see it only as a disorder of hyperactivity. Nevertheless, it is a real disorder with devastating consequences. It makes children suffer through the agony of working harder to focus, and it can ruin an adult's life. As we frequently say, if you rescue the child, you save the adult.

When ten-year-old Gerald was brought to our office, everyone, including teachers, parents, doctors, and family friends had labeled him ADHD. He was a classic case; he clearly met the diagnostic criteria of the DSM-IV. He was hyper, inattentive, and impulsive. He had poor school performance and poor behavioral control in public. It was very difficult to begin the neurofeedback training with Gerald because he could not sit still long enough to train.

Neurofeedback requires being hooked up to a computer with sensor wires. After five or six minutes of training, Gerald wanted to play with the sensor lead wires, sing, and ask dozens of questions. We must have heard "Are we through yet?" six or eight times a session. So we began by giving Gerald short sessions, limiting each to about ten minutes. As his brainwaves began to improve, we were gradually able to lengthen the session to twenty, then thirty minutes. Gerald made an excellent recovery, but it took several months and approximately sixty brainwave training sessions.

Gerald was an easy diagnosis compared to Karl, a fourteen-year-old truant. He was in trouble with school officials for fighting, had a brush with the law for petty vandalism, and was a chronic marijuana smoker. Karl was a skinny little tough guy and no one considered him ADHD. As it turned out, he used this tough, devil-may-care façade to cover his inability to focus and learn his schoolwork. Once during a training session, this young Mr. Tough Guy looked up and said pitifully, "I hope this stuff can help me. I don't want to be a dumb shit." Karl's treatment was successful and, as his grades improved, so did his school attendance. He became fun to be around and you had the sense that he was no longer on ready alert for a fight. He even developed friendships with peers whom he had once tormented and terrified.

Neurofeedback training is a treatment in which the patient's scalp is connected to a computer by sensor wires. The computer system reads and amplifies the brainwave signals and the computer monitor feeds back information about how well the brainwaves are functioning. By watching the information on the monitor, patients learn to change their brainwaves. When the changes are made incrementally, the level of arousal is improved and the ADHD symptoms are reduced. Gerald and Karl, as well as most other patients who seek out neurofeedback training, did very well. Their ADHD symptoms were dramatically reduced, their grades went up, and their social behavior improved.

Linda was the stereotypic ADHD child with hypoactivity. She sat in class daydreaming and doodling in her notebook. She would draw little cartoon characters and have them say funny things. Some cartoons were very clever, but the notepaper was void of any classroom notes. Linda was sweet, polite, and pretty. Her parents declared that she was smart but lazy; she was also failing every class. After a complete evaluation, she was diagnosed with ADHD, without hyperactivity, and we began brainwave training. She was wonderfully easy to work with because there were no purposeless movements and she cooperated completely. She had supportive parents who were willing to see that she got the treatment she needed. Linda improved nicely and she ended up passing every class with a C average. Academically, Linda may never be at the top of her class, but she is certainly capable of doing a little better than average work. She is also very creative and that will take her a long way in life. It would not surprise us if one day Linda ended up with a syndicated cartoon strip; she has the talent. Her endless hours of doodling may pay big dividends some day.

These are three examples of how ADHD presents with uniquely different behaviors. Although very different, each behavior is caused by the same type of brain dysregulation. We might add that not every case that presents with the symptoms in these examples is ADHD. There are many other disorders that must be ruled out before an ADHD diagnosis can be made and the training started. Disorders such as mild mental retardation, depression, anxiety, under- or overstimulation in a given environment, conduct disorder, abuse, grief, or anger should be considered before any treatment begins. Some of these disorders may be caused by over- or underaroused brainwave states, but the treatment protocol/regimen may be completely different from that of ADHD.

We need to know what we are dealing with before we start treatment. We almost always find that we are not dealing with a single problem, but a large cluster of problems that combine to make the situation more complex. This may necessitate a sequence of protocols to deal with all the symptoms.

Refining the Distinctions: All Is Not ADHD

I have talked with many teachers and parents who feel that just about all young children have ADHD and that there should be a Ritalin salt lick on the playground. Not everything that looks like ADHD is ADHD. Normal children and adults can have behavioral characteristics that resemble ADHD. We can all have bad days or even bad weeks. In our offices, if we juice up on coffee, our staffs threaten to treat us for hyperactivity and rapid-fire speech. Frequently, we will get on a new project and our enthusiasm and behavior resemble an excited twelve-year-old with ADHD, but then we finish the project and our mood and behavior settle down.

Linda Budd, PhD, a psychologist in St. Paul, Minnesota, labels many of these children "Active Alert" children. Dr. Budd publishes an excellent newsletter called the *Active Alerter.*[4] She suggests that many children who get labeled ADHD are just very active children who are alert to their surroundings. We generally agree; we see a number of children who are vibrantly alert and active but do not have brain dysfunction. There is also the probability that some children who get labeled "just active" are, in fact, children with ADHD.

We have on many occasions done a thorough evaluation of children who were labeled ADHD and concluded that they were not ADHD. We often recommend psychotherapy, behavioral training, family counseling, and even parent training to help these children. There are many different children and adults who come to our offices who must be reevaluated before we make a firm diagnosis and begin brainwave training. It is a common problem, once a diagnosis gets mentioned in the media, that people in all walks of life begin diagnosing others as having the problem. As Dr. Budd has pointed out so clearly, many bright, active children inappropriately get negative labels that can follow them for a long time. Let us be very clear: There is such a thing as ADHD and it is a very destructive disorder, affecting millions of children and adults. If left untreated, it can have profound consequences on adult life.

Summary

Perhaps this chapter seems a bit confusing; we wander back and forth between children, adolescents, and adults. Going from early childhood to adulthood is on a continuum and the disorder of ADHD can influence a life regardless of the stage. We just want to point out that it is the same disorder whether we are discussing an eight-year-old or a forty-five-year-old. Any observer of human behavior will agree that there are many adults who act like children and many children who act like adults, and most of this is dependent on brain function. Our job is to point out that there is a training that helps regulate brainwave function, regardless of age or gender.

The best predictor of future behavior is past behavior and since most children do not outgrow ADHD behavior, children usually take into adulthood the worst part of the disorder, attentional problems. So the reason we have included a discussion of adults with ADHD is because it is not just a childhood problem. ADHD is a pervasive disorder that starts in childhood, is carried through adolescence, and often becomes an adult disorder. We have spent a lot of time looking at how the disorder unfolds in individuals over decades; we have gotten a much broader picture of ADHD.

We now realize that this is a much larger problem than a child who cannot pay attention and who is in perpetual motion. Adults who continue to show signs of attentional problems are much more likely to have failed marriages, poor job success, more aggressive behavior, poor social skills, and problems with addictions. The next time you hear about someone with ADHD or see it firsthand, remember this is someone whose life is built on a telescoping history, and levels and layers of similar behavior stack up as the person advances in age.

4

You Don't Just Outgrow ADHD

People don't just outgrow ADHD; it is not like the "baby fat" we lose when we start getting taller. Many people will have it forever if not treated. Adult ADHD carries many of the same symptoms that children have and the stakes are higher, the ramifications of the problems much broader. There is a long-held misconception, even among some professionals, that children will grow out of their ADHD, thereby becoming "normal" adults. Look around you at the adults who cannot sustain attention and are easily distracted, unfocused, and disorganized. Chances are, they have been like that since early childhood and they did not outgrow the condition.

In reality, ADHD does not go away as effortlessly as some predict. Long-term follow-up studies on children with ADHD have found that as many as 80 percent of children with ADHD take their disorder into adulthood. Experts in the field indicate that 1 to 2 percent of the adult population have some degree of ADHD. This could mean that millions of adults have the disorder. The hyperactivity component usually disappears, but the majority of children with attentional difficulty take the problem into adulthood. This means we take the worst part of the disorder into the workday world, and unless someone is hyperactive, the problem may go unrecognized.

Hyperactive children tend to be a problem for everyone around them, but the children may be having fun. They do not realize there is a problem; they are into everything, having a great time. The attentional component of the disorder is what causes the individual to have difficulty with academic success, job performance, and relationships. So when it comes to something like schoolwork, the children suffer. Their poor academic performance is usually followed by low self-esteem, loss of motivation, and even depression.

Since the adult usually continues to have the attentional problems rather than the hyperactivity, the ramifications are far-reaching. Low self-esteem, poor motivation, lack of follow-through, trouble sustaining attention, and depression become serious problems in adulthood. ADHD interferes with every aspect of one's life. Let's look at how the adult with ADD may behave in the workday world.

One Big Idea after Another

Adults with ADHD are often very bright and come up with great ideas. As a matter of fact, it is like one big idea after another. They tell us about these ideas and we often get excited for them. They take off like a whirlwind, doing things, arranging things, setting things up. For those of us who love them, we feel they have finally found themselves. They're finally on track. They initially have boundless energy and cannot be stopped even by the most discouraging news. When they are in this phase, it is impressive, but as the project progresses, these individuals go flat as a pancake. The work stops, the idea doesn't seem so good, and they usually perceive their failure as somebody else's fault.

Once again, family and friends shake their heads in frustration. Adults with ADHD are usually good "idea people" but need to have the backup of steady workers. They are good for short projects that do not require much follow-through.

At our office, we frequently put a stopwatch on children and monitor how long they can look at a TV monitor or carry on a conversation before they break away. Surprisingly, there are consistent patterns in the individual. Some children can hold on for twenty or thirty seconds, but many of them are in the five- to fifteen-second range. Adults with ADHD are generally able to lengthen this time as a result of work experience, but they cannot always see projects through without a lot of help, encouragement, and supervision. Just like the children, they lose concentration and focus.

John was a thirty-nine-year-old independent contractor who built small single-family houses. He came to us because of a long history of ADHD, and he readily acknowledged that his disorder kept him from being more successful. He reported that he was sure his father had ADHD and perhaps one of his brothers. He wanted help. He came to us because we had treated a neighbor's child and he was impressed with the changes he saw. "Can you help a grown man?" he asked.

We told him that although there were no guarantees, we thought we could. We then discussed the treatment plan and the probable outcome. He knew it would take longer for an adult to change, but he was willing to commit to the treatment plan. It was not always easy working treatment times into his busy schedule; it took a lot of effort on his part.

The typical number of neurofeedback treatments for a child is thirty to forty. That usually translates to $2,000 to $2,500 for the total treatment at our office. John had almost fifty treatments before he began to report changes. First, his depression lifted and he began to feel better about himself. Finally, after sixty-five neurofeedback sessions, he reported he was "catching up" in his work. He was no longer leaving jobs before he was finished or starting new jobs that would go unfinished. He was finally able to stay with a job until it was completed. He said that before treatment, he would get "antsy" on a job and have to start something new. Although John ended up taking eighty sessions, he reported it was well worth the time and money it cost him. John spent nearly $4,000 on treatment, but it was successful, whereas everything else had failed. John said, "It was worth the money just to get rid of the depression." That was several years ago, and John still reports no depression and better job efficiency.

Oops! There Goes Another Job

People with ADHD can be great workers, but they usually lack staying power. They often change jobs because they see a new opportunity around every corner. Of course, new jobs do not always pan out the way they planned. People with ADHD have selective hearing; they may hear the part that says, "You can make more money," but miss the part that says "longer hours." If they have personality or character problems along with the ADHD, then it is always somebody else's fault. "He did me wrong," "They lied to me," or "I intimidated them with my abilities."

After they are hired, things go wrong. They make lots of mistakes that "weren't my fault," and they are likely to say something like "the part you bought doesn't fit," or "the paint wasn't put on correctly" (as in the case of one ADHD adult painter). There is no way to estimate the amount of money that is lost in the economy each year due to mistakes and inefficiency caused by ADHD. There are people with ADHD who are able to compensate well for it and be very productive, but many cannot, and struggle on a daily basis. They struggle with inattentiveness, easy distraction, excitability, poor focus, disorganization, and difficulty completing tasks. For those who do learn to compensate, the extra effort takes its toll; it takes much more energy and effort just to maintain a normal level of efficiency.

Studies indicate that adults with ADHD are less likely to fulfill work demands, work independently, and get along well with employers and supervisors. They are more likely to perceive the job as more difficult than non-ADHD adults do, so they quit their jobs more frequently. They are also fired more frequently. This correlates with early antisocial behavior. They tend to be more explosive and more difficult to deal with.

Perhaps one day some forward-thinking company will address this type of inefficiency, and neurofeedback training will be available to every employee. In the future, we might have "peak-efficiency" industries without poor performers or alcoholics, and "peak-efficiency" sports teams with no players who are in court or jail for off-the-field ADHD behaviors. People with ADHD are like radio receivers with all the channels open. They hear and see everything, paying attention to all the stimuli in their environment at the same time. Athletics is often the perfect outlet for aggressive, hyperactive, risk-taking behavior. But off the field, it is a different matter.

People with ADHD will frequently leave a job when they feel the pressure to perform at a level beyond their abilities. These individuals are usually bright but feel at some level that they don't match up. When they can't keep up, they are usually looking for a "better job." The adult work world becomes as frustrating as schoolwork was as a child; they may work hard, but the effort does not seem to pay off. For the spouse and family, it's one excuse after another, one disappointment after another. It is not easy for the person with ADHD or the family living with that person, as the following example shows.

Philip came in to see us because his wife was leaving him. He reported depression, anxiety, and anger toward his wife. When we asked why his wife was leaving him, he had "no idea." He said, "I guess she just doesn't love me." Further questioning revealed Philip had left eight jobs in ten years. The family had moved three times in the ten years, and there was one period of eight months in which he had no job. Philip disclosed that he had hated school and that his grades had been "average." His wife later reported to us that Philip had had great difficulty in school. She also disclosed that she felt she could never depend on him, that she lived in constant fear of his being out of work again.

After a thorough evaluation, Philip was diagnosed with adult ADD and concomitant depression. His treatment consisted of not only neurofeedback, but also marriage therapy. Throughout the treatment, we relied heavily on his wife's report of progress. It took several months for Philip's brain to begin to respond. It finally kicked in and became balanced and flexible. Only then was Philip successful at finding a suitable job. His wife stayed and she reports that things are "much better."

Please Don't Stand Up and Give a Talk

Adults with ADHD are too easily distracted to give good talks. They are often bright, enthusiastic, and witty, but they ramble; boy, can they ramble. It is impossible for them to stay on track. If someone does something distracting, they are lost. For example, if asked a question, their answer is likely to go off in multiple unrelated directions, and they may or may not get back to their original topic.

A few years ago, we attended a conference on healing. At one point, a physician (who we are convinced has ADHD) stood up to make a quick comment. He went on for ten minutes. The speaker tried politely to end the filibuster but was unsuccessful. The audience became so impatient there was a mass cry for him to shut up and sit down. He missed those cues just as he had probably missed most social cues in his life.

Yes, there are ADHD physicians. There are ADHD engineers, dentists, therapists, and, frightfully, there are probably ADHD airplane pilots. Many people are able to compensate quite well by using dogged determination. They become single-minded and hyper-focused, much like the child with ADHD who plays video games. When the game starts, they go into hyper-focus and it is hard to get their attention. You may ask them over and over to stop and do something else, but they cannot respond to your request. It is a perseverative quality that locks them in to one thing and it is extremely difficult for them to refocus quickly. In such cases, there is a lack of flexibility both in behavior and in brainwaves. Neurofeedback allows the brain to restore balance and flexibility.

ADHD in a Marriage—and Chaos Prevails

Adults with ADHD have many more divorces than those without ADHD. They go into marriage with the same zeal with which they come up with ideas. "This is perfect" or "This is what I've been waiting for," and then, "I can't understand why she wants a divorce."

ADHD individuals bring the same disorganized qualities to a marriage that they take to work. They forget birthdays and anniversaries and can't understand why their mate is upset. They are baffled at why their partners are not excited about their new jobs. They never seem to clean up their messes; they leave their clothes, shoes, cups, and golf clubs all over the house. A simple project takes forever and may never get completed. They never have the tool they need because they can't find it or it is in the other room, left there from the last project. Often, if they can't find the tool, somebody else lost it or misplaced it, or it was stolen.

Over time, the symptoms of ADHD may cause a person to become quiet, withdrawn, depressed, and exhibit a beaten-down kind of personality. But they still continue to be inefficient, forgetful, and easily distracted; they will probably have trouble completing tasks like mowing the grass or cleaning the house. Many adults with ADHD have the feeling of being abused by the world. To function normally requires more energy than some can muster. Consider the following case.

Because we have a general practice, people frequently do not come in for neurofeedback, even though their problem indicates that neurofeedback would be the most effective treatment. Ann and Tom came in for marital therapy at Tom's insistence. He was ready to leave Ann if things did not change. Tom reported Ann was smart, loving, and pretty, "But she is a mess. The house is always in a state of half cleaned; the laundry is always half done; dinner is always half fixed—everything is 'half.'" Ann could never finish anything she started; she was disorganized, bored, and unfocused.

For her part, Ann reported she had been this way as long as she could remember. "Tom thought it was cute at first, but over time he has become angry about it," she said. After the initial intake evaluation, Ann was diagnosed with adult ADHD. Treatment in this case included neurofeedback and marital therapy. Neurofeedback could remedy the ADHD, depression, and motivation problems, but it could not teach Tom and Ann how to communicate clearly with each other. As Ann's symptoms improved, the marriage became more fulfilling for both of them.

ADHD and Driving—A Recipe for Disaster

ADHD people are individuals who cannot see consequences. They have five times more auto accidents than people without ADHD. Imagine this scenario. A parent sends an adolescent driver out at night with no medication because if they get the medication, they can't sleep. So a 3,500-pound automobile that can travel at speeds greater than a hundred miles per hour is in the hands of someone who has poor attentional skills. We believe no child or adult with ADHD should have a driver's license, unless they get neurofeedback treatment.

If people are aware they have ADHD, they may exercise more caution. The responsible person with ADHD is a more methodical driver and will compensate for their inattention. Others do not compensate or even realize their driving style is risk taking. Many people who have ADHD are often too distracted even to know they have a problem, but they may be a driving nightmare for everyone else on the road. People with ADHD are significantly more likely to have automobile accidents than people without it because people with ADHD often have trouble controlling their angry impulses. ADHD is a likely component in what is now labeled "road rage." Individuals with ADHD have less impulse control, so if they are presented with a situation that makes them angry, they may act on that angry impulse rather than control it.

This is so important, let's go over it again. To give a person with ADHD a driver's license is to put behind the wheel of a vehicle someone who, in varying degrees, is disorganized, unfocused, forgetful, highly distractible, and possibly irritable. They have a low frustration tolerance and they may be hyperactive. They want to go quickly, do a lot, bounce from place to place, and they resent anyone slowing them down. These same symptoms apply to both teenagers and adults, and are likely to lead to problems behind the wheel, such as accidents, tickets, and road rage.

We have had countless conversations with parents of ADHD teenagers about driver's licenses. ADHD teenagers, like most other teens, want their driver's permits as soon as humanly possible. They also like other motorized vehicles such as four-wheelers and motorcycles. Our advice to both parent and teenager is always treatment first; when the behaviors improve, then get a driver's license. When it comes to four-wheelers and motorcycles, we never encourage use of these because of the high injury rates associated with them. When a parent disregards our advice on getting a driver's license for a teenager with ADHD, we then recommend long periods of supervised driving, always accompanied by a parent.

It is even more important for adolescents with ADHD to establish good driving habits early. When they start driving on their own, there need to be strictly enforced rules, such as no driving after dark and only one other adolescent in the car at one time. We have seen a disproportionate number of accidents and injuries, even deaths, from drivers with ADHD. So we recommend a very cautious path.

Julie wanted her driver's license as badly as any other adolescent. She lobbied, pleaded, and negotiated from the time she turned fourteen. She had been diagnosed with ADHD when she was in the fourth grade, and in spite of four years of medication, there was little change in her behavior. Julie's mother brought her in when she was fifteen because of poor high school grades. Her parents were afraid she would eventually quit school. Then the question came up about her driver's license.

We recommended treatment first, then getting the license. Her parents gave in to her constant pleading, and she got her learner's permit in a few weeks. On Julie's first drive, she had a single-car accident. The car was a wreck, but fortunately, Julie and her mother were not hurt. Julie came back to treatment with her confidence shaken. We were able to make more progress after the accident than we had before because Julie acknowledged she had difficulty concentrating. We were all relieved that the situation had not been worse; it could have been disastrous.

ADHD in Jails

Although this statement will probably invite challenge, we strongly contend that our jails, prisons, and juvenile detention centers are full of ADHD adolescents and adults. After all, we are talking about risk-takers, individuals who have no fear but who cannot foresee consequences. It is easy to see that there is a recipe for disaster in the ADHD cluster of behaviors. The child who is prone to get in trouble and prone to accidents because of taking risks is now a late adolescent or adult who takes a different risk. The adult risks are bigger and the consequences greater.

There are not as many good follow-up studies as we would like to see, but the ones that are available are consistent in their findings. Brown and Borden did a study in 1986 that indicated that between 22 and 30 percent of hyperactive people engage in antisocial behavior.[1] That statistic could mean five or six million, or even more, adolescents acting out in antisocial ways, and the best prediction for future behavior is past behavior. Gittelman and colleagues found that antisocial behavior may be present in 20 to 45 percent of ADHD children by the time they reach adulthood.[2] The significance of that study indicates that as many as 25 percent of adults with ADHD would meet the criteria for a psychiatric diagnosis of antisocial personality disorder. The DSM-IV states "the essential feature of Antisocial Personality Disorder is a pervasive pattern of disregard for, and violation of, the rights of others that begins in childhood or early adolescence and continues into adulthood." Behaviors of this disorder include lying, stealing, impulsivity, aggression, recklessness, and lack of remorse.

Weiss and Hechtman conducted a three-year study that looked at adults who had been diagnosed with ADHD in childhood.[3] They found that those adults had much more likelihood of having trouble with the law and ending up in court. Approximately 20 percent of these adults committed physical acts of aggression.

No single childhood factor has been pinpointed as the predictor of adult criminal activity; there are several factors that play a role. The chief factor to be considered is the diagnosis of ADHD. Other factors included childhood aggression, intelligence, hyperactivity, conditions in the home, and parenting. There are a number of factors that play a role in human development and some of these include genetics, environmental factors, and even physical and emotional injury.

Interestingly, the reason that many felons are behind bars is because they have ADHD-type behavior; it is often the ADHD qualities and behavior that get them caught. They are forgetful, they are disorganized, and they can't pay attention. They leave behind clues, forget what they said before, and, in general, give themselves away. Ironically, sometimes there are police officers with ADHD looking for lawbreakers with ADHD. In fact, there are individuals with ADHD in every profession. We repeat that this undiagnosed, untreated population costs society a lot of money, to say nothing of the problems people with ADHD cause and the pain experienced by all associated.

Drugs, Alcohol, and ADHD

Alcohol, drugs, and ADHD are frequent companions. Virtually every study we have seen supports this conclusion, and it certainly holds up in our clinical practice. Using alcohol and drugs is an "easy" way to cope with difficult situations. As one of our twenty-year-old patients put it, "If you are numb, failure ain't so painful." Alcohol and drugs slow down the racing mind and provide a sense of calm.

More children with ADHD develop problems with alcohol and drugs than do children without ADHD.[4] This destructive behavior frequently carries over into adulthood; most late-adolescent substance abusers become adult substance abusers. Retrospective views of the problem reveal that alcoholics frequently have a history of childhood hyperactivity.[5]

Dale Walters, PhD, former director of training for the Menninger Clinic in Topeka, Kansas, traversed the United States during the 1990s, teaching clinicians how to treat alcoholism and drug addiction with neurofeedback. He worked closely with Eugene Peniston, PhD, who developed a specialized treatment protocol for alcoholism. The treatment was later expanded to include drug addiction and to treat Vietnam veterans with posttraumatic stress disorder. This treatment protocol has been shown to be the most promising treatment for alcoholism and drug addiction to date, with an astoundingly low, 20 percent relapse rate. Prior to this neurofeedback protocol, a 20 percent relapse rate was unheard of in the treatment of addictions.[6-8]

In patients with alcoholism or drug addiction, it is a good practice to look for a history of ADHD. In patients with ADHD, it is a good practice to learn coping skills that preclude the use of drugs and alcohol. Add alcohol or drugs to someone who is already impaired with ADHD and there is potential for disaster. We seldom see an alcoholic who doesn't have a history of ADHD. This, of course, increases the chances of auto crashes, failed jobs, failed marriages, and failed lives.

David Miller and Kenneth Blum, PhD, have done an outstanding job of looking at ADHD and the addictive brain in their classic book, *Overload.*[9] We suggest this book go to the top of your reading list if there is any history of alcohol or ADHD in your family.

A Hard Road

When we look at the personal lives of individuals with ADHD, we often find them to be sad and frustrating. The child frequently has headaches, sleeps poorly, and generally doesn't feel well. These problems are dramatically worsened if the child is on the standard treatment, a prescription for stimulant medication.

Both children and adults with ADHD miss out on many things. They do not pick up the normal social cues. For example, when we recently ushered a twenty-nine-year-old male into our office for an evaluation, he took the doctor's chair at the desk. He never realized this was not where he was supposed to sit. Individuals with ADHD seldom realize their inappropriate behavior.

In sports, people with ADHD can be both brilliant athletes and court jesters. They are fearless, and get into the thick of the fray with no hesitation; they often barrel over their teammates to get to the ball. If they are not knocking everybody down, interrupting the natural order of the game, or making a sensational play with pure ability, they are looking at flowers or some other distraction on the playing field, completely missing the game.

Frequently, the only safe place for the ADHD person is on the playing field. If they are able to combine all that hyperactivity with natural talent, they can become gifted athletes. Unfortunately, their lives off the field may be a mess. We have had college coaches tell us that three-fourths of their team members have ADHD. The pro ranks are filled with adults with ADHD. This is one of the reasons that professional athletes often make negative headlines for off-the-field behavior.

Studies have estimated that 30 percent of people with ADHD are depressed, 30 percent have an anxiety disorder, and 50 percent have conduct problems. This does not make for a happy life. Those with ADHD usually receive a lot of criticism. It seems that someone is always critical of their behavior and performance. If it's not a parent, it's a teacher; if it's not a teacher, it's a sibling. Their peers even criticize them. This is one of the reasons for the high levels of depression and anxiety.

As a result, they either withdraw or develop a "stand-back-I'd-rather-do-it-myself" attitude, which, of course, generally gets them in more trouble. The constant criticism also produces a lot of anger and hostility, and when they act on those angry impulses, they get in even more trouble. They get tired of being seen as, or feeling like, "damaged goods," and they rebel. All of these problems, we emphasize, are a result of a dysregulated brain. By regulating the brain with neurofeedback, we see the collateral damage of depression, anxiety, and anger resolve.

The ADHD Solution

Regulating the brain to a more functional pattern may not fix the individual stresses in the life of the person with ADHD, but at least the brain can take a more active role in problem solving. Untreated, the individual may be driven ever deeper into nonfunctional and slow brainwave patterns.

Neurofeedback is a treatment that can normalize the dysfunctional or injured brain. For example, if the brain is too slowed down, causing a state of low arousal and ADHD-type symptoms, neurofeedback can train the brain to speed up its activity level. This is done by feeding back information to the brain about how the brain is functioning, and rewarding the person with a sound or score for any improvement. Teaching by rewarding appropriate behavior is called operant conditioning. With this simple operant conditioning procedure, the brain begins to regulate itself, and undesirable behaviors begin to modify. We discuss this training procedure in detail in chapter 17.

5

The Source of the Problem

The big question haunting researchers and professionals who treat ADHD is how does ADHD start in the first place? There have been a number of theories and hypotheses over the years, but they generally explain only a part of the problem. The theories have ranged from the silly to the scientific, each having its basis in the assumptions of the observer.

Popular Theories

Let's explore some of the more popular theories.

The Bad Child: The earliest description that characterized ADHD came at the turn of the twentieth century. In 1902, G. F. Still published an article in the British medical journal *Lancet*.[1] He described in detail children who exhibited symptoms of ADD/ADHD and labeled them as having "abnormal defects in moral control . . . and wanton mischievousness and destructiveness." This was the notion of the "bad child," born "bad," and there was nothing you could do about it.

Even today, one hundred years later, there are still those who believe that some children are born with "deficits in moral control." The only factor that would offer even an element of credibility to this early theory is genetics. If this is the case, then these children are destined to live out the genetic predisposition passed down to them. Regardless of genetics, a motto that every adult should consider is that if the child doesn't learn, then the adult has not taught. Adults cannot change the genetic code, but good teaching and good modeling can alter the life course of most children.

Family Discord: A second theory that has enjoyed a lot of support is the family discord model. The theory suggests that a chaotic family life or marital discord in the family causes the children affected by those stressors to become ADHD.[2-3] This is also the case when psychiatric problems in the parents are a factor in the marital discord. Children need a stable environment, predictability, and an element of constancy. Families that have chronic marital discord lack that sense of predictability, at least that sense of comfortable predictability. Often the children are left to parent themselves; the parents are too busy trying to take care of themselves and neglect the children. Emotional abandonment can be as bad as, if not worse than, physical abandonment. It is hard to grow up healthily in an unhealthy environment.

When the noise and chaos in a family reach a certain level, children are likely to tune it out. They do this by slowing down their brain; the slowed brain is less alert to and less impacted by what is going on. It is slow brainwave rhythms that characterize ADHD. In our clinics, we have seen the same slow brainwave patterns in children who are yelled at constantly. Not surprisingly, we have also seen this in verbally and physically abused spouses. It is possible to conclude that anyone who lives in chaos and discord could suffer an emotional brain injury and exhibit many classic ADHD-type symptoms.

No ADHD in the First Place: Perhaps the most disturbing theory of all is the theory that there is no such thing as ADHD. Even today in our clinic, we have people say, "There is nothing wrong with him; he just needs a good kick in the pants," or some other colorful phrase indicating there is no problem except not enough discipline. The idea that a child can be spanked out of this syndrome is not only offensive, but also ludicrous. Chronic verbal and corporal punishment just drives the brain deeper into a slow brainwave state.

This is a survival mechanism, but if it happens enough, it becomes the "new normal" and the brain loses its flexibility.

Contrary to the assertions in articles like Schmitt's 1975 "The Minimal Brain Dysfunction Myth,"[4] ADHD does exist. Schmitt even goes so far as to say that ADHD is a fabrication by distressed parents, teachers, and physicians to allow them to medicate disruptive children. We are the first to concede that thousands of children are needlessly medicated, but that does not mean that we are not dealing with the real issue of a dysregulated brain. Sadly, some children are actually medicated for the sake of adults, but ADHD is not a myth conjured up by distraught teachers, parents, and physicians. ADHD is identifiable by a well-designed checklist, and brain maps can show actual dysregulation in the brain.

Poor Parenting: The theory that has the most popular support as the cause of ADHD is that of poor parenting. It is difficult to discount the notion that poor parenting creates difficulties for children because, in fact, it does. Years of psychiatric and psychological work and countless research articles have been enough to convince us this is true. We the authors do not believe, however, that parents are the root of all evil. We have worked with ADHD children who had great parents as well as those who had less-than-adequate parents. We are convinced that it is highly unlikely that poor parenting is the causative factor.

Now, before we go further, we would like to point out that ADHD can become like a runaway train if parenting is inadequate. Good parenting skills can dramatically alter the course of a child with ADHD. This may be why ADHD children can grow up, go to college, and lead normal, functional lives. Good parenting is able to set boundaries and teach children how to compensate; it can instill good values and model good behavior. By contrast, poor and neglectful parenting gives the ADHD child a world with no boundaries in which risk taking escalates and respect is nonexistent.

In general, poor parenting can lead to children who are uncontrollable, disrespectful, undisciplined, and neurotic. Their brain dysfunction may be a result of the way they interpret the world based on how it was presented to them by dysfunctional parents. In some cases, we have seen ADHD behavior in children who did not have the typical slow-wave brain patterns seen in ADHD. Our conclusion is that poor parenting can dramatically affect the outcome of ADHD children in negative ways. We also concede that in some cases the brain injury may be due to a tragic home situation. Children who are abused can suffer the physical or emotional injuries that lead to classic ADHD-type behaviors. One of the greatest problems with poor parenting is that intolerant parents usually don't realize that they are bad parents. We have had many cases in which the parent(s) scream and yell how much they love their children and how important they are, and then they go home and scream and yell some more. The problem with dysfunctional people is that they usually don't know they are dysfunctional.

Environmental Influences: With the growing global awareness of how we are affected by toxins, synthetic substances, and pollutants in the environment comes the theory that ADHD is caused by environmental factors. At this point in time, this theory cannot be completely ruled out or completely supported because nowhere near all the data is in. This is a theory that will be examined and reexamined for a very long time to come. New understanding in molecular biology, toxicology, and human sensitivities may lead to deeper insights into ADHD as well as other disorders and diseases.

To say with confidence that sugar, food additives, dyes, preservatives, and other such products do not cause ADHD-type symptoms is scientific foolishness. We remember vividly an eight-year-old boy who was very physically aggressive. During the intake interview, we noticed a constant runny nose. When we asked his mother about it, she reported that he always had a runny nose. We recommended no dairy of any kind for two weeks. The mother was compliant, and she reported back to us that when he had no dairy, he had no runny nose, plus his aggression was dramatically improved. This is just one case in a complicated array of cases, but environmental agents can affect certain individuals.

We are just scratching the surface of how some individuals are affected by certain products. We are well aware of how humans and wildlife are affected by deadly toxins like lead, dioxin, and mercury, but we suspect that that is just the tip of the iceberg. Recent reports have revealed that water supplies contain dozens of prescription drugs in addition to toxins we have known about for years. We have no idea how these drugs will affect humans and other species, much less the vulnerable nervous systems of children.

The notion of allergies and toxic reactions causing problems such as ADHD got a big boost in the mid-1970s when Dr. Ben Feingold's book *Why Your Child Is Hyperactive* was published.[5] Since that time, the Feingold Association has done much to promote the idea of feeding children pure foods. We are in sympathy with this cause. Even if red dye #3 or some other product does not cause ADHD, it could be a contributing factor in some other diseases and disorders. Even if not causative, many drugs, chemicals, and toxins could exacerbate ADHD and autistic symptoms. The jury is still out on this connection, so in the meantime, we think it is best to keep our water, air, and food as pure as possible.

Meanwhile, theories of environmental causes for ADHD are receiving increasing interest. Though no single factor has clearly been shown to cause ADHD, ultimately some of the environmental factors may. Environmental theories include nutritional causes, toxic chemical exposure, TV, video games, video monitors, fluorescent lighting, chemical additives, and other environmental hazards. Even though we have no clear and direct cause-and-effect relationships at this time, we want to know as much as possible about the child's lifestyle, eating habits, and exposure to the aforementioned environmental factors before we initiate treatment in our clinics.

Knowing about these factors may help to direct our treatment protocols and parental recommendations. We hope all parents and treating professionals will examine not only the child's eating habits, but also such things as TV viewing, exposure to chemical additives, and other environmental factors.

Genetics: The idea that ADHD is a genetic disorder is well grounded in the scientific literature. We in the mental health field have long accepted the notion that certain psychological problems such as alcoholism, depression, anxiety, and antisocial problems run in families. Beginning in the 1970s, research data began to support this observation.[6-7] What is clear, though, is that the genetic relationship of ADHD is not as strong as the genetic relationship of conduct disorders and antisocial behavior. When you have a person with both ADHD and conduct disorder, the genetic relationship is a stronger one.

In a study examining the parents of fifty-nine hyperactive children, J. R. Morrison and M. A. Stewart concluded that fathers of ADHD children had a greater incidence of antisocial personality disorder when compared to the control group; mothers, on the other hand had a greater incidence of histrionic personality disorder.[8] Histrionic personality disorder is characterized by excessive emotions and attention-seeking behavior. There was a much higher incidence of alcoholism in both parents of ADHD children than in parents in the control group. This study lends support not only to the genetics theory, but also to the family discord and poor parenting theories.

Looking at brothers and sisters of ADHD children, there are a number of studies indicating that if one child is ADHD, there is approximately a 30 percent chance that brothers and sisters will be ADHD. Again, studies like this not only support the theory of genetic transmission, but they also leave open the question of learned behaviors. Did the child inherit the ADHD or conduct disorder, or did the child learn the behaviors from watching the parents and siblings exhibit such behaviors?

The most convincing evidence for the genetic theory comes from a large study of twins. Goodman and Stevenson compared 127 monozygotic (identical) with 111 dizygotic (fraternal) pairs of twins.[9] The researchers found 51 percent of the monozygotic twins to be hyperactive, compared with 33 percent of the dizygotic pairs.

We believe that genetics plays a role in ADHD. Not only can ADHD behaviors run in families, but the susceptibility to acquiring brain dysfunction can get passed from generation to generation. This susceptibility factor puts children at risk from a host of injuries, from trauma to a toxic family environment. In a disorder that is as disruptive and pervasive as ADHD, all types of injury and dysfunction must be considered.

In more thoroughly examining the case for genetics in ADHD, Dr. David Comings has written a classic work, *Tourette Syndrome and Human Behavior.*[10] Dr. Comings has taken our understanding of the role of genetics in these disorders to new heights. This is a complex text but is well worth reading, particularly for health professionals. Dr. Comings clearly outlines the role of genetics in ADHD as well as other disorders, including Tourette's syndrome, alcoholism, bad conduct, anxiety, depression, schizophrenia, obesity, sleep problems, and personality disorders. Many of these other disorders are closely associated with ADHD.

When working with children, we frequently spot ADHD in the parents, usually undiagnosed. Our staff frequently tells us which parent has the ADHD before we even see the child for evaluation.

Brain Injury: The last major theory, which has a strong scientific basis, holds that brain injury can cause ADHD-type behavior. This injury can be structural, functional, or both. A structural disorder is when the brain is physically damaged, as with a heavy blow to the head. These injuries usually show up on hospital diagnostic imaging such as MRIs. The functional injury relates to how the brain is functioning. For example, there may be no structural damage, but the brainwaves are dysregulated. These disorders usually do not show up on MRIs or CT scans. We believe that the functional type of injury is much more prominent in ADHD. The brain's physical structure may appear normal on conventional diagnostic imaging.

As a matter of fact, almost all of the ADHD patients we have seen over the years have had normal CT scans and normal EEGs. But when we break the EEG down into functional bandwidths (a specific range of the EEG) at specific sites on the head, we usually see abnormal patterns in people with ADHD as well as other disorders. Examples of abnormal patterns are often seen in the low bandwidth range of four to seven cycles per second or the higher bandwidth above eighteen cycles per second. The dominant frequency in a bandwidth will have a profound effect on the behavior of the individual.

A functional injury generally relates to the timing of the brain; the brain is not producing the appropriate brainwaves for the task at hand. What if the brain is slowed down or is too fast? How will this affect behavior? For example, what if the person is trying to go to sleep and the brain is producing a faster, alerting-type wave? What if a child is trying to pay attention in class and the brain is producing a slow, sleep-type wave? Will the person be able to accomplish the task at hand? Not likely. So, in a functional injury, although the structure of the brain appears normal, it is functioning at an inappropriate level. This would be much like having a new car in which the engine's timing is wrong. The car looks great, but it does not function properly.

The idea that ADHD is a manifestation of a brain injury, in our opinion, is the most productive theory about this disorder. This theory was reflected in the diagnostic term minimal brain dysfunction (MBD). We remind you that the term MBD was later changed to the descriptive term attention-deficit/hyperactivity disorder, to describe the nature of the dysfunction rather than to reflect the etiology of the disorder.

There are numerous causes of functional injury to the brain. The first and most common is physical trauma. We have seen many ADHD children with histories of head bangs, hits, falls, and accidents. One adult female with severe ADHD reported a concussion as a result of a minor motorcycle accident. After the accident, she became even more prone to take risks, and consequently suffered three additional head injuries. Most of the ADHD children we have seen did not report what we would term "significant head trauma," but many reported jolts, hits, and bangs that might have been sufficient to alter their brain's rhythmic functioning.

Other types of injury that could be responsible for functional problems are toxic exposure, nutritional deficiencies, hypoxic/anoxic trauma (an interruption in the flow of oxygen to the brain), genetics, difficult pregnancy or birth complications, and infections. The severe influenza epidemic of 1918 resulted in many children who developed influenza-related encephalitis. In the 1920s, researchers began to notice an increase in ADHD-type behavior and conduct disorders.[11] The increase in these two disorders was attributed to the influenza epidemic, and this gave credence to the idea of an infection-related brain injury. Often in our clinical work, parents report that their children with ADHD had, at some point in their lives, a severe infection, usually accompanied by high fever.

We contend that brain injury from toxic metals and other pollutant exposure is much more commonplace than is scientifically accepted. Toxic levels of such heavy metals as lead and mercury have long been known to cause behavioral problems in children. We discuss the implications of exposure to other toxic materials in chapter 19 and the role of nutrition in brain function in chapter 18.

Pregnancy and birth trauma have been suspected in this causative hunt for a long time. The research generally supports the theory that there is a higher incidence of ADHD-type behavior in children who have had problems during the gestational period or during delivery.[12] Our clinical findings indicate that the problems are often related to such phenomena as a difficult pregnancy, long or hard labor, fetal distress, forceps delivery, anoxia, and jaundice. Clinical findings are what the treating professional observes in the clinic, however, and are not always confirmed by research data.

Parents of our ADHD children often relate birth stories like "The cord was wrapped around his neck two times," "He was blue as could be," or "I was in hard labor for twenty-six hours." More often than not, the APGAR scores (a way of measuring a newborn's progress in terms of coloring, heart rate, respiration, reflexes, and muscle tone) were normal, but parents report that some kind of difficulty occurred during the birth. APGAR scores are given to newborns at one minute and five minutes after birth. The higher the APGAR score, the better the condition of the infant.

The fact that some children go through difficult births and have no problems whereas others experience difficulty and become ADHD may suggest a genetic predisposition or a vulnerability to such difficulty. The fact remains, however, that there is a greater incidence of ADHD in children who experienced birth difficulties.

Stress Injury: Stress may play a greater role in ADHD than previously considered. The EEGs of people under stress show that these individuals begin to produce faster brainwaves (15 Hz and higher) in the beta range. This busy activity is designed to problem-solve and reduce feelings of stress. In essence, the brain kicks into a higher gear, becoming more alert and aroused. If the brain adapts to the stressor or solves the problem, it appears to become more comfortable and moves down to a lower frequency range. This seems to be good for the ego; there is now an element of positive self-esteem in knowing one has solved the problem. There is a calming of the stress response, and the person produces more relaxed, alpha-type waves.

If, however, the brain does not adapt to the stressor but instead feels assaulted, it ceases its busy activity and slips far down the continuum to the very low frequency ranges. It goes into that foggy theta world (4–7 Hz range), which is the frequency of pre-sleep. In some cases, the brain keeps increasing its activity until the busy work becomes anxiety. So, under chronic unsolvable stress, the brain either slows down to pre-sleep and sleep waves or speeds up to the faster worry and anxiety waves. In the low-frequency ranges, we find reduced alertness, difficulty learning, reduced quality and quantity of thought, depression, attentional problems, and learning deficits. These are all consistent with the ADHD symptom picture. For a more thorough look at brainwave states and the correlating behavior, see figure 5.1 on page 88.

In our clinic, we see a recurring pattern, namely that children and adults who are constantly exposed to stress develop a pattern of low-frequency brainwaves. The brain begins to make more low-frequency (slow) brainwaves and fewer mid-range frequency (somewhat faster) brainwaves. As noted earlier, the brains of children and adults exposed to chronic yelling, threats, physical abuse, critical remarks, or tasks that seem overwhelming appear to go into low-frequency waves. In our clinical experience, it seems that exposure to chronic stress causes the human brain to either zone out or become hyper and anxious.

One day in the clinic, we decided to test the hypothesis that stress causes a slowing of brainwaves. We took two children with whom we were doing neurofeedback and asked their parents to assist with the training. We purposely selected two children who had what we considered demanding, autocratic parents. (Incidentally, both fathers were professionals, one an attorney and the other a physician.) We invited the parents to sit in on their children's training sessions.

A short time into the first training session, both children began to increase theta waves and decrease beta waves. This reflects a slowing down of brainwaves. Both parents "coached" their children with typical remarks like, "pay attention, sit up straight, don't talk, and don't look at me." This type of coaching went on for the entire training and it drove the children straight into theta. We concluded that in this slowed-down state, the children tuned out the obsessive-compulsive training style of their parents. This was obviously not a scientific experiment, but it did satisfy our hunch. Before we draw any hard and fast scientific conclusions, we would add that we have had many children, as well as adults, drift into the low ranges during training.

A milieu of continual demands and threats placed upon children and adults appears to dramatically exacerbate ADHD-type symptoms. It either makes them dull and unproductive or anxious and unproductive. Life is not fun in theta, but at least it is quiet and not particularly threatening.

We hypothesize that much of the depression and ADHD-type symptoms we see is a result of individuals feeling overwhelmed, threatened, or constantly faced with tasks that seem too large or too difficult. It is easier to let the brain slow down so the person can "zone out" or, as we call it, "go underground." Many children who feel overwhelmed become depressed over time, and they appear to have ADHD. They often end up diagnosed with ADHD and are prescribed a variety of medications, particularly stimulant medications, which can make their condition worse.

Earlier we talked about genetic injury to the brain. We would like to clarify what we mean by this. A genetic brain injury is an injury or a dysfunction that is passed from one generation to another. In working with ADHD children, we often feel we are working with second- or third-generation pathology. Because our office staff frequently gets to observe the parents while we are treating the child, it has become commonplace for us to ask them which parent of the ADHD child has ADHD. As mentioned, the office staff frequently observes ADHD-characteristic behavior in the parent(s) before we do.

Many times we have ended up treating both the child and the parent(s), and this usually produces a profound change in the family dynamics. After treatment, we no longer have a person with obvious ADHD symptoms parenting a child with ADHD. When we are able to treat all the family members with ADHD, things at home go more smoothly. In cases like this, we usually recommend brief family therapy or parent training to go along with the neurofeedback.

Rhythms Tell the ADHD Story

Since there appear to be no differences in the brain structure of people with and without ADHD,[13] how does the injury show up, other than in their behavior? In 1938, Jasper, Solomon, and Bradley published an article demonstrating that there were abnormalities in the brainwaves of minimal brain dysfunction children.[14] This was the first evidence of a functional injury as opposed to structural damage. Over the next thirty years, there were a number of articles indicating that the EEGs of people with ADHD and conduct disorders were abnormal. The general findings were that they had brainwaves similar to people with epileptic seizures and a generalized slowing of the brainwaves, meaning that the brain was slowed down, not as active or alert as it should be.

The idea that the brainwaves of people with ADHD are slower than non-ADHD individuals helped to explain why children were improved when Bradley administered the stimulant amphetamine sulfate.[15] Even today, that is the basis for administering amphetamine drugs such as Ritalin to people with ADHD. There is a generalized slowing of the brainwaves in people with this disorder, so amphetamines speed up the brain and the problem is temporarily "solved." But of course, it is not solved at all.

It was not until 1971, when Satterfield and colleagues proposed the "low-arousal hypothesis," that other treatment modalities were looked at seriously.[16-17] The low-arousal hypothesis basically says that hyperactive children are in a low state of arousal, not very awake or aware of what is going on around them, so they tend to be hyperactive to wake up, to be in the world.

Dr. Barry Sterman's work had a profound impact on the development of a theoretical model for ADHD. His work consisted of using neurofeedback to train people with seizure disorders to produce different brainwaves, thereby reducing their seizure activity. Dr. Sterman demonstrated that people with the low-frequency brainwave burst that produces seizures can be trained to produce higher-frequency brainwaves. Rather than producing excessive brainwaves in the slow four- to seven-hertz range, they were trained to produce more brainwaves in the area of fourteen hertz. Since there are some brainwave features common to both seizure disorders and ADHD, Dr. Sterman's work added more credibility to the theory that ADHD is a functional disorder, involving the timing of the brain[18-23] (see figure 5.1).

Dr. Joel Lubar at the University of Tennessee saw this relationship very clearly and, after working with Dr. Sterman for several months, began applying his model to children with ADHD. Dr. Lubar and his wife, Judith, began training children using brainwave biofeedback to reduce the four- to seven-hertz range and increase the brainwaves above fourteen hertz. When the ADHD children learned this, there was a significant reduction in ADHD-type symptoms. The implications of this early research were profound. This research added credibility to the low-arousal hypothesis and pointed to the idea that ADHD was a functional disorder, not a structural disorder, and was caused by dysfunctional brain rhythms.[24-26]

Figure 5.1. Brainwave Frequency Bands and Related Behaviors

cps = cycles per second, or Hertz

DELTA Less than 4 cps	THETA 4–8 cps	ALPHA 8–12 cps	SMR 12–15 cps	BETA 15–18 cps	HIGH BETA more than 19 cps
Sleep	Drowsy	Relaxed Focus	Relaxed Thought	Active Thinking	Excited

Depression, ADHD, and seizure activity in this range.

We train the brain to move into this range to modify symptoms of depression, ADHD, and improve seizure activity.

After All Is Said and Done, What Is the Cause?

After all this research, what is the cause of ADHD and ADHD-related behavior? We have concluded that it is an injury of some sort. It may be a genetic predisposition to brain injury passed from one generation to another. It may be a traumatic brain injury caused by a kick, knock, bang, hit, or fall. It may be a result of some injury sustained in utero or during delivery. It may be an injury sustained during exposure to a toxic environmental element. It could also be emotional injury resulting from growing up in a family where stress and chaos reign. ADHD and ADHD-type symptoms are manifestations of a slowing of the brainwaves, and this slowing is a result of some type of injury.

Practitioners

Everyone with good training in neurofeedback is taught how to treat ADHD. So in most cases of ADHD, any properly licensed neurofeedback provider is capable of treating this disorder competently. This is not to say ADHD is a simple disorder; it is an extremely complex disorder. It is standard, however, to train new neurofeedback therapists in the treatment of ADHD. There are now, all over the United States, neurofeedback providers who can reach the "unreachable" child. We would, however, like to introduce you to a few outstanding providers with whom we have had the pleasure of working or whom we know by their outstanding reputations.

Lynda Thompson, PhD, is a child psychologist in Toronto, Canada. In addition to being the director of the ADD Centre in Toronto, she is the coauthor with William Sears, MD, of *The A.D.D. Book,* a rich and informative must-read for anyone dealing with this pervasive disorder. Other practitioners who have come to our attention are Rob Coben of Massapequa Park, New York; Larry Hirshberg of Providence, Rhode Island; Gary Schummer of Torrance, California; Roger deBeus of Asheville, North Carolina; Randy Lyle of San Antonio, Texas; Barbara Muller-Ackerman at the Parsippany Counseling Center in Parsippany, New Jersey; and Sue and Siegfried Othmer at the EEG Institute (www.eeginfo.com). These are just a very few members of the rapidly growing field of neurofeedback who provide services to people with ADHD and other dysregulation disorders.

We would like to recognize two of the earliest pioneers in the field treating ADHD and other dysregulation disorders. The first person we would like to present is psychologist Douglas A. Quirk. He did pioneering work in the field of biofeedback and neurofeedback in Toronto, Canada, in the 1950s and 1960s. Douglas Quirk is no longer with us, but it was his work that demonstrated that the field of neurofeedback was safe and effective. Without his work, the development of this treatment would have occurred much more slowly. He developed what he called Stimulus Condition Autonomic Repression. When he worked at the Ontario Corrections Institute, he saw a total of 2,776 inmates and his treatment dramatically reduced the rate of recidivism.

George Von Hilsheimer, PhD, was a close associate of Douglas Quirk and he has continued to do neurofeedback work. Dr. Von Hilsheimer and Douglas Quirk were using biofeedback and neurofeedback long before most of us were even aware of some of the techniques. He has had a most distinguished career and has contributed three books to the field: *How to Live with Your Special Child, Is There a Science of Behavior?* and *Allergy, Toxins, and the Learning-Disabled Child.* Dr. Von Hilsheimer has retired from his very busy practice, but as he says, "I keep two machines at home and I still see a few people." Neurofeedback is very powerful and most of us cannot let it go because it is so effective and exciting.

Though Dr. Von Hilsheimer is no longer in practice, his "practice" is in his home in Maitland, Florida.

6

Checklists for Assessing Difficulties and Following Progress

When a person receives treatment for any disorder, they should know, with some degree of certainty, whether the treatment had any effect, positive or negative. All too often, people receive treatment for some problem and end up just guessing as to whether or not it helped. In order to help diagnose the childhood disorders we have been discussing and to evaluate the progress of treatments, we developed checklists for most of the disorders. It was important for us to know how good this new treatment was. We wanted simple checklists that would give us a clear picture of the problem areas and assess the severity of each problem. We also wanted to be able to follow related problems in the cluster.

With much trial and error, we have developed checklists that can be used by parents and health-care professionals. Our checklists are always a work in progress. We have modified them a number of times and we are sure they will continue to evolve. Our checklists were not designed to replace the DSM-IV, but rather to augment it and to give concerned individuals and treating professionals a picture of what they are dealing with and how symptoms interact and change with treatment. In *Getting Rid of Ritalin*, we had the checklist in one long two-sided sheet. Many people reported to us that this was too cumbersome and even overwhelming to some people. So in this book, we have broken the checklists down problem by problem. After each problem section, you will find a brief checklist(s) related specifically to the target area. What we encourage you to do is to fill out each separate checklist just to make sure that the area we are discussing is not a collateral problem in a wide cluster of problems. At the end of this section, you will find a summary sheet. List all the percentages from the individual checklists; this will give you a visual picture of the difficulties in areas of the cluster.

Efficiency in the treatment is one thing we work hard on, so a checklist is invaluable. We use the checklists to help us determine the starting positions for the neurofeedback and use them again and again to determine how the feedback protocols change. As a general rule, we redo the checklists at least every ten training sessions. It takes more time on our part and for the patient, but it usually pays off in the long run by reducing the number of sessions needed to ameliorate the problem.

There are several good checklists available, but they are usually very specific and relate to only one problem. We wanted to cover not only the main problems, but also problems in the greater cluster. We wanted a broader picture of what was going on, so we decided to develop our own. We sat down with the files of the people we had treated with neurofeedback. This was about eight years' worth of charts. We separated them into diagnostic categories; then we started listing the symptoms and arranging the symptoms under specific diagnostic categories. This was most enlightening because we began to see how a single diagnosis was accompanied by symptoms from multiple diagnostic categories. It really reinforced our idea of cluster groups or what we refer to as global dysregulation. Doing it this way, for example, we could see how ADHD children had clusters groups that included things like depression, anxiety, oppositional/defiant, and other disorders all mingled under a single diagnostic category. Many children could qualify for any one of several diagnoses. Seeing the picture from this perspective often caused us to grapple with what to treat first. Did the depression cause the anxiety or were patients depressed because they had been anxious for a long time? There were many times we did not know what came first, "the chicken or the egg." In the end, however, it worked out okay because with neurofeedback protocols we were always treating the cluster and not a single problem.

We decided to design a checklist that gave us percentages rather than cutoff scores. Checklists with cutoff scores are more absolute; that is, if the score is above a certain number, you have the disorder, and if the score is below that number, you do not have the disorder. We never liked the absoluteness of these checklists. If a person misses the cutoff by one point, does that mean the person is not affected by the symptoms he or she listed? By using a percentage score, you can more easily assess the severity of the problem. For example, if a person has a score of 85 percent on the impulsivity category, you can conclude the problem is severe. Whereas, if the score was only 27 percent, you can conclude there is some impulsivity, but it is not severe. In our opinion, a 27 percent score does not mean we can ignore the symptoms listed there; it just means that that will not be our primary focus. Our primary focus will most likely be on the 85 percent categories, but we will monitor all the other categories with lower percentages. This is because, as treatment progresses, the picture changes. A tic disorder may be what the child was brought in for, but as the tics resolve, you begin to see that there are serious problems with attention, impulsivity, or anxiety.

We also wanted a checklist that gave a broader overview of how the person is functioning in many different areas of life. The checklists are simple to use and they are usually completed by parents, guardians, and the treating professional. The consistent pattern that emerged in our clinic is that Mom rated the child worse than did Dad, who did not see as many problems. This seemed to relate directly to time spent with the child: The more time a parent spent with a child, the worse the rating. Occasionally, if you have an absentee parent, as in a noninterested, noncustodial parent who was paying for the treatment, that parent may see very little wrong with the child. These are often the cases in which parents are blaming each other for being poor parents. Neurotherapists tend to have the most accurate ratings because they see many cases of each disorder and therefore have something with which to compare each case. There are some unusual circumstances in which we have someone other than a parent fill out the checklists. For example, in the case of an adult ADHD patient, we may have the spouse or even a sibling fill out the checklists.

Instructions for using the checklists are simple: Each category is scored on a scale of "not present (0)," "very mild (1)," "mild (2)," "moderate (3)," "severe (4)," or "very severe (5)." Tally the score in the category by adding all the numbers in the blocks together, and then figure the percentage for each category. For example, if you end up with a score of 70 points in the ADHD checklist, which has a maximum of 110 points, by dividing 70 by 110, you have a 63 percent problem rating. This gives you a reasonable idea of the severity of the ADHD symptoms. If 100 percent is very severe, the 63 percent figure is in the moderate range. If the score is 22 percent, that is in the very mild range. If the score is 93 percent, the symptoms are very severe. Although this is subjective scoring, it gives you an idea of the level of severity you are working with in each category. The neurofeedback training protocols determine where the sensors are placed on the scalp and what brainwave bandwidth is reinforced and inhibited. By seeing the percentage scores of the checklists, the therapist gathers more information for determining which protocols are used.

The repeating of the checklist is also an excellent way of measuring progress. For example, if we are treating a person with endogenous depression, we look carefully at the depression checklist. If the depression is going down, it is reasonable to assume we are using the correct protocol. If depression is unchanged, however, but the anxiety percentage is going up, we can conclude we are using the wrong protocol. We occasionally have parents who complain that their child has made no progress, for example, "He still doesn't do his homework." By looking at the entire cluster of symptoms, we might see that he no longer has all the tics he came in with and has not been in a fight for weeks. When we do this, parents often acknowledge that they had completely forgotten about certain symptoms. It is easy to forget about symptoms when they are no longer seen on a daily basis. And remember that parents sometimes have problems of their own and may miss things that are going on with their children. It is easy to miss the problems your children are dealing with if you are busy dealing with your own issues.

When you are initially filling out the checklist, you do not need to figure the percentages to know there is a problem. Just "eyeball" the numbers and you will see the areas of dysfunction. You also do not need to be told the child's problem. You can see everything for yourself. This checklist provides a graphic representation of the symptoms. As you progress through each checklist, however, it is helpful to figure the percentages and transfer them to the master sheet at the end of this section. This will give you and your therapist a good baseline to work from.

This scoring method is not beneficial in tic disorders or developmental and learning disorders. If a child has any tic, consider it severe and make sure it is addressed. For example, if a child licks his lips until they are red and sore, that is a severe or very severe problem. Parents and therapist alike must use judgment and look at the checklists sensibly. If the checklists are completed at home, take them to the physician and/or to the nearest neurofeedback therapist. The checklists will help your physician if there are medications to be prescribed; they will give clues to your neurofeedback therapist as to where to place the EEG sensors and what EEG brainwave frequency or frequency bands they want to increase or decrease. Figure 6.1 on the next page is an example of a completed checklist.

Now is a good time to begin filling out checklists. We start with the checklists related to ADHD. These include attention deficit, hyperactivity, and impulsivity. Fill out these three checklists and record the results on the checklist summary chart (see figures 6.2–3). There is a checklist at the end of most sections in the following chapter. After filling each out, score it, and record the percentage in the master sheet below. This will give you a global picture of the problems you are dealing with.

Figure 6.1. Sample Checklists

I - Attention Deficit

	not present 0	very mild 1	mild 2	mod. 3	severe 4	very severe 5
Does not seem to listen when spoken to				✓		
Makes careless errors in schoolwork				✓		
Avoids or dislikes tasks requiring sustained attention				✓		
Short attention span					✓	
Disorganised				✓		
Loses things				✓		
Trouble keeping up with personal property				✓		
Easily distracted					✓	
Forgetful in daily activity			✓			
Difficulty completing tasks				✓		
Gets bored easily				✓		
Stares into space/daydreaming					✓	
Low energy, sluggish or drowsy		✓				
Apathetic or unmotivated			✓			
Frequently switches from one activity to another					✓	
Trouble concentrating					✓	
Falls asleep doing work		✓				
Failure to hand in work					✓	
Trouble doing homework					✓	
Trouble following directions				✓		
Excited in the beginning but doesn't finish				✓		
Difficulty learning				✓		
TOTAL	0	3	10	24	16	0

53/110 = 48%

II - Hyperactivity

	not present 0	very mild 1	mild 2	mod. 3	severe 4	very severe 5
Fidgets with hands and feet					✓	
Squirms in seat					✓	
Frequently leaves seat inappropriately					✓	
Runs, climbs or moves excessively					✓	
Difficulty working or playing quietly					✓	
On the go					✓	
Driven					✓	
Talks excessively					✓	
Can't sustain eye contact				✓		
Needs a lot of supervision				✓		
Pays attention to everything				✓		
Frequently "rocks"			✓			
Excitability				✓		
Lacks patience					✓	
In trouble frequently				✓		
Restless					✓	
TOTAL	0	1	6	4	36	0

47/80 = 58%

III - Impulsivity

	not present 0	very mild 1	mild 2	mod. 3	severe 4	very severe 5
Cannot see consequences of behavior					✓	
Blurts out answers or comments					✓	
Difficulty waiting turn					✓	
Frequently interrupts					✓	
Butts into others' conversation						✓
Engages in physically dangerous activity				✓		
Acts before thinking				✓		
Frequently takes risks				✓		
Takes all dares					✓	
Frustrated easily					✓	
TOTAL	0	0	6	6	12	5

29/50 = 58%

At a glance, you will be able to determine the problem areas and the severity of the problems in these categories. The three checklists are taken from the chart of a nine-year-old patient seen in our clinic. The Attention-Deficit checklist had a raw score of 53 points out of a possible 110, giving him a 48 percent score. This score falls roughly in the moderate range of Attention Deficit and is certainly in the range requiring treatment. On the Hyperactivity checklist, he had a raw score of 47 points out of a possible 80, giving him a 58 percent score. Lastly, on the Impulsivity checklist, there was a raw score of 29 out of a possible 50 points, yielding a percentage score of 58 percent. It is obvious that this child had slightly more difficulty with hyperactivity and impulsivity than he did with attention. Both the hyperactivity and impulsivity clustered in the severe range. We can also see that there are attentional deficiencies. Knowing the raw score and the percentage helps the therapist determine the starting protocol to be used in treatment.

*Figure 6.2. The Attention-Deficit, Hyperactivity,
and Impulsivity Checklists*

I - **Attention Deficit**	not present 0	very mild 1	mild 2	mod- erate 3	severe 4	very severe 5
Does not seem to listen when spoken to						
Makes careless errors						
Avoids or dislikes tasks requiring sustained attention						
Short attention span						
Disorganized						
Loses things						
Procrastinates						
Easily distracted						
Forgetful in daily activity						
Difficulty completing tasks						
Gets bored easily						
Stares into space/daydreaming						
Low energy, sluggish or drowsy						
Apathetic or unmotivated						
Frequently switches from one activity to another						
Trouble concentrating						
Falls asleep doing work						
Failure to meet deadlines						
Underachiever						
Trouble following directions						
Excited in the beginning but doesn't finish						
Difficulty learning/remembering						
Works best under deadlines/pressure						
TOTAL						

$$\overline{115} = \underline{\quad}\%$$

II - Hyperactivity

	not present 0	very mild 1	mild 2	mod-erate 3	severe 4	very severe 5
Fidgets with hands and feet						
Squirms in seat						
Frequently leaves seat inappropriately						
Moves excessively						
Difficulty working quietly						
On the go						
Driven						
Talks excessively						
Can't sustain eye contact						
Needs a lot of supervision						
Pays attention to everything						
Frequently "rocks"						
Excitability						
Lacks patience						
In trouble frequently						
Restless						
TOTAL						

80 = ___%

III - Impulsivity

	not present 0	very mild 1	mild 2	mod-erate 3	severe 4	very severe 5
Cannot see consequences of behavior						
Blurts out comments						
Difficulty waiting turn						
Frequently interrupts						
Butts into others' conversation						
Engages in physically dangerous activity						
Acts before thinking						
Frequently takes risks						
Takes all dares						
Frustrated easily						
TOTAL						

50 = ___%

Figure 6.3. Checklist Summary Chart

Name_____

Date_____Age _____

Rater _____

    I. Attention Deficit   _____%

   II. Hyperactivity   _____%

  III. Impulsivity   _____%

  IV. Immaturity   _____%

   V. Oppositional Behavior   _____%

  VI. Aggressive/Sadistic Behavior _____%

 VII. Tic Disorders   _____%

VIII. Depression   _____%

  IX. Anxiety   _____%

   X. Low Self-Esteem   _____%

  XI. Sleep   _____%

 XII. Others   _____%

                  Total   _____%

Before a treatment plan can be developed and protocols selected, the therapist will need to look at the complete checklist summary chart. There may be categories with much higher percentages than ADHD. By looking at the entire group of checklists, the therapist can prioritize the treatment plan, focusing on the most severe complaints first.

7

Other Disorders and Checklists

Now we'll have a look at other disorders that can benefit from neurofeedback therapy. Most sections will have a checklist at the end.

Epilepsy

Perhaps one of the most interesting issues in using neurofeedback to treat disorders is the fact that almost all of our early research was on the treatment of drug-refractory cases of epilepsy; now, most neurofeedback therapists see very few cases of epilepsy. It is hard for us to imagine that one of our most successfully treated disorders is seldom treated with brainwave training. It all got started with epilepsy. Research has clearly demonstrated that many, if not all, animal species exhibit a particular brainwave frequency band, that of twelve- to fourteen-hertz rhythm, over an area of the brain called the Rolandic or sensorimotor cortex. This is a band or strip-type formation that runs across the brain, basically from ear to ear. This strip plays a major role in the treatment of most disorders, as you will see later.

We owe a lot to cats because the specific frequency, which is now labeled sensorimotor rhythm (SMR), was first observed in, you guessed it, cats. Dr. Barry Sterman and others observed that when cats produced this rhythm, there was less motor activity. So when you see a cat sitting still, perhaps waiting for a mouse, nothing is moving aside from an occasional flick of the tail, and they seem to be quite relaxed, then they are probably making a lot of SMR brainwaves. The same is true for humans; when we are quite relaxed and yet not in a fog, we are probably making an increased amount of SMR. It is a state of controlled relaxed focus. Controlled is a key word. When we are in control, there are no seizures, no anxiety, no hyperactivity, and so forth. In this state, the brain is balanced and in control of all of its functions. Out of control, there is a cascade of problems from neurological to endocrine issues.

Seizures are caused by abnormal and excessive amplitude brainwave spiking. The spikes are known as epileptiform discharges. That means that you get a very high spike(s) in the brainwaves. It is like a strong burst of energy in a particular area of the brain that overrides all the other brainwaves. It is like a strong electrical surge to your computer that disrupts everything. The frequency band where these abnormal firings occur is in the low-frequency range, usually between six and nine hertz. There is less of what we term "cortical control" when there is an excess of low-frequency waves. We have to have a sufficient amount of mid-range brainwaves in order for the brain to monitor and control unconscious processes. We find this is true in a number of unconscious processes, such as sleep, apnea, and snoring. Therefore the therapeutic strategy for treating epilepsy is to train the patient to make more SMR, twelve to fifteen hertz, which is a "calm, relaxed, and focused," frequency band, and to inhibit or train down the low-frequency band, six to nine hertz.

This may sound like an awesome task, but Dr. Sterman and his colleagues were able to train cats to make more SMR. This is not fantasy or magic, it is simply a training program. If we give the brain information about how inside-the-skin events are occurring, we can modify those events. We might not know exactly how we do this, but we know we can.

It is still amazing that a cat can be trained through the use of reinforcements to change its brainwaves. Once it was demonstrated that cats could learn to increase their SMR, thereby becoming more seizure resistant, we moved on to work with humans. It has now been demonstrated and replicated many times that by training human beings to make more SMR and inhibiting the low frequencies, their seizure threshold increases. That translates to fewer seizures and less intensity when a seizure occurs. Many patients learn to stop a seizure when they feel the first signs of an onset.

Even more remarkable than being able to successfully treat seizures with neurofeedback is the fact that this knowledge has been available for more than thirty years and it is still not mainstream medicine. We are still treating patients with powerful drugs that could possibly be eliminated with neurofeedback and we are still allowing drug-refractory cases of epilepsy to suffer through multiple daily seizures.

At this point, we would like to make a political comment. There should be a government agency in charge of investigating every reported treatment for every disorder and disease and when one proves successful, it should be mandated for use in the medical mainstream and covered by insurance companies. In the long run, it would save millions and probably billions of health-care dollars.

Over the thirty years that neurofeedback has been used in the treatment of epilepsy, there have been a stream of reports and dozens of studies indicating that brainwave training reduces the number and intensity of seizures. Drs. Sterman and Friar published a single case study in 1972, in which they reported that not only was there a dramatic reduction in seizures, but there was also a positive personality change. The young subject became more confident and outgoing and her sleep improved. This reflects the idea of a cluster of problems resolving with a single treatment modality. We are not basing our judgment on a single case; the same results have been replicated many times with similar results.

Depression

We don't normally think of children being depressed, but depression knows no social, economic, gender, or age boundaries. There are many children with dysregulated brains who manifest symptoms of depression. Many children diagnosed with ADHD and other disorders are actually depressed, and if you clear the depression, the attentional and behavioral problems disappear. Depression can manifest at any age. Once again, if we rescue the child, we save the adult. If brainwaves are not regulated in childhood, they may carry those dysregulated brainwaves into adulthood. We know of no specific clinical studies confirming that treatment of children for depression precludes depressive patterns in adulthood, but in our clinical practices, this idea seems to hold up.

Often children do not demonstrate the typical signs we think of as depressive signals; instead, some children become more irritable and defiant. They are often angry about not feeling well and so they act out or show irritability or impulsivity. They get labeled as stubborn, disobedient, oppositional, or mean, when, in fact, they just feel lousy and are mad about it. Depression produces unhappy feeling and often severe emotional pain. No one wants a child to live in a chronic state of unhappiness. Brainwave training can help even with severe symptoms. If a child or an adult is on antidepressant medications when they come for neurofeedback, they are usually trained while they are on the medication. As the symptoms improve, the medication is titrated down.

Physiological processes are homeostatic in nature, which means that they work to stay in balance. Systems are turned on and off in order to maintain balance. Pharmacological treatments are designed to bring systems into that balance state, but they often dysregulate some other area, causing it to be out of balance, which is what we often call side effects. Brainwave training brings the "central processing unit" (the brain) into balance. If you bring the brain into homeostasis, all systems then function more normally. This is why multiple symptoms in the cluster begin to disappear.

It has long been known that there is a diffused reduction in cerebral activity in depressive patients. So practically all known treatment modalities work to keep the brain more active. This is precisely what brainwave training does without negative side effects.

We have seen a large number of children who were brought in for ADHD and turned out to be depressed. Once the depression was resolved, the attentional component was no longer a problem.

We were referred a fourteen-year-old girl with ADHD. She was from one of the very rural counties near Abingdon, Virginia. When she came in, she looked very much like ADHD without the hyperactive dimension. She was daydreamy, never smiled, and could not focus on our questions and her responses were often inappropriate. Before we began the brainwave training, however, we referred her to one of our therapists for an evaluation. The therapist was unsure of what was going on, so she wanted to see her several times before we started brainwave training. What began to unravel was a two-and-a-half-year scenario of sexual abuse by an uncle who had moved in with the family. The uncle had a brush with the law and was forced to leave his home out of state and so he had moved in with this family. It wasn't long before he had manipulated this then-twelve-year-old girl into an inappropriate relationship.

Prior to the introduction of the uncle, this young lady was doing okay in school and had good social skills. Shortly after the uncle moved in, she changed schools and her new teachers saw a young lady who was unengaged and disinterested. They did not have the advantage of seeing her before the abuse started. Her parents just thought it was a new school environment and adolescent changes and did not take her for treatment. The girl would not disclose anything to the school authorities, so when the guidance counselor saw her, she determined that there were symptoms of ADHD without the hyperactivity and some mild depression. She was referred to our clinic for treatment.

As it turns out, this patient was not ADHD. The abuse caused her to present in ways that resemble ADHD with some concomitant depression. Once the entire story was revealed, the situation in the home was quickly resolved, the uncle was put in the care of the state, and we worked with the girl. With a combination of psychotherapy and brainwave biofeedback, she was restored to her pre-abuse social/emotional functioning and her academic performance improved because of better attentional skills.

Another patient, Tim, was an only child whose parents divorced when he was thirteen. Well, it wasn't just divorce; it was World War III. There was a custody fight and multiple trips back to court over

alimony and child support requests. There was also a lot of screaming and crying on his mother's part, and door slamming and cursing on his father's part. Tim had been an average student who
showed some athletic promise, but all of that seemed to fade as
the fighting went on. He became withdrawn, his grades dropped,
and he became increasingly more irritable. He got in trouble with
teachers because of outburst and conduct disturbances.

Tim was referred to us because of ADHD and conduct disorder.
It didn't take long to determine that he was not ADHD, but that the
chronic stress of his family situation was taking a heavy emotional
toll. With the use of psychotherapy and regular biofeedback, Tim
was able to regain some control. Occasionally, one parent or the
other came in with Tim for his treatment sessions, and over time
both parents realized that their outrageous behavior was seriously
hurting their son. Things got a lot better for Tim; grades improved
and he played a couple of sports. But his parent's behavior had a
dreadful impact on him; no doubt he will have memories of his
experiences as long as he lives.

It is one thing for parents to reach the point they cannot live
with one other and finally divorce. It is, however, quite a different
story when there is outright warfare and the children are used as a
weapon against one parent or both. It has been our clinical experience that when parents are able to adjust in healthy ways to a
divorce, the children will adjust as well. When the war goes on years
after the divorce, however, the children suffer dreadful effects from
their parent's neurotic behavior. Depression and anxiety are the
most common things we see in children of dysfunctional parents.

Divorce is not the only reason for depression in children. The
precipitating factor can be a number of things. There are a lot of
dysfunctional families that somehow get along, yet some of them
are over the top and are very disruptive to the life of a child. If we
were to list all the factors that have contributed to depression in the
patients we have seen, the list would be very lengthy. There are,
however, some major factors that often trigger depression. These
include economic difficulties, physical disabilities, being different
in any way, illness in the family, death in the family, and any type

of significant loss. We would propose that loss is one of the most significant factors. If you dig around in the life of a person who is depressed, you will likely find some significant loss. This ranges from loss of an important relationship to the loss of self-esteem. Like most disorders, depression knows no social, economic, gender, or age barrier. It can conceivably happen to almost any person; given enough stress, almost anyone can break. This certainly includes children.

We use traditional therapeutic treatment modalities for depression, but in almost every case, at some point, we begin brainwave training. We find the results are often profound and the time of treatment is significantly shorter. Conventional treatment for depression can go on indefinitely, even for a lifetime. With neurofeedback, we think in term of months, as opposed to years, and the results are seldom dependent on staying on medication for years. In terms of cost, we cannot estimate the enormous amount of money that would be saved if neurofeedback became the treatment of choice for depression.

The Rationale for Using Brainwave Training for Depression

There are basically three types of depression seen by mental health professionals: reactive depression (exogenous), endogenous depression, and chronic low-grade depression. Reactive or exogenous depression is a result of some external stressor. It could be an injury, death in the family, or some other great loss. If dealt with, this type of depression usually lifts fairly quickly. If it is not dealt with appropriately, it can manifest into long-term depression. Endogenous depression is a different matter. Many people are depressed for no external reason. This type of depression is often more difficult to deal with and is usually long term. The last type of depression is a chronic low-grade depression. This type of depression is called a dysthymic disorder.

Situational depression is usually best dealt with through psychotherapy and some type of situational resolution. Endogenous depression and dysthymia, however, respond very well to brainwave training (neurotherapy). This sophisticated form of biofeedback training impacts the basic mechanism by which the brain controls physiological and mood states. Depression is a state of underarousal. By using the brainwave training, the person learns to regulate a normal state of arousal. With brainwave training, we see the symptoms of depression begin to normalize. For example, the person may begin to sleep normally, the quality of thought improves, and the person becomes more appropriately active, in general more functional. The normal range of behavior and affect begins to return. The return to normal happens quickly with brainwave training, which is in sharp contrast to years of therapy and sometimes countless drug trials.

At this time, it appears that brainwave biofeedback training is effective against depression regardless of how the person became depressed, that is, whether it is a genetic predisposition, from early childhood trauma, or the result of a deep emotional experience. The same finding seems to be true regardless of how long the tenure of the depression. Generally speaking, we usually find that, as the training proceeds, the patient no longer requires antidepressant medication, or at the very least, the medication can be reduced.

Brainwave training for depression is a process whereby we feed back to patients information about the way their brainwaves are functioning. By getting immediate feedback, they are able to learn how to control their various brainwave states. This is a learning process that helps patients establish self-control. After training, they have the ability to consciously change brainwave activity, which will reflect a change in behaviors and emotions. The patients' emotions are no longer at the mercy of all of the external events going on in their lives.

There is evidence that once the patient experiences a depressive episode, subsequent episodes are more likely to occur. Training the brainwaves to reduce the low cerebral activity has a beneficial effect, reducing the likelihood of recurrences. When we train young brains to produce healthy brainwave activity, we not only reduce the depression, we also improve the chances of a healthier and happier adulthood.

Most well-trained practitioners of brainwave biofeedback can treat depression. It is a common diagnosis seen in clinical practice. When it comes to the more complicated conditions such as bipolar disorder, however, seek someone with a wide range of experience. It is far more complicated than unipolar depression.

VIII - Depression	not present 0	very mild 1	mild 2	mod-erate 3	severe 4	very severe 5
Seems sad, does not smile very much						
Seems unusually quiet						
Poor sense of humor						
Grouchy, irritable						
Sullen						
Looks flat						
Withdrawal from family/activities						
Tearful						
Frequently seems lonely						
Moodiness,unpredictable moodswings						
A loner, withdrawn						
Depressed						
No interest						
Problems with sleep						
Thinks about death or dying						
Suicidal						
TOTAL						

80 = ___%

Bipolar Disorder

Bipolar disorder used to be called manic depression because along with depressive symptoms, patients have at least one bout of a manic phase. Bipolar disorder is a serious mental disorder and should not be treated casually. This disorder is characterized by both depressive and manic behavior and can include psychotic phases. Without a comprehensive evaluation and/or time in a therapeutic relationship, one phase or the other may not be observed or disclosed.

Bipolar disorder is not something to be left to the new practitioner, so if you or someone you care about has this disorder, seek an experienced practitioner. Early on in neurofeedback, practitioners spent their time chasing symptoms and this was not always in the best interest of the patient. Over the years, we have become more knowledgeable about the disorder and the use of neurofeedback. Now there are experts in the field who specialize in treating bipolar disorder.

Depression is characterized by a slowing of the brain, generally producing a picture of sadness and lethargy; bipolar disorder, on the other hand, may look very different. That is because it is characterized by instability in brainwave functioning. The practitioner must tread lightly when treating bipolar so as not to swing the brain into an opposite phase. There are specific neurofeedback protocols for treating bipolar that are different from those for other disorders and it takes training and talent to get the desired results.

When we get a bipolar patient, we usually refer to the Pisgah Institute in Asheville, North Carolina, which is just over the mountain from us. Dr. Ed Hamlin, the clinical director at Pisgah, is a recognized expert in the field and has a remarkable track record in helping these patients. He and Dr. Roger deBeus do a wonderful job of brain mapping, diagnosing, and treating serious disorders. Over many years, Dr. Hamlin developed protocols to help stabilize the mood swings of clients with bipolar disorder. His protocols are now being used in a number of clinics in the United States and other countries. Drs. Hamlin and deBeus not only do neurofeedback, but they are also expert in the use of qEEG and brain maps. They use these tools to pinpoint problems.

If you are seeking treatment for bipolar disorder, make sure you seek professionals who do this type of work and have plenty of experience. If you cannot travel to some place like the Pisgah Institute, make sure that your neurofeedback practitioner is supervised by someone who is well trained in the disorder with which you are dealing.

Anxiety and Panic Attacks

Imagine if you will, living in a state of constant worry. Sometimes it is just a sense of uneasiness; at other times, it is a chronic state of fear; and at still other times, it is a paralysis of will. There are people who spend their entire life bracing for what could happen. Some individuals are in constant dread of some event that may or may not happen. Others have episodic dread and even panic. Technically speaking, this exaggerated fear response is a result of an overexcited limbic system. That is a part of the brain that responds to emotions.

We often refer to anxiety and panic attacks as the disorder of "what if." What if this happens, what if that happens, what if I get sick, what if they die, what if the sky falls, Henny Penny? Most of us are not paralyzed by the future. Sure, things can happen and we could suffer the insults of life, but we will deal with it when it happens. For others, however, their entire lives are predicated on what could happen; the thoughts and images they conjure are not very pleasant. They are living almost exclusively in the future, which means that they have abdicated the *now*. There is very little danger in the now. If people stopped to look realistically at the now, they would find that they are in no immediate danger of death, starvation, mutilation, or any of the other awful fears they have. The now is usually very safe, but patients with anxiety and panic don't live in the now because they are too busy fighting with the future. Neurofeedback calms the overexcited limbic system and helps them focus on living in the now.

We have seen a wide variety of patients who have benefited greatly from brainwave biofeedback. The patients have varied enormously, from the physician who had a belt phobia (true) to the child with generalized anxiety, from test phobias to panic attacks and everything in between. Anxiety, like depression and most other emotional disorders, does not know boundaries.

We had a close personal friend who developed daily panic attacks. She decided to quit work rather than receive treatment because she never wanted to admit she had a problem. We repeatedly offered treatment, but she refused. She readily admitted that other people with panic attacks needed treatment and that brainwave training helped hundreds of sufferers get over it, but she had convinced herself that her problem was strictly hormonal and that she didn't need treatment. "It's good for other people, but I don't need it." So she quit her job, went home, and not only did the panic attacks get worse, she developed agoraphobia. Her husband pleaded with her to come in for treatment, but she could not allow herself to believe that she had a "psychological problem." She once said, "I worked all my life without any problems. I don't need a shrink," and she said, "I just need to get my hormones straight." Hormone replacement therapy was used, but it did not help her agoraphobia. The last we heard of her she was housebound and "very happy staying home and being a housewife."

The reason we shared that example is because there is still a stigma associated with mental health disorders. Many individuals see mental health treatment as something that detracts from one's character, intelligence, or reputation. In some families, there is the perception that mental health treatment reflects disgrace on the entire family. Instead of admitting to a need for help, people will disguise the situation with comments like, "Oh, she is just high-strung" or "That is just the way he is." Most mental health issues can be resolved or, at the very least, improved, and this is certainly true of anxiety and panic.

The broad term "anxiety" represents a wide variety of disorders. It includes panic attack, obsessive-compulsive disorder, generalized anxiety, posttraumatic stress disorder, and numerous phobias. We have general clinics and, like most clinics, we see a little bit of everything. We have helped people prepare to give speeches and get over driving phobias. We have seen brainwave training calm the most nervous patient and fearful, withdrawn children become socially active. We have had combat veterans thank us for saving their lives, but most of it is due to simple biofeedback procedures. We are not wizards; we just have a wonderful tool in brainwave training.

Anxiety is a very pervasive disorder that also knows no boundaries. Anxieties are prevalent in every nook and cranny of this and every other country, and they are not limited to age, gender, or socioeconomic status.

Children frequently have anxieties about the broad new world they are facing; fortunately for most children, these are just stages that they grow through. For some children, however, anxiety becomes a way of life and many of their anxieties are carried into adulthood. Anxieties also tend to generalize from one worry to another, to another. Many of our adult patients report that they were "worriers" for as long as they could remember. We frequently hear childhood stories of anxieties that persist even into the late stages of adult life. If we can work with the children before these "worries" become entrenched, we can save a lot of pain in later years.

Cynthia is now in graduate school and she recently phoned the clinic to thank us for helping her get out of high school. Her test anxiety was generalizing to the rest of her life. She was convinced she would never get a high school diploma and would end up "cleaning the streets for a living." She started out with high hopes; she wanted to be an engineer, but her fear of failure grew out of control. When we first saw her, perhaps ten years ago, she was considering dropping out of school because she couldn't stand the constant fear of failure. She panicked before every test to the point that she was "sick" all the time and couldn't go to school. Her mother was exasperated with her. "She is so intelligent. I can't stand the thought of her being a dropout," the mother would say.

When we first hooked up Cynthia to the EEG machine, she was afraid she would be electrocuted. It took some powerful persuasion and several demonstrations for her to allow the hookup. We had trouble convincing her that the sensors to the biofeedback machine were not putting anything into her brain. She could relate to the idea that the sensors were like little stethoscopes and they were just listening, not inputting anything. Being the engineering type, she soon learned to read the oscilloscope, and before long, she was telling us what her brainwaves were doing. The greater her improvement, the greater salesperson she became for brainwave training. By the time Cynthia left treatment, she was claiming that one day, even after she became an engineer, she would build her own EEG biofeedback machine just to keep training herself. She laughed about that over the phone the last time we talked. She said it was still a good idea, but she had other things she wanted to work on.

One person who has made a special contribution to the field of relaxation and focusing is Les Fehmi, PhD. He has developed some creative ways to teach people to relax, focus, and deal with a variety of problems, not just anxiety. His technique is called Open Focus. Dr. Fehmi runs the Princeton Biofeedback Center in New Jersey, where he treats a wide variety of disorders. There are hundreds of neurofeedback providers who treat anxiety and panic disorder and you will find them on the websites listed at the end of the book.

Rationale

The most common use of biofeedback over the past thirty or forty years has been for relaxation and stress management. We have long realized that both chronic and acute stress can lead to various anxiety states. Anxiety can manifest in a number of different ways, from a severe panic attack to phobias. It can also manifest in less severe cases such as performance anxiety or stage fright. The single most important function of brainwave training is its effect on the overexcited limbic system. When you calm the central system (the brain), you are calming the entire system, internally and externally.

When an individual feels threatened in some way, the brain reacts by being in an overly heightened condition. In other words, it speeds up; it is no longer relaxed and comfortable. The brain is making an excessive number of fast-frequency waves; these are not the waves that are conducive to being calm and in control. The problem can compound and the person becomes increasingly out of control. It can finally reach the point where the person becomes frozen, unable to function. Anxiety can become a self-fulfilling prophecy; I see myself becoming anxious and I fear becoming more anxious, so I do. The more I observe myself and worry about the future, the worse my condition becomes. So it is, in part, the self-observation and self-attention that drive the person deeper into anxiety. For example, the person begins to notice her heart beating rapidly or feel other autonomic changes, so she pays more and more attention to the physiological changes. Fearing the worse, things do get worse, until it reaches the point at which the autonomic nervous system is out of control. At this point, the person has gone from a state of anxiety to a full-blown panic attack. The anxiety is paralyzing. If this continues to happen, before long, the self-fulfilling prophecy takes on a life of its own. Remembering earlier panic attacks can actually lead to chronic recurrence.

We see anxiety as just one of many manifestations of the dys-regulated brain. Instead of being in homeostasis, the brain is out of balance. In depression, the brain exhibits an excess number of slow-frequency brainwaves, whereas in anxiety there are excessive fast-frequency waves. There can also be instability in the brain-waves; the brain is vacillating between fast and slow. When the brain is really racing, it is often visible on the EEG screen. As for less acute anxieties, they are not always as easily seen but can be identified over time.

By teaching the brain to regulate itself better, it subsequently functions better, not only in anxiety states, but also in life's normal challenges. Once patients have been trained to self-regulate brain-wave states, they are no longer as vulnerable to the downward and upward spirals of anxiety and depression.

The training process for anxiety, as well as for a wide variety of other disorders, involves showing the patient information derived from his EEG. Through multiple training sessions, the patient learns to bring certain aspects of his brainwaves under voluntary control; muscles begin to relax, the mind starts to calm, and a sense of control exists. Soon the patient learns to generalize this control in his everyday life. In the course of training, the patient receives repeated challenges to improve, and it is this training that promotes the regulatory process. Think of it as weight training for the brain; once the brain shows the slightest movement toward balance, it is challenged again to move even closer to homeostasis.

We learn many skills at an unconscious level and this is true of brainwave training. In general, we have little or no awareness of the mechanisms by which the brain regulates its own activities, but we do know that through operant conditioning the brain can be trained. As the patient becomes more proficient at changing the brainwaves, the process enhances self-confidence. Toward the end of training, the patient has gained the ability to control and regulate the various brainwave states. We find that most patients who undertake the training gain significantly in their ability to control anxiety and panic states. They can generally do this to the point that these anxious states no longer interfere with the conduct of their normal lives. Finally, by the end of the training process, the brain is self-regulating and requires no effort on the part of the patient. The brain is a self-regulating organism and once the neurofeedback gets the brainwaves closer to a normal balance, the brain takes over and begins to regulate itself.

One very important aspect of the training is that the patient is there in the room focusing on the training. There is no future in the room, only the now. The brain can really have only one thought at a time, so if you are thinking about the training, you cannot be fearful of six months into the future. As patients become more skilled at focusing in the now, in the training room, this generalizes to the world outside the training room. Neurofeedback providers train people to focus with a higher level of intensity, which precludes being somewhere else at the same time.

When we see anxiety patients for the first time, we often conceptualize their bodies being in the room, but their thoughts are days, weeks, or months into the future. While they are answering our questions, they are internally "what if-ing" way down the road. We can almost hear them: "What if this doesn't work, what if I get worse, what if I make a fool of myself today?" Once we start the training, we help them to focus on the feedback they are receiving and to develop an ability to dismiss the fearful future. The process is repetitious and we do it until focusing on the now becomes an automatic process. Once they learn the skill, they take it with them to work, the grocery store, and everywhere else they may find themselves.

After completing the training, which may take twenty to forty training sessions (more in severe cases), no continuing willful effort is required to control anxiety or panic attacks. Once the brain is regulated, the normal brain flexibility is restored and the brain automatically adjusts to prevent these out-of-control states. Since brainwave training is a learning process, it is unlikely to require follow-up sessions after the completion of the training.

IX - Anxiety	not present 0	very mild 1	mild 2	mod-erate 3	severe 4	very severe 5
Panic attack type symptoms						
Frequently nervous						
Often upset						
Generally fearful						
Fearful of losing control						
Fearful of a specific object or event						
Jumpy, hypervigilance						
Timid						
Worries excessively						
Persistent thoughts						
Repetitive behaviors (hand washing, counting)						
Exaggerated startled response						
Shaking, trembling						
Tearful						
Fear of death or dying						
Tense muscles						
Always on edge						
TOTAL						

85 = ____%

Diaphragmatic Breathing

Patients are always asking if there is something they can do between their neurofeedback sessions. The answer of course is yes. There are a number of relaxation techniques that are helpful in controlling the out-of-control feelings. Temperature biofeedback is an excellent way of dealing with stress and anxiety, but a temperature trainer is not always available when patients are feeling anxious or panicky, so we teach a technique of diaphragmatic breathing.

Breathing is one of our most important functions and yet we seldom pay any attention to how we are breathing, unless of course we are scared and notice it. Ideally, our breathing is slow, rhythmic, and deep. In times of stress, however, breathing tends to be shallow, quick, and often erratic. This is opposite to our natural bodily rhythms. Because the entire autonomic nervous system is entrained, when we calm one function, it tends to calm all the functions. If, however, one function, like breathing, becomes anxious and jittery, the rest of the systems tend to be anxious and jittery. By learning to calm our breathing, we can have an effect on other systems such as blood pressure, heart rate, and peripheral coldness (i.e., cold hands and feet). When we learn temperature training, for example, by warming the hands, we affect breathing. If we take the time to learn any of the biofeedback techniques, we can gain control of the entire autonomic nervous system.

Diaphragmatic breathing relieves stress, calms the nervous system and promotes the body's natural healing processes. There are basically two types of breathing: costal and abdominal. Costal or chest breathing tends to be shallow; it is characterized by an outward and upward movement. Abdominal breathing is very different, characterized by a downward, outward movement. We have seen many patients, children and adult, who breathe so shallowly and high in the chest we refer to them as neck breathers. Take a deep breath; if your chest goes out and it seems to rise toward the upper chest and neck, then the breathing pattern is wrong. If on the other hand, your stomach tends to push down and outward, then you are probably breathing correctly. We frequently ask patients to put one hand on their chest and the other on their stomach and breathe. We tell them that they should feel very little movement in the hand on the chest and much more movement in the hand on the stomach.

The principal muscle of abdominal breathing is the diaphragm, a strong, horizontal, dome-shaped muscle. It divides the thoracic cavity, containing the heart and lungs, from the abdominal cavity, containing the organs of digestion, elimination, and reproduction. The muscles of the abdomen work in cooperation with the diaphragm. The diaphragmatic breathing has three important effects on the body. First, unlike shallow breathing, diaphragmatic breathing fills the lungs completely, providing the entire body with sufficient oxygen. Second, diaphragmatic breathing forces the waste product of the respiratory system (carbon dioxide) from the lungs, leaving them cleaner. Lastly, the gentle up-and-down motion of diaphragmatic breathing gently massages the abdominal organs, increasing circulation and promoting better health.

Diaphragmatic breathing uses minimum effort to receive the maximum amount of oxygen for the human body. The process is simple. Lie on your back with feet and arms positioned comfortably. Have your arms at your sides and your legs uncrossed and slightly separated. Close your eyes. Place an object directly over your stomach; it can be a book or some other object of sufficient weight so you feel a slight pressure on the abdominal muscles. At our offices, we use a "breathing bag,"* which is a rectangular bag filled with sand. We have eight-pound bags for adults and four-pound bags for children.

With the bag or other weight securely placed on the stomach, begin to inhale and exhale through the nostrils, slowly, smoothly, and deeply. There should be no jerky motions or pauses in the breathing. Slightly exaggerate the inhalation until you feel the abdominal muscles rise. Do not push the bag upward with the stomach muscles; let the breath do the job. There should be little or no chest movement when you take a breath. If this happens the way we describe it, you are breathing correctly.

Practice this technique several times a day, five to ten minutes a session. Soon the technique will become automatic; it will be

---

*Breathing bags can be simply constructed by filling an old pillowcase with a few pounds of sand, sewing it together about six to eight inches above the bottom, and then cutting the remaining material off just above the stitching. You end up with something like a six-by-eighteen-inch bag filled with a few pounds of sand. The bag is excellent for learning to breathe correctly because it does not slide off when the stomach rises. Other objects like a book tend to fall off and you have to keep putting it back on.

second nature to breathe slowly and deeply. One of the beautiful benefits of this technique is that you will be able to use it in the grocery store, at work, and in any stressful situation simply by placing a hand over your stomach and making sure you are breathing into the abdominal cavity and not in the upper chest and neck.

Of all the techniques developed for managing stress and anxiety, diaphragmatic breathing remains one of the best, and you can carry it with you wherever you happen to be. This is an ability that we once possessed and have lost; for the first few years of life, abdominal breathing is a natural function, but over time we are taught to stand up straight, suck our stomachs in, and stick out our chests. Somewhere around the age of four, we switch from diaphragmatic breathing to costal or chest breathing.

Self-Esteem

There is nothing more important than feeling positive about yourself and having a sense that you are of value. Perhaps the most important personal characteristic a human being can have is that of good self-esteem. The greatest attack on self-esteem comes from a dysregulation disorder. Not only do those with such disorders realize they are not like others, but others also label them as having a problem.

The task of children and adolescents is to discover who they are and determine how the world environment relates to them. This is no simple task and some people never acquire a positive sense of self-worth. We have all met adults who have not solved this riddle. Discovering who we are and how we fit in depends partially on our culture and subculture, and on a deeply personal level, it depends on the family and friends that directly surround us. Most people grow up relatively healthy, but not everyone is that fortunate. Some people grow up in situations that are too threatening and they spend their life waiting for "the other shoe to drop." There are other situations that are so bad that individuals grow up depressed, withdrawn, and alone. Helping people find themselves in relationship to their environment and then actualize in that environment has been the task of therapists. Sometimes it requires helping clients make significant changes and that can be frightening, particularly for children.

Self-esteem is that quality of having a pleasing self-identity and being able to fulfill at least some of our intentions and desires. Too often we see boys following in the footsteps of their fathers and girls ending up exactly like their mothers, neither having a personal sense of identity. The process of growing up involves separating from our parents' identities in appropriate ways and, for lack of a better term, "finding ourselves." Acquiring an identity, hence self-esteem, is a process that takes place in stages.

Good parenting is the process of programming for success; it is also a process of reinforcing, supporting, and teaching how to deal with difficult situations. In a good parenting situation, the child will be taught how to think through life scenarios and make informed life decisions. The parent will carefully encourage children to do age-related tasks and yet protect them from problems that are above their maturity level. When possible, we should expose children to the world at a level they can process and make sense of. The single most important responsibility of adults is that of protecting children from parasitic people who are giving in to their own unhealthy desires and fulfilling their own agenda. There are those who use children for their own end or who are too immature themselves to be trusted. The good parent is the parent who guides the child to be his or her own best self.

Even in the best of situations, young people can develop an identity based on lies. If you are constantly told you are stupid or not very pretty, you may begin to believe the lie. Several years ago, a forty-year-old woman receiving treatment in our office told the therapist, "My momma always told me that I was the smart one and I always knew this was because she didn't think I was as pretty as my sister. She thought she was helping me, but it really hurt. I wanted to be pretty too." We have spent a lot of time helping adults go back to earlier times and identify the lies they grew up with. As the old saying goes, "It is never too late to have a happy childhood."

The messages we give to young people are often carried into adult life, even into old age. The mother in the last scenario was surely trying to help her daughter, but it turned out to have a negative impact. Young children are not always capable of realizing one talent is equal to another. To a ten-year-old girl, being smart is seldom as good as being pretty. Backhanded complements, subtle putdowns, and runner-up comments are like subliminal messages that get encoded in our consciousness over time. It can take years or even a lifetime to break through a negative self-image and create ourselves anew.

There are other things that contribute to our self-esteem, like our body image. After all, the one thing that we see on a regular basis is our image in the mirror. We are constantly comparing that image to people around us, so our body image and appearance relate to how we feel about ourselves. Other things that play a role are our peer relationships, our sex role identity, and our self-expression. We can be skinny and pimply faced, but if the people around us like us and include us, our self-image is not wounded. It often takes children a while to recognize that we all have talents in different areas. Children may see themselves as fat and ugly and only later appreciate their academic or athletic abilities. In the meantime, there is the potential for low self-esteem, even depression.

Self-esteem is a positive attribute that does not include arrogance. Often people confuse arrogance and narcissism with self-esteem. Arrogance and narcissism are double-edged swords. Underneath the verbosity associated with them are usually feelings of inadequacy. Their buoyancy is usually a compensation for fears and a sense of unworthiness. For example, there are some smart people who tend to put down and look down on others because of their lack of IQ points. They often forget that we are all brilliant in our own way. Besides, IQ points do not necessarily reflect creativity and certainly do not take into account desire and drive. Smart people often forget that there are a lot of other people who are smart.

Now, getting back to the main topic of poor self-esteem, many children and adults do not realize their potential because they do not recognize their worth. Most individuals with problems in this area have other problems that overlie the problem of self-esteem. For example, most children who have the diagnosis of ADHD or a specific learning disability often end up with low self-worth. If you are always disorganized and unfocused and have trouble concentrating, you will eventually realize you are not like the people you compare yourself with. Soon you will begin to believe you are not as good or as smart as others, even though this may be untrue. If you seem always to be failing at something, you are likely to attribute it to a lack of ability rather than to a brain that is just making too many slow-frequency brainwaves. If there is a specific problem, such as difficulty reading, you are likely to label yourself as not as smart as others.

Being different in any way, whether in looks, thoughts, or abilities, certainly invites teasing, and teasing does not help the self-image. Things tend to compound and the negative self-image grows. Children can be very cruel to one another and adults are not always aware of the difficulties their children face.

Over time, low self-worth can lead to depression. The opposite side of that situation is the fact that depression can lead to low self-esteem. These two problems feed off each other, each one driving the other element deeper. The good news is that if you begin to pull one element up, the other element is positively influenced. If you help depressed individuals start feeling better, their self-esteem rises. It works the other way as well; give them reasons to feel better about themselves and the depression begins to lift. We almost always find low self-esteem incorporated in the diagnosis of depression. And with both disorders, we find there is a tendency to have an excess of low-frequency brainwaves. When you treat one, you are treating the other element in the cluster of problems.

We have seen children of all ages, sizes, races, and certainly both sexes who have self-esteem problems. Girls with acne, short boys, bookworms, unathletic children, and boys with hair that can't be combed can have self-esteem problems. Overweight children, girls with no "girly" figure, and boys with no muscles can have self-esteem issues. Tall kids, short kids, and thin and lanky kids can have self-esteem problems. Puberty can bring on a cascade of self-esteem issues. The simple fact is that what is important to one child or adult may be completely insignificant to other people. So if one child gets a pimple, his "life is ruined," whereas other children may not even notice a pimple.

Personal issues always get compounded when someone teases a child or an adult about something that is important to them. Children, in particular, tend to believe the teasers. If peers or an older sibling constantly tell a child he is stupid, he may start believing the lie. The lie can be carried into adulthood. We never run out of adults telling us that they believed all their lives that they were ugly or stupid. We once had a forty-year-old woman bring in her adolescent pictures and say that when she looked at the pictures, she realized that she was not a fat teenager. "All my life I thought I was fat in high school, but I'm not fat in these pictures," she said. A little psychotherapy and twenty-five brainwave training sessions sent this woman on to a high-paying job promotion she was initially afraid to try for. Once her self-esteem was restored, she felt worthy of a better job and a better life.

Siblings are notorious for picking on siblings and this sometimes leaves lifelong scars. Parenting is crucial in early stages of life for building good self-esteem. If parents are absent, critical, aloof, demanding, or just plain uncaring, children suffer the consequences. Do not misinterpret what we are saying; we do not believe that all people's problems come from their parents. Some do, of course. There is no such thing as a perfectly functioning family, which means that all families are dysfunctional in some way. Regardless of our childhood situation, at some point in time we have to take responsibility for our own happiness and well-being. That means that, at some point in our lives, we have to stop blaming and start living. The golden rule of parenting is be kind, firm, consistent, and, above all, loving.

Rationale

At this point you may be wondering how neurofeedback can help with self-esteem. Brainwave training for low self-esteem is much like the training for depression. There is usually too much low-frequency, high-amplitude, slow-wave activity. The patient is trained to bring up the mid-range waves. This brings the brain into a new homeostasis. The positive benefits include not only improved self-esteem, but also an overall improvement in brain functioning. Cluster problems begin to lessen with increased training. Time and again, we have patients lessen their dependence on medications and become more independent and proactive in their life. Human potential is virtually untapped, so when people improve, they expand their potential, often doing things of which they had only dreamed.

If you improve people's abilities, you improve their self-outlook. For example, a child with deficits in math will frequently fail math tests. If he fails enough, he will begin to believe negative things about himself. If the brainwaves are regulated, however, and he starts doing better in math, that negative self-image can start to

X - Low Self-Esteem	not present 0	very mild 1	mild 2	mod-erate 3	severe 4	very severe 5
Doesn't trust self						
Frequently puts self down						
Refuses to try new things						
Poor performance even when they have the ability						
Always takes a back-seat position						
Timid and reserved						
Often shy around others						
Trouble answering questions in front of others						
Sees the worst in self						
Hangs around with less capable friends						
Easily embarrassed						
Seems satisfied with poor performance						
Does not compete with others						
Gives up easily/expects failure						
Shows no self confidence						
TOTAL						

75 = ____%

improve. Once a negative self-image is entrenched, you can tell him he is smart ten thousand times and it probably won't get through. If, on the other hand, he starts passing math, he can see that he has abilities he didn't realize. Time and again in our offices, we have seen children who came in sad, angry, or depressed change before our eyes as we begin to regulate their brainwaves. When you can focus, concentrate, and think more clearly, you can see your talents and abilities. We really do see frowns turn to smiles.

Attachment Disorder

There are children who, before the age of five, begin to exhibit an inability to make appropriate social attachment to others. Since the symptoms are often similar to other disorders, it takes some skill and energy to distinguish this inability to make attachments from other disorders like autism, mental retardation, and even early signs of ADHD. The specific DSM-IV diagnostic name for this disorder is "reactive attachment disorder of infancy or early childhood." We live in a world filled with other people and it is not only desirable but also necessary to be able to attach and relate to others. When we don't, there is a cascade of emotional problems.

Early life isn't always easy, but most children can adjust to difficult situations. There are, however, certain children who cannot make social connections. They are in a world alone. The inability to make attachments is associated with early child care that is pathological. By that we mean care that is so poor that it does not foster an ability to form relationships. In general, children who lack the ability to make proper attachments usually have parents that fail to supply any of their necessary emotional, comfort, and affection needs. Parents who fail to supply their children with their basic needs have severe problems of their own. These parents are usually incapable of supplying a stable emotional environment and appropriate verbal communications and are themselves incapable of healthy relationships.

Children with attachment disorder give the appearance that they have no self and they do not recognize others as having any relationship to them. They are distant, aloof, and fearful; their facial appearance is often blank. One therapist described a child he was treating as having "a thousand yard stare." They don't react to others, they are inflexible and closed, and they show no interest or empathy toward others. It is an appearance of "not being there."

Our nervous system should react and interact with our environment. When it doesn't, there is no regulated affect. We need contact with the world in order to have appropriate affect. We need people and we need to interact with them and that requires that our affect be regulated to supply the appropriate affect for the time and situation. It is our response to others that gives us our sense of self. It is like a self-observation model. We find out who we are by the way we react; if there is no reaction, we don't know who we are. To further explain this, if I am always eating ice cream and I observe this, I can conclude that one of my traits is that I like ice cream. With both autistic children and children with attachment disorders, we always feel that we need to free them because they are "trapped inside" that body of theirs; they cannot get out and no one can get in. We always have the feeling that they should wear a sign that says, "Help, I'm trapped in here."

In thinking about this disorder, we must give some time to the idea of states and traits. Our traits come from our interactions with our environment. Interacting with the world around us causes us to develop specific traits. If I like the reaction of others when I say something funny, I may start saying funny things all the time and one of the traits I develop is a sense of humor. Over time these traits become stable. It is our stable traits that give us our personality. Children who do not interact do not end up with positive stable traits; hence they lack an orderly, predictable personality. It is only when we begin to make attachments that our personality begins to manifest. States, on the other hand, are momentary and fleeting events. States would be things like embarrassment over an offending comment or an angry outburst in response to an unexpected insult. If a state is replicated often enough, it can become a stable trait. For example, if a person is constantly in a state of frustration, anger may become a stable trait.

Empathy is a trait that is missing from children with attachment disorder. They have no capacity for feeling what others feel. They cannot "walk in the shoes" of anyone else. They are scarcely able to feel any feelings at all and, certainly, they cannot relate to the feelings of others. Empathy is a product of regulated emotions. Empathy comes from attaching and relating to others. If I cannot attach, then I cannot relate. If I can't relate, then I can't feel anything for others. Emotions are trained over time to be in accordance with the social situation. Affect regulation is a necessary emotional component of being in the world. We can never be in the world unless we participate in the world, and we can never have appropriate emotions unless we are attached to other.

Self-esteem can only develop out of a sense of self. If a person is not attached to other, there can be no sense of self. When the self begins to emerge, self-esteem can begin to develop. The fear that can develop from pathological parenting and the subsequent withdrawal because of that fear play a vital role in the inability to form attachments. After all, if I am frightened or rejected by my parents, how could I ever be accepted by others? Neurofeedback can play an important role in allowing the self to unfold because brainwave biofeedback helps to regulate the fear that keeps the self repressed. It cracks the shell of isolation as you increase the arousal level. This enables the child to recognize other and be capable of realizing that her actions impact others and their actions impact her. The only way to have self-esteem is to recognize that we fit in the world and the world is a part of us.

Fortunately, attachment disorder is rare and the severity depends on several factors, including the hardiness of the child, the quality of caregiving, and the duration of the time spent in the situation of rejection and deprivation. If appropriate treatment is received early, the damage can be limited. If treatment is not available, the disorder can have a lasting influence. This is one of those disorders for which it is true that if we rescue the child, we save the adult. There are a number of treatments that help with the disorder, including: play therapy, art therapy, music therapy, group and family therapy, parent and family education and training, and cognitive behavioral therapy. Other things that have been used in the treatment of this disorder are cranial sacral therapy and systematic desensitization. Neurofeedback has recently emerged as an important treatment for this disorder because the regulation of brainwaves can dramatically impact the regulation of affect. When we retrain their brainwaves, children begin to emerge from their own little world and interact with the larger world.

There is a direct relationship between attachment failure and early childhood emotional trauma. In trauma, a likely scenario is that the brain goes into a defensive posture and slows down; it is a way to deal with the underlying fear. There is very little joy in a very low level of consciousness, but there is also less fear. Fear affects our state, and continuing to be in a state ultimately impacts our traits. The objective in brainwave regulation is to move the brain out of the fear state. This is why neurofeedback is an effective treatment in affect regulation. When we reduce the fear, we improve the interaction with others, thereby allowing the self to develop. Neurofeedback improves the ability to discriminate and this is critical in society. We need to be able to discriminate those who can hurt us from those who love and protect us. We can only improve discrimination by changing the arousal level.

Neurofeedback is not a quick fix, but over time the personality begins to emerge as fear is quieted. The mechanism by which the personality emerges is the ability to develop "cause and effect thinking." With the ability to think in a "cause and effect" way, we can learn to discriminate and also learn appropriate affective responses. This enables the child to develop a capacity for remorse and empathy. Neurofeedback affects frequencies, which in turn affect the state of arousal. By changing the level of arousal, we are able to modify the state and, over time, the trait. Retraining brainwave frequencies and intensities changes the level of arousal, lifting the brain out of a defensive state and allowing it to once again become flexible and reactive to the environment. When the brain is "parked" in one place, it is unable to respond appropriately to the environment; the flexible brain is a healthy brain.

We have seen very few cases of reactive attachment disorder, but there are neurofeedback therapists who see a lot of it. Our good friend Sebern Fisher focuses her neurofeedback practice in Northampton, Massachusetts, on attachment problems, developmental trauma, and posttraumatic stress disorder (PTSD). She has become convinced that fear is a core issue. She uses neurofeedback primarily to teach the brain what it has not learned to do on its own, that is, regulate affect. She combines neurofeedback with psychotherapy; she feels that neurofeedback greatly enhances the therapeutic process. With years of clinical experience, Sebern Fisher has witnessed the powerful impact of neurofeedback on affect, fear, state, trait, and personality.

Another practice that has demonstrated the power of neurofeedback in the treatments of trauma and attachment disorder is the Institute for Children and Families in Lancaster, Pennsylvania. The founder and CEO of the institute is Lark Eshleman, PhD. She and her husband, Bob Patterson, developed a treatment modality they call Synergistic Trauma and Attachment Therapy (STAT). Other providers in the field that have achieved recognition are Stephen Gray of Colorado Springs, Colorado; Lori DiRicco, RN, BSN, of Chattaroy, Washington; and Vicki Moss, PhD, and Robert Rafael, PhD, at Delta Consultants West in Johnston, Rhode Island.

Sleep Disorders

The primary sleep disorder that every parent should be concerned about is sleep deprivation. Both children and adults in our frantic society are sleep deprived. Sleep deprivation is usually a fallout of poor lifestyle management. Sleep should be a priority, but it is usually way down the list of priorities in many families. The average adult sleeps about 6.7 hours when they should be getting seven and a half to eight hours' nightly sleep. Sleep-deprived children get less than seven hours when they should be getting nine to ten hours. A young brain needs more sleep time because it is growing, maturing, and reorganizing.

The effects of sleep deprivation are cumulative and have profound effects on memory, learning, reasoning, reaction time, and what we label "executive functioning." How can you pay attention, think, and remember if you are exhausted? It has been found that many children who were labeled ADHD were actually sleep-deprived children. When these children start sleeping the appropriate length of time, many of the ADHD symptoms go away. Reports of sleep problems are common for children with ADHD. When we treat ADHD with neurofeedback, we usually see the poor sleep patterns disappear. We are always surprised at how many children fall asleep the minute we start the neurofeedback training; it is usually because they are sleep deprived to start with. We know it seems contradictory to say a hyperactive child may be sleep deprived, but that is often the way they stay awake. Constant movement precludes falling asleep. Anyone who has tried to get a young child to go to sleep and they keep moving, talking, singing, and so on knows that their movement is purposely to avoid sleep. Sometimes childhood sleep problems are carried into adulthood.

Adult sleep deprivation can have a negative impact on the family, society, and the workplace. Sleep-deprived adults are very inefficient and at times unsafe. We would like to have a nickel for every sleep-deprived adult that says "Oh, I've adapted." They just think they have, but the sleep-deprived brain is in a constant state of insult. Sleep-deprived adults have more accidents, lose productive work time, and have even been known to cause disasters in industrial settings. Sleep-deprived adults as well as children often get the label of lazy; many of these individuals are not lazy, just exhausted.

Night-shift workers are a perfect example of what we are talking about; they have a higher rate of physical illnesses such as heart disease, obesity, miscarriages, and breast and colon cancer. They also have more accidents and are generally not as productive as their daytime counterparts. In addition, sleep deprivation is a contributing factor to depression and anxiety and it will likely exacerbate bipolar disorder. By the way, it is a myth that the elderly need less sleep. They may sleep less due to a number of other factors, but they need the same amount of slow-wave sleep as the rest of us. There have even been studies that support the idea that very short sleepers (four or five hours a night) and very long sleepers (more than ten hours) actually have shorter than normal life spans.

The basic function of sleep is to rest the body and the mind. There is an old saying in psychology that we sleep to rest the body and we dream to rest the mind. You cannot dream enough unless you sleep enough. In the process of sleep, we recover cognitive abilities such as memory, reasoning, and learning. Also in the sleep process, we recover our emotional stamina and stability. Individuals with emotional difficulties become increasing more unstable with less and less sleep. During parts of the sleep cycle, our immune system recovers so we can defend ourselves against disease-causing germs and viruses. Basically, without sleep, we physically and mentally deteriorate, and it is cumulative and progressive.

One of the more common complaints we hear in our clinics is that the child is impossible to get to bed, and when they do get in bed, it is twenty questions: "Can I have a drink of water? "Will you tell me a story?" The other strategy is "I'm scared." In fact, they may feel threatened, so it is often a balancing act for the parents. We need to be understanding and yet firm. The use of a temperature trainer (which we will discuss later) is often very helpful. It gives the child something to focus on, eliminating those extraneous and fearful thoughts. We frequently recommend the use of a temperature trainer to people when they are doing neurofeedback. Not only is it a good ancillary tool, it gives them something to practice on between the brainwave training sessions. As inexpensive as a temperature trainer is, they are good to have around the house for managing everyday stress. It is amazing how de-stressed you can get by just training the hand temperature to elevate.

There are three specific sleep complaints we hear: can't go to sleep; can't stay asleep; and can't go to sleep or stay asleep. We look at all three of these problems differently. They each require a different brainwave training procedure. Though we do not want to go into all of the physiological/neurological mechanisms involved, we would like to give you a general idea of what is happening.

"Can't go to sleep"—we hear this a lot. Parents report that the child will lie there for hours with eyes wide open, sometimes fighting sleep. Some patients report that their mind races, while others say that they weren't thinking of anything important. Regardless, they cannot initiate sleep. Usually, people report that they finally went to sleep in the wee hours of the morning. As a result of not sleeping, they consequently have trouble getting up or feel in a fog all day. In general, an inability to initiate sleep falls in the general category of an anxiety problem and generally requires right-hemisphere training. Basically, the person is keyed up and unable to relax, so the brainwave training slows down the activity that is causing the failure to sleep.

"Can't maintain asleep"—well, the way patients usually phrase it is "I keep waking up; sometimes I go back to sleep, but then I wake up again." This is paradoxical, but here is how it works: We have to be awake enough to go to sleep. The entire time we are sleeping, our brain is monitoring important functions such as heart rate and respiration. Some people sleep so deeply that they cannot monitor life support functions. They wake up frequently to ensure that these functions are continuous and safe. Sleep apnea is an example of this. As strange as it may seem, we wake the brain up a bit in order to sleep. This ensures that the brain can monitor all the life processes that need attention. The primary objective in brainwave training in this type of sleep disorder is to increase the amplitude of mid-range waves, primarily in the front left hemispheric region of the brain.

Now, this leaves us with the third and more complicated sleep problem. There are people who can neither go to sleep nor stay asleep when they finally manage to fall asleep. You might say that they are in both anxious and depressed categories at the same time. In fact, they have instability in their brainwave functioning. There is generally no such thing as a depression without a little anxiety or anxiety without a bit of depression, and it is easy to see why. In an unstable situation, the brain fluctuates. Therefore one mood element is more dominant, but it can easily shift. In cases like this, the brainwave functioning must be stabilized, so we use specific protocols that have been shown to stop the shifting back and forth. One of the things we find occasionally is that once we lessen the instability, the brain seems to settle into one pattern. At that point, we have to shift the training either to speed up the brainwaves or to slow them down, depending on what is needed.

We have seen lots of sleep disorders and they usually resolve very quickly, but there are some cases that are quite difficult and require a great deal of brainwave training as well as behavioral changes. There is one other thing we should mention. We also see sleep apnea and snoring. Snoring is usually quickly resolved but may occasionally need refresher training. Snoring and apnea are both disorders in which the brain is too asleep to monitor its functioning. When it comes to sleep apnea, losing weight is often the most successful treatment. When weight loss is combined with other treatments such as brainwave training, there is a high probability of a good resolution.

Your biofeedback therapist will need to do a complete evaluation to determine your exact sleep problem and to understand all the factors playing a role. Once this is accomplished, a preliminary plan is formulated and the training begins. Keeping good records will be very helpful to the therapist because your reports on nightly sleep help determine what protocols to use. The protocol will include which brainwaves need to be increased and which ones need to be inhibited. The placement of the electrodes is also a critical factor in treating any disorder.

In addition to neurofeedback, there are things that can help the process of improving sleep. We need good sleep and good dreaming; both are important for good health. Almost all of us experience some difficulty sleeping during some period of our lives, but sleep is particularly disturbed when we are experiencing stressful situations or other difficulties such as a physical disorder. So to complement neurofeedback, consider the following.

Regular Schedule: Set a regular schedule with a specific bedtime and a specific time to get up. With a lot of activities, bedtimes can get shuffled around; this may be okay occasionally for a mature person, but it is not good for children. Young brains need a good routine.

Naps: Naps can be very important, even necessary for younger children, but don't make them too late in the day. Any person can get days and nights mixed up so that they want to sleep all day and lie awake all night. We have had many patients who take naps late in the day and wonder why they cannot initiate sleep at bedtime. Make sure that napping is not a substitute for not getting sufficient sleep at night; there is no substitute for a good night's sleep.

Exercise: The right type of exercise is wonderful for sleep, but the wrong kind of exercise is a sleep disaster. The right type of exercise burns up stored energy and allows you to turn emotional tension loose. Regular aerobic exercise will aid your overall well-ness. It is always a good idea to consult your physician before you start any exercise program.

Sleep Exercises: Sleep exercises are different from other types of exercise. Aerobic exercise should be avoided in the evening. As a guideline, we recommend no aerobic exercise at least three hours before bedtime. Sleep exercises are gentle stretching exercises like yoga or tai chi. Stretch very slowly and gently allow all tension, tightness, and stiffness to leave the body. Focus on each muscle you are stretching so that it gets your undivided attention. This is the time when you are completely in touch with your own body.

Use the sleep checklist to determine the specific sleep problem

XI - Sleep	not present 0	very mild 1	mild 2	moderate 3	severe 4	very severe 5
Difficulty going to bed						
Difficulty going to sleep						
Wakes up frequently						
Early awakening						
Restless sleep						
Talking in sleep						
Walking in sleep						
Wakes up in terror						
Restless legs						
Night sweats/Hot flashes						
Nightmares						
TOTAL						

55 = ____%

as well as the severity of the problem. Use it in concert with the other checklists to find out where sleep ranks in the cluster of symptoms. This will help your neurofeedback therapist develop your treatment plan.

Immaturity

We have seen a large number of children who were very immature. Often children act two or three years younger than their chronological age. On a few occasions, we agreed that the problem was due to parents who, at some level, wanted their child to stay a baby. Our approach in these cases was to work with the parents on letting the child resume normal developmental stages.

Perhaps the most prominent reason for immaturity is delayed development. The brain is like any other part of the body. There is a gradual unfolding of maturity; it develops, generally at a predictable rate. In some cases, however, it develops more slowly than expected. In ADHD, for example, some parts of the brain develop more slowly than other parts. The parts that lag in development are usually those that relate to actions and thoughts. In these children, we see behaviors that would usually be attributed to younger children. If there are delays, you are likely to see immature behavior, a lack of focus and attention, and an inability to remember things. The parts of the brain that are the slowest to mature in ADHD children are the front and side regions of the brain that integrate information with sensory input and that involve our higher functioning. We often refer to these functions as "executive functioning." Executive functioning involves decision-making, organization, and attention. Parents of these children have to go over things multiple times and still the lessons don't seem to last.

We had one fourteen-year-old in the office who insisted on sitting as close to his mother as humanly possible. When we discussed things with his mother, he was there, holding her hand. He wanted her to come with him to the session and it took some time before he would separate. It was a type of anxiety, but more than that, he acted like a very young child. Unfortunately, the mother colluded in the poor development. She seemed comfortable with his "cuddly" demands. In addition, she constantly talked "baby talk" to him. Over time, it was obvious that with this particular child there were some sexual identity issues. Neither the mother nor the son was comfortable with the psychotherapy or the neurofeedback and soon, we should say "he" dropped out but more appropriately, "they" dropped out. Therapy of any type can only work, if the person is there. We found out later that it was not the mother or the son's wish to receive treatment; they were only there at the insistence of other family members. We can want to help, but they must want the help. We often think about these cases and worry about the eventual outcome for the child, but therapy is not mandatory.

We also see the other side of the coin. In these cases, the parent is unengaged, disinterested, or dismissive. Sometimes we feel like the parent is just dropping the child off and, in essence, saying, "You fix him and I'll pick him up when you are through." Neurofeedback is a very strong and positive treatment, but it is not magic. It is certainly aided by a supportive environment.

We occasionally find parents who resent their children for a wide variety of reasons, but basically because the child has altered their life. On one occasion, we felt that the child was acting in a very childlike fashion to acquire the love an infant might get. There are people who deal very well with babies and can interact normally with adults but have no clue as to how to cope with a teenager. These cases require more than neurofeedback; parenting skills, family therapy, and sometimes intensive psychotherapy are needed to resolve the problem. We frequently have to rearrange the family dynamic to facilitate a good ending.

We have had frustrated parents who complain that they have to leave younger children in charge of things because the older sibling can't remember or acts far younger than younger siblings. Parents in these cases are afraid the child will neglectfully burn down the house or not be able to deal with an emergency. This is not an uncommon situation. There are many younger siblings who are much more capable of handling the necessaries of the day. Immature children usually seek out younger friends, play with younger toys, and, in general, shy away from age-appropriate activities. They are developmentally slow in the area of maturity.

Brainwave biofeedback is very useful in these conditions because it appears to help the brain mature more quickly. This is one of the reasons therapist are reluctant to treat very young children for disorders like ADHD. Often the brain in some of these children matures slowly, but by the time they are seven or eight, they start to catch up. In some of the more serious cases, however, we have treated children so young that their mothers held them while we trained them.

Children who show signs of immaturity can suffer profound consequences as they age. Not only do their peers tease them, they also begin to develop the attitude that they will never fit in. Their younger friends mature and they are left without friends again. Parents eventually grow frustrated because they expect behaviors that never materialize. If children are out of step with their peers, they are vulnerable to a host of potential problems such as isolation, depression, anxiety, and, later on, substance abuse. We also have to be cognizant of the potential for self-harm when any child or adult feels isolated and alone.

Parents of these children can buy them all the appropriate toys for their age, but the children will likely not relate to them. The goal of any therapeutic process is change and, generally speaking, these children must change or they will grow into immature, isolated, and disappointed adults.

There are definitely biological maturation differences in children and, as a result, we see children exhibit behaviors that are not age appropriate. Some immature children grow out of the condition as their brain matures, but this is not always the case. Usually, immaturity is one of the cluster symptoms in such disorders as ADHD and autism. So when we treat the cluster, we observe a normalization of most, if not all, the symptoms in the cluster. We remember vividly the mother who seemed awestruck when she said, "She actually helped me clean the house. She has never helped in any way." Her thirteen-year-old daughter acted very much like an eight-year-old when she first came in for treatment and, though it took a while, she started maturing as we watched. We always have to rule out mental retardation and other disorders, but there are many, many children who are very bright, just socially immature. It does take neurofeedback time and often some type of additional therapy, but it is very gratifying when we see the whole child come together in an integrated self.

We have a short checklist for immaturity. Do not examine it alone; use it in combination with other checklists in the book such as that for ADHD, impulsivity, and hyperactivity to get a complete picture of the problems in the cluster.

IV - Immaturity	not present 0	very mild 1	mild 2	mod-erate 3	severe 4	very severe 5
Delayed physical development						
Prefers to be with younger people						
Buys "things" below age level						
Behavior resembles a younger age						
Immature responses to situations						
Talks "silly"						
Whining and clinging						
Inappropriately messy						
Difficulty accepting responsibility						
TOTAL						

45 = ____ %

Tic Disorder/Tourette's Syndrome

One of the most disconcerting of all disorders is that of tic disorders, or Tourette's syndrome. Tourette's syndrome, or for that matter any tic, can create severe social problems. Tics usually make others uncomfortable; oftentimes people with tics do not realize they have a tic. Tics are a constant repetition of an annoying behavior or a group of annoying behaviors. Sometimes the behaviors are subtle, like a constant coughing or sniffing; other times the behaviors are dramatic, like barking, lip licking, spitting, or cursing. We once had an individual working in our office who constantly cleared his throat. While it was very distracting for us, he did not realize he was doing it. He would clear his throat every minute or so. We finally brought it to his attention, but it seemed uncontrollable. He decided against treatment and eventually moved on to another job, taking his throat-clearing with him.

The overwhelming numbers of tic behaviors that we have seen in our offices have been related to other disorders such as ADHD. Approximately half of the children diagnosed with ADHD have some tic behavior, but the tics are often subtle. The ADHD behaviors are often so obvious that coughs or sniffs are obscured by the hyperactivity. It is like the old saying, "The squeaky wheel gets the grease." If there is a child who is very hyper and disruptive, a minor tic like hair flipping is completely lost in the management of the child. There is a lot of overlap of Tourette's syndrome symptoms and the symptoms of other disorders, such as ADHD, bipolar disorder, and obsessive-compulsive disorder, just to mention three. There is also some evidence relating some of the stimulant medications to tics, either as causative or enhancing.

What we can tell you from clinical experience is that tics are usually one of the first problems in a cluster of problems to be eliminated, but we would add that this is not always the case. It is not uncommon to see the tics go away while we are still trying to get attentional skills improved. We have seen a wide variety of tics and there is a long list of them. To our recollection, all of our patients who completed treatment eliminated or at least lessened their purposeless movements. We have had parents complain that their child is not making any progress because they are still failing math or they are still hyper. When we remind them of the tics that are no longer there, they realize we are progressing. Many of these childhood problems take time, but in our opinion it is better to spend the time than it is to be on medication "for life."

There are basically two types of tics. There are the motor tics, which involve the purposeless movements such as eye blinks, spitting, kicking, tapping, and hitting oneself. Often tics are not recognized as tics. We remember one mother who was shocked when we told her that her son's picking of his skin and chronic popping of his knuckles were tics. After she watched her son for a week, she added a number of things to the list. She said, "I saw him doing all these things like moving his fingers all the time and grimacing for no reason, but I didn't know they were tics. I really just thought

VII - Tic Disorders

Motor Tics (sudden jerky type motions)	not present 0	very mild 1	mild 2	mod-erate 3	severe 4	very severe 5
Facial tic: eye blinking, eye rolls, squinting, grimacing, lip licking, biting tongue, grinding teeth						
Head and neck: hair out of the eyes, neck jerking, tossing head around, shoulder shrugging						
Arms and hands: Flailing arms, extending arms, biting nails, finger signs, flexing fingers, picking skin, popping knuckles						
Diaphragm: unusual inhale, exhale, gasping for breath						
Legs: Kicking, hopping, skipping, jumping, bending, stooping, stepping backward						
Feet: tapping, shaking, toe curling, tripping, turning feet						
Others: blowing, smelling, twirling hair, jerking, kissing, hitting self, chewing, scratching, shivering, pulling						
Vocal Tics						
Throat clearing, coughing						
Grunting, snorting, animal noises						
Yelling, screaming						
Sniffing, burping						
Barking, honking						
Motor or jet noise						
Spitting						
Squeaking, "huh"						
Humming						
Stuttering						
Deep breathing, sucking breath in						
Repetitive cursing, "fu", "sh"						
TOTAL						

95 = ___%

they were normal behaviors, but now that you point it out, he does these things constantly. His fingers won't stay still. And he makes sounds that I never noticed before."

This brings up the second type of tic: vocal tics. Vocal tics can be as subtle as clearing the throat and as pronounced as repetitive cursing. These tics often go unnoticed because many of the behaviors like coughing or taking a deep breath are normal everyday behaviors. The thing that separates a normal behavior from an abnormal behavior is the repetitive and often intrusive nature of the behavior. If we have a little grass allergy, we might cough for a few days and that is normal, but if we cough constantly over a long period of time, that might be a tic. It is easy to dismiss such behaviors with the justification "Oh, he has allergies." Perhaps he does have allergies, but he may also have a tic. It may take the observations of a professional to pick up subtle tics. Once we are convinced we are dealing with tic behavior, we carefully chart the progress.

If you suspect tic behavior, then you must become the keen observer. Take the checklist and begin noticing your child's behavior. You could even record the number of times you see the same behavior repeated. Unfortunately, even many professionals will dismiss a cough, sniffles, humming, or stuttering as not being a tic when they actually may be. After you have observed your child for a while, then record the behaviors on the checklist and see if there are consistent patterns to your child's behavior. The checklist will be very helpful to your doctor, especially to your neurofeedback therapist.

8

Headaches

Headaches are generally not considered an emotional problem, although they can be brought on by emotional stress. We discuss them because neurofeedback therapists frequently treat children with headaches. Although there are different types of headaches and a variety of causes, the headaches that we generally see come in three types. The first type is a migraine headache; the second type is a stress, or tension, headache; and the third type is an "I have a headache and I'm too sick to go to school" headache. The third type may actually be a headache, but sometimes it is a defense mechanism against something "out there."

Migraine Headaches

To simplify the problem, migraines are due to the dilatation of the scalp arteries, in other words, there is too much blood in the scalp arteries. This type of headache usually starts with vasoconstriction (a narrowing of arteries that reduces the blood flow). Then there is a rebound effect in which the scalp arteries overdilate, putting too much blood into the area. Most patients describe the pain as nearly unbearable. The traditional view of migraines is that they are vascular; however, some experts feel that migraines are neurological rather than vascular. Migraines exhibit brainwave patterns associated with the brainwaves seen in seizure-type patterns. For this reason, some brain scientists characterize migraines as a slow form of seizure. There have been cases in our clinics in which the migraine was so severe it was accompanied by nausea and vomiting. There is almost always sensitivity to light and sound. Most of the children we see for migraines are ten years of age or older.

Migraines are characterized by hyperexcitability of the central nervous system, and since the nervous system responds to bio-feedback in general, brainwave biofeedback is successful in treating this type of headache. The studies that have been done, as well as clinical reports, indicate that approximately 70 percent of the people treated with neurofeedback experience at least a 50 percent reduction in the frequency of their migraines. In our clinics, we usually use brainwave training for migraines in concert with dietary suggestions, hand warming, and stress management strategies.

When blood is restricted from the brain, the migraine sufferer often has visual disturbance just before the onset of pain; the visual disturbance is called the "aura." There is some evidence that migraines have a genetic component, whereas others seem to have a specific trigger, such as cheese and, in adults, wine. The common ingredient in these two foods is called tyramine. Most patients are well aware that stress plays a role in triggering a migraine, so we work hard to teach techniques to manage stressors. In what we label as common migraines, the patient does not have the warning sign of the aura before the headache starts. We seldom fail to either eliminate the headache or drastically reduce the frequency, intensity, and/or duration of the headache with brainwave biofeedback.

The earliest biofeedback treatment for migraines was discovered by Elmer and Alyce Green of the world-famous Menninger Clinic in Topeka, Kansas. They started using simple thermometers to measure the skin temperature of the fingers. This early form of biofeedback taught the patient to warm the fingers by creating a biofeedback loop, which allowed some voluntary control of blood flow. They found that by increasing the skin temperature of the fingers, migraine pain lessened and was eventually controlled. As it turns out, the earliest recorded treatment for migraines was in an ancient Egyptian papyrus that instructed the sufferer to warm the hands in hot water to relieve the pain. Now that we understand that migraines are a result of excessive blood in the scalp arteries, we can recommend warming the hands to pull blood away from the scalp and into the periphery, thus reducing head pain. We still use thermal biofeedback to treat many disorders, but by using brainwave biofeedback, we train the central processing unit (the brain) to change the homeostatic balance, rather than train peripheral arteries. Neurofeedback and thermal biofeedback together are extremely effective tools.

The economic impact of migraine headaches on the U.S. economy in 2007 was an estimated twelve billion dollars. This places a greater importance on treatments that eliminate or reduce this type of pain without the ongoing expense of medication. Biofeedback remains the most effective method for putting what was previously thought an involuntary process under the control of human consciousness. Self-regulation is now an integral part of mainstream medicine, but more important, it is another step in awakening human potential.

Tension Headaches

The second type of headache we see is the tension headache. We generally approach this type of head pain similarly to the way we approach stress and anxiety. The muscle contraction, or tension, headache is different from the migraine. It is usually experienced as a dull and often persistent head pain. It is seldom as intense as the migraine, but it can be rather constant. There is often soreness and tenderness in the neck, face, and head where the muscles attach to the bones. Patients report that it feels like the muscles are in knots.

Muscles can tighten without movement. Tension headaches result from stress, either physical or emotional. The physical stressor may be a result of poor posture, injury, work or sports activity, or some other physical strain. Emotional stress usually causes us to stay physically tense and "on guard." Either way, the muscles are held in a tightened state. The neck and jaw are particularly sensitive to stress because the skeletal muscles (striate muscles) attach to bone; therefore, tension headaches are quite common. Tense muscles can actually pull bones out of alignment, pinching nerves and causing additional pain. An estimated 40 percent of the population has tension headaches. So brainwave biofeedback therapists see their share of this common disorder.

Stress can affect us in a number of ways. Sometimes the result is temporary, but other times it is chronic. If the stressors are not dealt with in healthy ways, stress-related conditions can worsen over time. Adults often feel that "kids get over things quickly," but we believe that children are more vulnerable to stressors than previously thought. Once again, we believe that if we can deal with disorders in childhood, they will not manifest more severely in adulthood.

To follow up on what was expressed in the section on migraines, we can also treat tension headaches with thermal biofeedback. By simply warming the hands, there is a reduction in muscle tension, which eases the associated head pain. We can also use a form of biofeedback known as electromyography. In training using an electromyogram (EMG), sensors tell us the level of muscle tension in a particular area of the body. Sometimes the therapist puts the sensors on the forehead or even the forearm flexor muscles; when these muscles relax, there is a cascading effect and other muscles start to relax.

The autonomic nervous system of the human body actually has two opponent nervous system responses: sympathetic and parasympathetic. The sympathetic nervous system responses are physiological changes that enable the human to be on "high alert." When the sympathetic nervous system is activated, some of the following things occur: dilated pupils, increased heart rate, abnormal shallow breathing, digestive system shutdown, dryness of throat and mouth, muscle contraction, clenching of jaw, cold hands and feet, and brainwave alterations. This alerting nervous system response allows us to respond to emergencies. It is a defensive system against danger. The autonomic nervous system is "entrained," which means these responses are connected to each other. So when one symptom appears, a cascade of events occur, producing other symptoms. It also works in reverse. If you change one symptom in the system positively, other symptoms begin to change. For example, if we warm the hands with biofeedback, the heart rate and blood pressure begin to go down.

The other part of the autonomic nervous system is the parasympathetic system. This is the opponent of the sympathetic system and reverses the stress response, or the "fight-flight" response. The blood pressure goes down, hands warm, breathing normalizes, brainwaves normalize, and so forth. We can train the autonomic nervous system to allow the parasympathetic system to govern the state of the body by using several different biofeedback techniques. By using brainwave biofeedback, however, we normalize brainwave functioning, which in turn regulates and normalizes bodily functions centrally. Neurofeedback is quick, relatively inexpensive, and, unlike medications, can be discontinued once the brain is in balance.

"I Have a Headache and Can't Go to School"

Children are vulnerable to all types of stress, from school to their home environment. If home is safe, but school is threatening, then they will find ways to avoid school. If on the other hand, school is safe and home is painful, they will find all kinds of ways to avoid going home. We have seen many children from both categories. "Headaches" can be a way of avoiding school and they can also be a way to distract fighting parents. They may also just be headaches. For this reason, we spend a lot of time trying to figure out which process may be driving the complaint. In any case, brainwave biofeedback can help.

There are many times when we are seeing children for problems such as headaches that we are able to engage the parent(s) and treat them also. No one is immune from contemporary stressors. Whether it is marital difficulties or the economy, everyone feels some type of pressure. Children are often overwhelmed by the difficulties of their parents; they don't miss much. If parents are stressed, children have a unique ability to sense that something is wrong and they often respond by being injured in some way.

Neurotherapy, or brainwave biofeedback, addresses both the physical and emotional component of many disorders. It brings the dysregulated brain into a new homeostasis and the result is a more relaxed physiology and a more stable emotional state.

There is no checklist for headaches; you either have them or you don't. If you are dealing with headaches, it is best to seek professional help rather than rely on the continual use of over-the-counter medications. A frequent occurrence in our clinics is that someone will call in to cancel an appointment because they have a headache. Neurofeedback can usually eliminate a headache while it is in progress, so it is advisable to come in when you have a headache. We can usually eliminate or, at the least, lessen the severity of the headache (even if it is a migraine) in a single biofeedback session.

Approximately 70 percent of all headaches are tension headaches and the treatment of choice should be some type of behavioral therapy. We recommend biofeedback. Biofeedback is not an instant cure, but it has been our experience that it is the most effective treatment in eliminating and controlling the various types of headaches. Brainwave biofeedback potentially offers relief to millions of people, whether it is migraine, tension, or mixed head pain.

We liken family dynamics to an old set of bedsprings. If one area of the family is shaking, the whole thing is shaking. If you calm one area, the entire system tends to calm down. We have trained a lot of children whose families were in complete chaos. Once we had the child calm and in self-control, the entire family seemed to be calmer and more in control. We have even seen cases in which the children became like the parents and the out-of-control parents like children.

Neurofeedback and other therapeutic processes are not magic; they take time, effort, and energy on the part of the parents and the children. For many families, it seems far too easy to "take a pill," but that is, for the most part, like putting your finger in the dike. Stop or miss the medication and the problems are still there, whereas with biofeedback you are actually training away the symptoms. The overwhelming numbers of patients, both children and adults, never have to be seen again after the training is complete.

9

Temperature Training

Temperature training is a relatively easy and definitely inexpensive treatment. The first thing you must do is acquire a temperature trainer. This is simply a thermometer that will register in the normal human temperature ranges. You want the trainer to go from approximately seventy degrees to a hundred plus. We say a hundred plus because we have had youngsters who could raise the skin temperature of a single finger to 104 + degrees with practice.

Many drugstores and electrical component stores have trainers for ten to twenty-five dollars. They might not call them trainers; they may just call them thermometers. A good trainer has a two- to three-foot cord with a sensor on the end that attaches to a digital readout. This way you can set the trainer in front of you on a table or desk and tape the sensor to your fingers. You can also buy very good trainers on the Internet for twenty-five to thirty-five dollars. Most biomedical stores carry something you can use. Professional models used in clinics can cost upward of a thousand dollars.

Now for the training: Find a "safe" place. By this we mean a place that is quiet, peaceful, and where you will not be disturbed. It can be a room that is seldom used by others. Put a "do not disturb" sign on the door if necessary. Sit comfortably in a chair. If it is a recliner, be careful that you don't make yourself too comfortable; we want you to train, not go to sleep. Place both feet flat on the floor, do not cross your arms, and make sure that your head and neck are comfortable.

Attach the trainer to the inside of your middle finger, on the dominant hand, at the second digit; any household tape will serve to hold it in place. We usually start with the dominant hand because it is more responsive to internal commands. Now look at the reading and make a mental note of where you start. At this point, you start to imagine your hands warming. Some people visualize they are holding their hands over a warm fire or soaking their hands in warm water. Whatever your image, make it pleasant and warm. Keep checking the trainer reading so you can see if the temperature is moving up or down. If the temperature is moving down, that is an indication that you are becoming tenser. If the reading is going up, then you are relaxing. Eventually, you will develop a kinetic image. This means that you can actually feel the temperature rising and will know how to "turn it on."

As a guideline, if your temperature is in the seventies, then we would consider you very stressed; temperature in the eighties indicates moderately stressed. Your goal is to be able to reach the midnineties in about ten to fifteen minutes and maintain that temperature for a period of time. If you are training with the hands separated, you should achieve ninety-two to ninety-four degrees. If you cup the training hand in the other hand, then you should be able to achieve a temperature of ninety-five degrees and higher. If you are past the age of middle teens, do not expect the hundred-degree temperature range; this would be rare. Once you can get the temperature of one hand moving upward consistently, switch to the other hand. You eventually want to be able to warm either hand easily and quickly. Over time, the baseline and ending temperature will increase.

Most children can raise their hand temperature on the first try, but the overwhelming majority of adults fail miserably on the first few tries. This is because adults have been trained to self-doubt. They develop a quick case of performance anxiety. We often hear expressions like "I can't do this" or "This is embarrassing" or "This is too hard." Negative thoughts and depreciating statements will echo through their noggin. Most children, on the other hand, will jump at the chance to try this. They are excited to try something new. They see tasks like hand warming as a challenging game rather than a reflection of their inabilities. They are usually ready for the challenge and can't get to it fast enough. The moral of that story is to relax and remember it is a training, not a skill you already have. If you already had the skill, you wouldn't be having headaches.

Record your starting temperature and your ending temperature each time you train. Train at least once a day, twice if possible. The training session should last about thirty minutes. You may need to build up to this time because if you do have headaches, you probably don't sit very much and therefore thirty minutes of quiet is uncomfortable. If you cannot train for thirty minutes, train for the time you have, even if it is only ten minutes, but do it consistently.

Over time you should see a gradual climbing of both your starting temperature and your ending temperature. Chart both temperatures in different-colored ink and you can actually see the progress you are making. It usually takes about three months before you can elevate the temperature quickly and consistently, so don't get in a hurry. Once you have the ability to relax and hand warm, you can handle most of life's stressors and the head pain will be under voluntary control.

This does not usually apply to children, but when we use temperature training for borderline hypertension, it usually takes eighteen to twenty weeks to get the blood pressure under control. After hand warming is mastered, the sensors are placed on the big toe. As soon as the patient begins to elevate the temperature of one foot, we alternate the training between the big toes of both feet. It takes a lot more effort and concentration to train the feet to warm, but it is very successful in treating hypertension. We also use the hand warming to treat Raynaud's phenomenon and disease, conditions in which the arterioles of the fingers and hands go into spasm. When the spasms occur, the hands and fingers become cold and discolored. Using biofeedback to warm the hands lessens the severity of the spasms.

10

Closed Head Injury

Head injuries come in a variety of forms. Head trauma can have external causes, as in the case of a car crash, or internal injuries, as in the case of a stroke. Though the brain is incredibly tough, it is also quite delicate. It does not take much of a blow to cause the brain to dysregulate. It can be a fall, an unexpected baseball, a fight, or any kind of a hit or bang. Children are just as vulnerable as adults, if not more so, to head injuries. Yes, much to the surprise of many people, children even have strokes; sometimes the stroke can occur in utero. Neurofeedback has been demonstrated to be an effective treatment for minor brain injury. It is particularly effective when the organic damage is relatively minor. The types of brain injury that respond to neurofeedback include birth trauma, abuse, central nervous system exposure to toxic chemicals, concussion, stroke, central nervous system infection, whiplash, and cerebral palsy. In some instances, the injury does not show up on conventional imaging but can be seen when the neurofeedback practitioner looks at specific brainwave frequency bands at specific locations on the scalp. Clinicians across the country have successfully treated a variety of closed head injuries.

No neurotherapist in the country did more to demonstrate the power of neurofeedback in the treatment of closed head injuries than Margaret Ayers (1981, 1983, 1987, 1991, 1993, 1995).[1-6]

Margaret treated a wide variety of injuries: head and neck trauma, right- and left-hemispheric closed head injuries, seizure disorders, and pediatric and adult stroke. Before her untimely death in 2008, Margaret Ayers successfully treated a number of coma patients. In one case, the patient had been in a coma for approximately eight years.

In the case of stroke patients, it is generally accepted that the limits of recovery are within the first eighteen months. We have seen additional recovery occur, however, years after the stroke event by using neurofeedback. We saw an elderly gentleman seven years after his stroke. He could walk but seldom did; he could talk but said very little. After three weeks of training, his wife came in with him and told us the following story. When he came home from the last neurofeedback session, he sat down on the porch. She went inside to start cooking. After a little time had passed, she went to check on him and he was nowhere to be found. In a panic, she started searching the neighborhood and calling everyone she could think of. She finally reached a neighbor several blocks away who told her that he was at her house. The story unfolded as follows. He had walked to the homes of several neighbors to have conversations. He was bright-eyed, energetic, and very talkative. One neighbor said, "He nearly talked my ears off." The longer we treated him, the more improvement he achieved. His affected arm was never completely functional because over time the arm had fallen out of the socket at the shoulder, but everything else improved dramatically.

Whether it is a child or adult, mild closed head injuries are difficult to deal with and often go undiagnosed. The symptoms of minor head injury include headaches, dizziness, fatigue, poor concentration, poor memory, mood changes, insomnia, irritability, poor hearing or slurred speech, and, of course, depression and anxiety. We remember one case in which the patient seemed like a typical depressive until he walked into the restroom. Our offices are carpeted, but the restrooms have a bold black-and-white checkerboard vinyl. The minute the patient walked into the checkerboard room, he became extremely dizzy and nauseous. That was an important clue in recognizing his closed head injury. He had worked in a plant and he finally recalled the time a piece of pipe fell off a rack and struck him on the head. He reported that after a few days he was fine and never thought of the incident again; however, he became increasingly more depressed. When we treated the head injury, the depression went away.

As we have mentioned before, we believe that many cases of ADHD, epilepsy, hyperactivity, and aggressive behaviors are the result of an undiagnosed head injury. This is one of the reasons for the cluster of problems that encompass the primary diagnosis. We are always on the lookout for past head traumas that may present as other disorders. We take great pains in our intake interview and testing to make sure we know what we are dealing with.

Head injuries are like so many other disorders we have discussed, and often produce anomalous EEG patterns. The most common problem is the existence of excessive low-frequency brainwaves. In seizure activity we see abnormal spiking, usually referred to as epileptiform patterns or activity. In the case of head injuries we see excessive low-frequency waves, but they are usually even lower than we normally expect, often in the three- to four-hertz range. It is not uncommon to see four-hertz spikes when someone has suffered a head injury. Under stress, the brain retreats to the low-frequency ranges as a defense, but after a time the brainwaves become parked in the pattern. The brain establishes a new set point, or a new homeostatic point, if it parks for any length of time. Rather than retain its normal flexibility, it is now frozen in a dysregulated pattern. Neurofeedback breaks up the dysregulation, allowing the brain to restore its flexibility and adaptability. Restoring the brain's normal rhythms restores normal functioning.

In cases of traumatic brain injury, we frequently turn to Harold Burke, PhD, a neurophysiologist in Westlake Village, California. Among his many duties, Dr. Burke writes a monthly column in the EEG Spectrum newsletter *The Synapse*. The only problem we have with the column *Dr. Burke on the Brain* is that we wish it were weekly rather than monthly. Psychology psychiatrists, neuropsychologists, and some neurologists across the country have incorporated neurofeedback into their practices. The board-certified neurologist Jonathan Walker, MD, of Dallas, Texas, has successfully treated patients with multiple sclerosis (MS). He reports that the neurofeedback does not repair the damage done by MS, but he feels that he trains adjacent brain tissue to pick up the work of the damaged area. This noninvasive, nonmedication modality has demonstrated efficacy in a large number of "unreachable" children and adults.

Sherene McGee, a neurotherapist in Allen, Texas, has developed a unique way of providing neurofeedback. She calls it SweetSpot Therapy. She basically looks for the individual client's specific frequencies that restore the brain to balance. Every client gets a highly customized protocol based on her or his "sweet spot." When you achieve the sweet spot, the brain is able to filter out all the extraneous noise that is interfering with recovery. When you accomplish this, the brain is able to return to what she terms the "original factory setting." Sherene loves to work with postconcussion syndrome, but she also works with autism, Asperger's, stroke, and a variety of emotional disorders.

She recently related the story of a twenty-year-old man she had just treated. He came to her six weeks after a left-hemisphere stroke left him unable to speak clearly; the stroke was the result of a recent surgery. Prior to coming to Sherene's neurotherapy office, he had gone to several specialists, including a speech therapist, but he had seen very little progress. When he came to her office, his speech was almost unrecognizably garbled and he was very frustrated. This young man was a pre-law student and he frequently gave talks to youth groups. After the stroke, he cancelled all of his speaking engagements. After the intake evaluation, Sherene hooked him up to the neurofeedback machine and started the session. Not only was she training the brain, but she also made him talk during the session. Over the course of the first session, she noted slight incremental improvements. By the fifth training session, the young man's plans changed again; he was ready to resume his speaking engagements. His speech was clear and his life was back to normal. When you balance the brainwaves and strengthen the neural connections, you restore normal function. Whether the problem is due to head trauma or emotional trauma, neurofeedback is a cost-effective, noninvasive treatment.

One of the most interesting cases of head trauma is that of "Grandma Luge." Anne Abernathy has competed in six winter Olympic games. When she was just forty years of age, much older than her teammates on the U.S. Olympic luge team, she earned the nickname Grandma Luge. While competing, she suffered a severe closed head injury, which was believed severe enough to end her career. Determined to compete in the Olympics once again, she sought the services of Mitch Hopkins, DC, who was trained in brain mapping and neurofeedback. He decided to take the case, but he promised to work only as hard as she worked. Together they broke the medical barrier that many said would keep her from Olympic competition. At the time she began working with him, athletic trainers would not take her as a client until she was more stable. After a long and arduous process, she recovered and was able to compete, once again, in her sixth winter Olympics in 2006. At age fifty-two, she has raced against competitors as young as sixteen. She is still out there, thanks to a well-trained, dedicated doctor and Herculean effort on her part. Neurofeedback enabled her to fulfill her dream of returning to the Olympics as the oldest competitor in the demanding and dangerous sport of luge.

There is a treatment modality other than neurofeedback with which we have been impressed. It is Magnetic Molecular Energizing (MME). Larry Pearce, MD, and his colleagues at the Advanced Magnetic Research Institute (www.amri-nc.com) offer a treatment method consisting of the application of high (3000–5000 gauss) direct current electromagnetic fields. We have visited his clinic and observed some of his successful patients. I, Robert Hill, have actually been through the noninvasive treatment and found it very helpful. MME has been shown to successfully treat autism, cerebral palsy, spina bifida, stroke, and a host of other disorders. Dr. Pearce is a board-certified neurologist with a background in the research and treatment of neurological problems. Dr. Pearce's clinic is located in

Mocksville, North Carolina. There are several other MME clinics in the United States and Canada that provide this service.

Dr. Castro offers several complementary treatments to the neurofeedback. His clinic in Trout Dale, Virginia, offers hyperbaric oxygen therapy, chelation of toxic metals, and treatments for yeast overgrowth.

11

Addictions

No one did more to awaken us to the potential of neurofeed-back in the treatment of addictions than Peniston and Kulkosky (1989, 1990, and 1991).[1-3] They developed their now famous alpha-theta protocol for treating addictions. Their 20 percent relapse rate shocked the field of addiction treatment. Never before had alcohol and drug treatment specialists even dreamed of an 80 percent success at a year post-treatment. Their studies have now been replicated many times, with similar success. It is obvious that our earlier attempts to treat addiction with stress reduction and relaxation techniques were on the right track, but it took the power of neurofeedback to realize success.

The neurofeedback treatment for addictions actually got started as a result of a course on biofeedback at the Menninger Clinic in Topeka, Kansas. Eugene Peniston attended the course and was exposed to the idea of using neurofeedback to treat a variety of disorders. He went back to his Veteran's Administration hospital and the idea rolled around in his head for a time; then he decided he could use this modality to treat alcoholism. Peniston and Kulkosky put together a complete protocol using neuro-feedback and imagery. When they ran their first trial, they got an 80 percent success rate. This level of success was unheard of in alcohol/drug treatment literature. The staff at Menninger was so amazed they sent Dr. Dale Walters to review the findings and interview some of the participants in the study. Based on his review, the Menninger Clinic then sent Dr. Walters all over the country to teach practitioners how to use this new protocol. The result of his efforts has been that practitioners throughout the United States and many foreign countries now treat alcoholism, drug addiction, and PTSD successfully with neurofeedback. As for the VA hospital, we don't know the whole story, but we do know that Dr. Peniston was told to put his machines away and stop his treatment protocol. Why?

As we stated earlier, children with dysregulation disorders are more likely to demonstrate addictive behaviors than children without dysregulation disorders. Not only do drugs and alcohol reduce the constant swirl of thoughts, these addictive substances also have a numbing effect. There are other significant factors to be considered. For one thing, there is evidence that addictive drugs have the ability to cause a sudden release of dopamine. Dopamine makes us feel happier. Another factor is the idea of pleasure centers in the brain. Lastly, of course, the use of substances takes us away from the day-to-day stress of life.

In the early 1950s, Olds and Milner discovered that there are pleasure centers in the brain. These are areas that are rich in dopamine receptor sites. One of the problems in children with dysregulation disorders such as tic disorder or ADHD is low levels of serotonin, which is a neurotransmitter associated with mood. When addictive drugs are taken, there is a release of dopamine in the pleasure centers. If there is a predisposition for impulsive or compulsive behavior, as in the case of ADHD, then we have a prescription for addiction.

The problem, of course, is the fact that there is a surge of pleasure when these substances are ingested, and then there is a rebound from the drugs. The rebound is caused by a decrease in neurotransmitters; this, in turn, causes a craving for more drugs. So there is a dramatic seesaw effect to the addiction cycle. We can apply this same principle to drugs, alcohol, cigarettes, food, and sex. The oscillation is visible to everyone involved. One of the strengths of neurofeedback is its effectiveness in training the brain-waves in the areas that are filled with dopamine receptor sites.

Neurofeedback has the ability to stabilize the brainwaves, making the person less vulnerable to stress and influences. We have successfully treated alcoholics with neurofeedback protocols other than the alpha-theta protocols. Simply by regulating the brain's normal functioning, executive functioning is improved. Executive functioning involves our decision-making ability and neurofeedback strengthens the personality.

We treated a seventeen-year-old alcoholic who was in constant trouble with school officials. He came to our attention only after being suspended from school for being drunk on the school grounds. He was "plastered" when his mother brought him to our office. He was much too drunk to begin any training and it took a lot of time to clean up his constant vomiting, but we did get to work with him a few days later. He did fifty-one neurofeedback sessions before treatment ended. He completely quit drinking, his grades improved, and he got and held down a good part-time job. He finished high school and, to our knowledge, he is still clean and sober some twelve or thirteen years later. He is now a very stable young man.

Neurofeedback has shown positive results not only for people abusing alcohol, but also using the hardest of drugs. Drug addiction in our country and around the world is a growing problem, and neurofeedback offers relief from the pain and destruction of addiction.

12

Obesity

We would be remiss if we didn't at least take a quick look at the possibility of using brainwave biofeedback in treating obesity. Childhood obesity has reached epidemic proportions in this country. It is estimated that childhood obesity has now reached 30 percent. The Food and Drug Administration (FDA) has approved the use of cholesterol-lowering drugs in children as young as eight years of age. With a tool as powerful as neurofeedback that successfully treats addictions and impulsive behavior, we cannot ignore this growing health concern.

Though we have never specifically treated a child for obesity, it is not uncommon for an overweight child to lose weight while being treated for another disorder with brainwave training. Neurofeedback is a powerful tool for reducing the level of anxiety and depression, as well as improving impulse control.

There are multiple reasons for obesity and they vary from fats in fast foods to a sedentary lifestyle. All disorders have a stress component, however, and obesity is no exception. It is our belief that obese children, as well as adults, could be helped with this treatment. After all, we have been treating obesity for a long time with traditional biofeedback and it has been a solid ancillary tool. By reducing the stress level, we impact the stress eating and the unconscious grabbing of food.

Many children have poor impulse control and grabbing food is an automatic response. One of the things we have done with temperature biofeedback is have the patient warm their hands before they eat and image themselves taking the healthy foods and leaving the fattening foods. Dr. Eugene Peniston, in his work with alcoholics and drug addicts, uses neurofeedback with remarkable success. He and other practitioners use an imaging technique with their patients while they are actually doing the brainwave training. Since alcoholism has a strong impulse control factor, it seems only logical that we would gain some benefit by replicating this type of treatment with obese children.

If you improve impulse control, you could not only reduce the impulsive grabbing of food, but also assist in the motivational component of exercise. With ADHD children, we are constantly working to get them motivated to improve their skills. If we can improve academic motivation, we should be able to improve the motivation to eat better and exercise. When the brain is working better, the "will" improves.

Many children with dysregulation disorders have eating disorders. The most common problem is compulsive eating. Obsessive and compulsive behaviors are often seen in the clusters of problems that accompany other dysregulation disorders such as ADHD, depression, and anxiety. The genetic predisposition is often for compulsive eating and obesity in females and compulsive drinking and alcoholism in males.

As for children who are eating because of depression and anxiety, we know quite well that neurofeedback improves mood. If we improve the mood, then logically they will not have to eat to deal with their anxiety or depression. Food often eases feelings of inadequacy and aloneness. With brainwave training, we improve self-esteem. With a healthier self-image, there will be less inclination to put on pounds.

13

Peak Performance

Peak performance training is designed to make the already functional individual perform at a much higher level. The difference between two equally gifted athletes, one who excels and one who "also ran," is more than likely the ability to perform at their peak when it counts. Two equally gifted children in school may not have the same grade point average and that could obviously be for a lot of reasons. We feel that the primary reason for this type of disparity is that one of the children is likely functioning closer to peak performance than the other child. We would all like to perform at our maximum potential in whatever we do, but that is not always the case. If the brain is slightly dysregulated, it is probably more easily distracted and focus and concentration are not as sharp.

A golfer, football player, stockbroker, and high school student taking a test will all do better if they have maximum concentration. Unfortunately, concentration is a problem for a lot of people. If the brain is making too many slow-frequency waves, the brain is too sluggish for pinpoint concentration. If, on the other hand, the brain is racing, as in the case of anxiety, it cannot focus singularly on the task at hand. We need the midrange EEG waves to achieve optimum performance.

Since the 1950s, there have been several arousal theories that have attracted the attention of psychologists and others interested in human behavior. They all have one thing in common and that is that we need a perfect level of arousal to achieve our maximum potential. Most of these theories have been presented in the form of a bell curve. At the lowest end of the starting point is sleep; this represents our slowest brainwaves at 0.05 to four hertz. At this level, we are incapable of focusing on anything. As we begin to wake up to four to seven hertz, we are foggy or in a daze. If we keep waking up, we go up to eight to twelve hertz; this is the state commonly known as alpha. We are in a semi-focused, very dreamy state. Then moving up to the next level of brainwaves, we end up in the twelve- to fifteen-hertz range, which is relaxed focus. As we reach fifteen to eighteen hertz, our focus improves even more.

Till this point, our focus has been improving more and more, but what happens as we continue is that the level of arousal increases past the point of being productive. Now, as the dominant frequency reaches into the twenty-plus hertz range, there is deterioration in our ability to focus and concentrate. If it keeps climbing, there will be increasing emotional disturbance, even anxiety and/or panic.

What these theories demonstrate is that the degree of arousal is an important component in our ability to focus and concentrate. Arousal generates energy, so without arousal we are listless, and with too much energy we cannot settle down. So, it goes without saying, an optimum level of arousal is required to focus well, and with too much arousal we lose the ability to focus and concentrate.

The level of arousal can be seen very clearly on an electroencephalogram (EEG). Neurofeedback is simply biological feedback on the EEG. The EEG is a recording of the electrical activity of millions of functioning nerve cells in the brain. These very small recording and voltage changes, in the range of millionths of a volt, of electrical activity are picked up by little sensors and amplified; then they are presented in some way to the individual who is training. The feedback can be presented visually with a game or chart or with a sound such as a tone or music. It can even be presented in a tactile form, but in a way that the trainee can tell if there are changes in the EEG and in which direction the changes have occurred.

Competitive athletes at all levels, business executives, and students are beginning to understand the value of learning to perform at peak levels; consequently, people from all walks of life are seeking out neurotherapy centers. An increasing number of neurotherapists are adding peak performance training to their practices. We are frequently asked who could benefit from peak performance training and our answer is always a resounding "everyone." You do not have to be an Olympic-level athlete to want to play better or a Nobel laureate to want crisply focused thinking. Doctors, pilots, accountants, third-graders, and high school sophomores can all benefit from having their brains sharpened. Another thing to keep in mind, as we age there is a natural slowing of the brain and we just don't think as quickly and precisely as we did when our brains were younger. I (Robert Hill) have trained several lawyers, doctors, and other professionals who just wanted to brighten their brain. I have also trained a number of athletes who wanted to stay at the top of their game. We both continue to train our own brains on a regular basis, simply so we don't allow our brains to turn to mush.

One of the leaders in the field of peak performance is Rae Tattenbaum, MS. Her practice is in West Hartford, Connecticut. She not only focuses on helping individuals achieve optimum performance, she also teaches other practitioners how to provide this service. Another leader in the field is Jim Hardt, PhD, who runs the Biocybernaut Institute in San Francisco, California. He has done some very interesting work in creativity and altered states of consciousness.

14

Medications

The use of drugs is another topic that could be organized around a good, bad, and ugly scenario. Drugs for children with autism, ADHD, depression, anxiety, or headaches can be a mixed blessing.[1] They can cause serious adverse reactions.[2–3] And the whole issue of when to use drugs is influenced by the business demands of huge multinational corporations, where concerns about the bottom line trump concerns about health.[4–11]

The major benefit of using medication for children is that the drugs can reduce distressing symptoms or disruptive or harmful behaviors quickly and effectively. They can provide the window of opportunity that parents need to institute treatments that address the core of the child's problems. They can also give great relief to the child. Some children are able to perform well at school, to make friends, or participate in group activities like sports or dance. They may communicate, sleep, or eat.

Oftentimes drugs do not work this well. They may provide only partial benefit. If they are free of untoward effects, they can be useful and desirable. Frequently, however, the effects of drugs, commonly called side effects because they are not intended but are direct effects from the drugs nonetheless, present a dilemma: Continue for the benefit seen or discontinue due to the very real problems they are producing? There are also the associated puzzles:

Change the dose? Change the medication? Add another medication to see if it helps?

Too often, prescribed drugs produce no clear benefit, but they are continued as though it might be better than not doing anything. And of course, sometimes drugs have serious adverse effects, including death. They absolutely require the large and costly, carefully controlled studies before they are put on the market. Drugs are substances that do not occur in nature so can present significant biochemical difficulties as to how they are processed by the body. This is true for their metabolic by-products as well.

We should keep in mind that there are very real limitations to the studies that are done, impressive as they may be otherwise. They are no assurance of safety. Hundreds of drugs have been recalled, many have been Class 1 recalls, where there is excessive risk of serious harm or death.

Another limitation to drug studies is that, if the drug meets the safety standards, it only has to show greater benefit than placebo to be approved. That may not be much, not even a 50 percent likelihood of benefit. This is where the company statisticians earn their keep. Different sophisticated statistical tools can be employed to analyze data. One tool may emphasize the difference between two groups of numbers, which is useful for showing what appear to be greater benefits from the drug over placebo. Another tool may minimize differences, useful for appearing to minimize a drug's adverse effects when compared to placebo. And the reported improvements from the drug are as though there is no placebo effect in the drug group. They may report that 74 percent improve with the drug; but if 30 percent improved with placebo, the drug is benefiting 44 percent, not 74 percent.

Even drugs that have been correctly prescribed, dispensed, and taken can be dangerous. Adverse reactions to such drugs is the fourth leading cause of death in the United States with more than one hundred thousand deaths per year over the last several years. This is not to mention medication errors, with one and a half million people being harmed per year. Children are somewhat more at risk because of the general unfamiliarity of their dosing limits among nonpediatric hospital personnel.

There is also the seamy side of the pharmaceutical industry. Big Pharma, the thirty or so pharmaceutical companies that are multinational goliaths, uses deceptive practices. These include the suppression of negative clinical findings about drugs, heavy funding for researchers who have ties to drug companies, buying the silence of people who have been harmed by drugs, and the funneling of tax-funded research dollars which were intended for basic medical research but were instead used for identifying potential drugs Even when Big Pharma is not engaging in deception, the simple fact that they spend more on marketing than they do on research and development speaks volumes. We must not be passive consumers when it comes to making decisions about medication but informed participants in the decision-making. It is a double-edged sword with the potential for good or harm.

The major categories of drugs that are prescribed for children with the disorders we discuss in this book are the following.

Stimulants

This category of drugs is commonly used for children with attention problems, hyperactivity, impulsivity, and motor restlessness. Stimulants increase alertness, vigilance, and energy. Factory workers and long-distance drivers use them; they are used for the elderly, and the military is constantly researching their use in combat troops. The paradoxical improvement in children who are already energetic and hyperactive is due to their abnormally slow brainwave activity and low arousal levels in their brains. When these drugs raise the arousal level to an appropriate one, they sit quietly and are able to pay attention. The drugs typically work quickly. When they do, it is beautiful to see. Do not try to tell the parents of children who respond like this that children should not be taking drugs. They bite. Many teachers see the characteristic behaviors of ADHD improve dramatically when a child is prescribed stimulants, so they urge parents to seek a trial of medication for virtually any disruptive behaviors.[12] We do not disagree with a trial of medication, but these children also deserve to have their nutritional deficiencies corrected and food additives removed to see if drugs can be avoided.[13]

One group of stimulants contains methylphenidate, and includes Focalin, Ritalin, and its slow release forms, Concerta, Methylin ER, Metadate CD, Ritalin LA, and the patch, Daytrana. The other group of stimulants contains amphetamincs, and includes Dexedrine, Adderall, and Vyvanase. When drugs are called for, we prefer to start with one from the methylphenidate group.

Stimulants are often more useful when the attention problem is due to a short attention span; they are less frequently useful when a child is inattentive. Often, stimulants are used on any child who is overly energetic. If a child who has a short attention span, is inattentive, or is energetic does not show a recognizable improvement in behavior or school performance, it should not be continued; there is no other, unseen benefit the child is getting. Do not fall into the trap of feeling the need to do something for your child. Too many pediatricians and psychiatrists fall into wanting desperately to help. Parents need to be highly objective about these decisions. And continually pushing the doses up when there is no improvement after a reasonable trial is madness.

The slow release forms can help a child whose behavior tends to deteriorate later in the day when the drug effects are wearing off. Also, the slow release forms are somewhat less desirable for recreational use, so make sure your teenager is on a slow release form—less likelihood of being stolen, sold, or abused. There is rampant abuse of stimulant drugs by young people.

Children commonly require a lower dose as they grow up; their brains are further developed and need less help to function well. If your child had done very well on a medication and now is not doing as well, perhaps more irritable or moody, he or she may well need a lower dose, not more or other drugs. Autism and ADHD do not get worse as children grow, unless there are additional insults to the brain. If anything, they get somewhat better over time.

The best use of stimulants is to get a brisk improvement in a child's behavior and schoolwork while he or she undergoes neurofeedback to correct the problem. It is rare for a child who has had a course of neurofeedback not to be able to reduce the stimulant dose drastically, and it is common after neurofeedback training to be able to discontinue drugs altogether.

An alternative to drugs for some children is DMAE. Years ago, when we were in training, DMAE was a prescription drug, called Deanol or Deaner, and was used for what was called hyperkinetic syndrome, a rare disorder in children with hyperactivity, impulsivity, and poor attention.[14] In 1983, the FDA called for more studies to show its efficacy, but the manufacturers did not do these studies because the condition it treated, what we call ADHD today, was not common enough for the drug to be profitable. The FDA had it pulled from the shelves, but later DMAE was determined to be a safe nutrient and is available over the counter. It often has a milder effect than the prescription stimulants, so is perfect for some kids, and not useful for others. It is used for improved alertness, vigilance, and mood, and by the elderly for improved memory. Many adults use it instead of caffeine; it has a smoother onset and lasts longer than a cup of coffee.

Antidepressants

The antidepressants that are by far most prescribed for children are SSRIs, selective serotonin reuptake inhibitors. They significantly increase the activity of the neurotransmitter serotonin in the body. Included in this group are Celexa, Lexapro, Luvox, Paxil, Pexeva, Prozac, and Zoloft. Not all are FDA approved for children, but they are commonly used nonetheless. They can be useful for depression, obsessive-compulsive disorder, eating disorders, insomnia, anxiety, panic disorder, and sometimes for migraine headaches. These are the drugs most often prescribed for children in the autistic spectrum.

If an antidepressant helps, its effectiveness seldom becomes evident for a week or two, and a full six-week trial is necessary to evaluate its usefulness. Be patient. If, after an adequate trial, there is not a clear improvement in symptoms or behavior, discontinue it. There is no benefit to your child "being on it" if it is not evident.

Drug effects can include gastrointestinal problems of any type, headaches, dizziness, and either sedation or agitation. Some children gain weight. If there is benefit and the undesirable effects are manageable, the child should continue on the drug, but not if there is agitation, increased anxiety, or restlessness. The presence of these significantly increases a child's risk for self-injury, suicidal thinking, and suicidal behavior. It is the same if a child becomes gloomy and avoidant. The FDA started looking at antidepressants one by one to see if certain ones were worse than others, but it soon became clear that they all increase risks.[15–16] The concern was sufficient to require the dreaded "black box warning" on the labels of antidepressants, warning about increased risk of suicidal behavior in children and adolescents. This type warning is the strongest the FDA issues on prescription drugs.

An option to drugs is S-adenosylmethionine (SAMe). It enhances a crucial reaction in the body: methylation. Several processes that are dependent on methylation improve, including the formation of many neurotransmitters, connective tissues, and one of the important types of detoxification by the liver. It was used in Europe as an antidepressant for mild to moderate depression for years before practitioners in the United States became aware of that use for it. SAMe has been used in this country for a long time for arthritis and to enhance liver detoxification.

Side effects usually only occur in someone who is taking an antidepressant and adds SAMe, so a gradual increase while tapering the antidepressant down is a good idea. Anyone with bipolar disorder needs to be extremely cautious. Some find it is energizing, so avoid taking it at night.

In studies on depression, SAMe showed a quicker onset than antidepressants, one to two weeks, not two to six.[17–18] It appears to improve depression and avoid side effects by optimizing the levels of a number of neurotransmitters, not just excessively increasing the activity of one.

Another option, and one easier to use in children who have difficulty taking pills, is inositol. Inositol is a nutrient that we eat and that our bodies produce; it can be safely taken in high doses. Since the dose for depression (also for obsessive-compulsive disorder) is ten to twenty grams per day, it is more convenient to use powder. It has no taste, so it may be introduced into a child's food easily.[19–20]

Antipsychotics

These heavy hitters are used for treating psychotic episodes, as occur with schizophrenia or mania. They are used in tranquilizer guns to bring down bears. In very different doses, they are used for children who exhibit behaviors that are dangerous or extremely disruptive to themselves and others—aggression, self-injury, and severe hyperactivity. They can be a godsend.

The antipsychotics most used in children are Abilify, Clozaril, Haldol, and Risperdal. There are many others. The older drug, Haldol, may be more likely to produce undesirable effects, but they all can cause excessive sedation, lethargy, and loss of interest. They may constipate, which is terrible for a child who has a heavy toxic load, so this must be promptly corrected. If a child develops anxiety or restlessness, we discontinue these drugs unless they are lessening dangerous behavior.

As with stimulants, the best use is to give the opportunity for other treatment options that address the underlying condition to be instituted, and not rely on the drug for long-term behavioral control.

Anticonvulsants

Anticonvulsants usually work well for seizures, and they are also used for recurrent depressions, bipolar disorder, and, increasingly, for any mood problem. They are often the go-to drug when the usual drugs are not working, and sometimes in those situations, they turn out to be the answer. Again, there a number of these drugs; the ones more commonly used for children include Depakote, Dilantin, Keppra, Lamictal, Neurontin, and Tegretol. They appear to work by stabilizing areas of the brain.

Undesirable effects from this group are usually neurological—dizziness, blurred vision, impairments in coordination, and sedation. Gastrointestinal complaints—nausea and abdominal pain—are not uncommon.

A different anticonvulsant, Klonopin, is in the tranquilizer class of drugs, so is very useful when a child has anxiety, fearfulness, or insomnia. Although all medications should be tapered when they are being discontinued, an even slower tapering is necessary for Klonopin.

There is a tendency that once these drugs are started, if effective, they are continued long term. If a child has stabilized on one of these drugs for six months or longer, we believe there should be trial at a lower dose, and then discontinuation if possible. If a child begins to deteriorate, it is clear what to do. But if a child does well for months to years before another episode, we believe it is worth having that period of time off the drug. If symptoms do redevelop down the road, we already know the effective dose and undesirable effect profile, and can institute treatment quickly. These drugs work the second time around.

Although there is no guarantee with any treatment, when we treat a child who is responding well to one of the anticonvulsants with neurofeedback, we fully expect an excellent result. Neurofeedback stabilizes and balances the brain. And we know that seizure threshold goes up after neurofeedback training. Dr. Sterman demonstrated this more than forty years ago on neurofeedback-trained cats that became resistant to seizures even when they were injected with a massive dose of a convulsant.

Based on the previous discussion, here is our thinking regarding medications:

- If the severity of the child's problems is disruptive to daily activities, relationships, or school performance, a trial of medication is called for.

- If the benefits clearly outweigh the drawbacks, it should be continued as long as this is so.

- If both benefits and undesirable effects are present, the drug should only be continued if parents feel the problems the drug is producing are manageable.

- It should also be continued if the drug makes possible the instituting of a treatment that addresses the cause of the problem, such as dietary changes, neurofeedback, or antifungal medication; in this case, the effort to tolerate undesirable effects should be greater.

- If there is no clear improvement from the drug, it should be discontinued.

- A second drug should not be used to treat bad effects from the first; this has a very low likelihood of overall benefit.

- If a drug helps a child resolve an episodic problem, it does not need to be continued indefinitely, unless demonstrated otherwise by lowering and attempting to discontinue the drug after a period of extended stability.

- Drugs should only be introduced one at a time.

- The use of more than one drug at a time in a child should be avoided if possible.

We give a plea to parents for whom a drug has been the answer to a prayer for their children to consider neurofeedback for their children as well. An ADHD child who does beautifully on a stimulant, at the end of the day, still has ADHD. If that child gets neurofeedback, he or she has a good chance of the ADHD resolving. The difference will impact that child's life immeasurably.

15

The Healing Power of Neurofeedback

Neurofeedback, often known as brainwave biofeedback or EEG biofeedback, is a sophisticated form of biofeedback. Biofeedback is one of these terms that most people have heard but may not understand what it actually means.

Eavesdropping on Events inside Your Body

Biological systems in the human body are constantly sending us messages. We don't usually pay attention to them until they become so loud we can't avoid them. For example, if we run up three flights of stairs, we notice we are breathing hard and sweating, and our hearts are pounding. We hear the message loud and clear, and we slow down, rest, and recover.

The internal messages are always there, but unless we exaggerate them or specifically go looking for them, they generally go unnoticed. When your doctor checks your pulse, she is listening in on biological information; hence, what she gets is biofeedback. If your doctor uses a stethoscope to listen to your heart and lungs, she is using a simple biofeedback instrument.

It is only in the past few decades, however, that technology has provided us with machines sophisticated enough to detect, amplify, and record the more subtle biological signals. Being able to do this started a revolution in medicine. We soon learned that by getting feedback on internal processes, we could change internal activity.

Biofeedback is like eavesdropping on our body's internal conversations. When these inside-the-skin events are detected and fed back to us through electrical signals using sight, sound, or touch, we can learn to use this information to change unwanted patterns that are contributing to poor physical and/or mental health. That's because our bodies are a sea of information and communication. Every organ is talking and listening to every other organ. This seems to be important for the health of the whole. We are a complexity of many organ systems and trillions of cells that are completely dependent on one another for life itself. If communication breaks down, or a system becomes dysregulated, it affects all other systems.

The idea that there is such a strong mind-body connection in healing has produced an entirely new field of medical study, psychoneuroimmunology (PNI). The term "psychoneuroimmunology" connects the mind *(psycho)*, the nervous system *(neuro)*, and the body's natural defenses *(immuno)*. We know that these three systems carry on a constant dialogue, particularly the brain and nervous system, and this is where neurofeedback plays a major role.

Inside-the-skin events have often been ignored because they are subtle and often difficult to detect. Now, with the development of small, affordable computers, we are more capable than ever of listening in, amplifying, recording, and getting feedback information on biological events. This is revolutionizing the way we look at the whole body as a functioning system. The feedback may be in the form of sight, sound, or physical stimulation. With the latest advances in technology, the feedback can come in the form of sophisticated computer games. With practice, we can begin to change inside-the-body events to make us healthier.

The quieter messages that otherwise go unnoticed until we have a medical or emotional problem are now available for study. With biofeedback, it is a relatively simple process to teach a person to change inside-the-skin activities. We can change things such as temperature, heart rate, blood pressure, muscle tension, chemical responses, and even brainwaves.

To illustrate the effectiveness of biofeedback, we will share with you a wonderful story that Dr. Elmer Green tells. Dr. Green is one of the early pioneers in biofeedback and has contributed as much to the field as anyone in its history. Dr. Green would bring individuals with unusual talents for self-regulation to the Menninger Clinic in Topeka, Kansas, where they would be studied. On one of his trips to Menninger, the Swami Rama demonstrated that he could create a ten-degree temperature differential just two inches apart on the palm of his hand. This, in anyone's opinion, would be extraordinary. Swami Rama said it took thirteen years to learn this. His biofeedback was the skin color of his hand. The swami would watch the palm of his hand to get his biological feedback. When a part of the body heats up, the area turns red. This is easily seen when a person is embarrassed and the skin flushes. The face, ears, and upper chest turn deep pink to bright red.

So Swami Rama would observe his hand and focus on making one spot red and the cooler spot a grey color. When the one spot turned red, he knew that it was hotter than the surrounding area. This was obviously a result of changes in blood flow. A graduate student working with two temperature biofeedback machines was able to accomplish this task in two weeks. So with appropriate biofeedback technology, the graduate student was able to learn the task more than three hundred times faster than Swami Rama. This reinforces the notion that we can change any organ system quickly if we provide it with appropriate information.

Biofeedback is simple and painless. The therapist attaches small sensory monitors to the scalp or skin, like placing tiny stethoscopes to listen to inside-the-skin events. The patient then sits back, usually in a comfortable chair, and begins to relax. The machines then show how a particular body system is functioning and feeds back information as the patient works to change that system. The patient may be trying to relax a group of muscles for back pain or increase skin temperature of a finger to help in Raynaud's disease.

Raynaud's disease is a painful phenomenon in which the small arteries in the finger go into spasm, cutting off the blood flow. The fingers turn white and/or purple due to loss of blood flow.

As the patient becomes more proficient in the use of a biofeedback instrument, he becomes more aware of how a particular body system is functioning. This helps the patient bring that system under more voluntary control. Until recent decades, Western medicine believed that systems under the control of the autonomic nervous system functioned involuntarily, that we had no control over them. Yet yogis in the East had demonstrated for millennia that they could control such processes. It was only through biofeedback that we were able to change the belief system of Western medicine.

Now, in biofeedback practices all over the world, we routinely train people to change those "involuntary" processes, bringing them under voluntary control. Once patients learn to regulate a system, they no longer need the biofeedback equipment. While training, they develop a sensory image. This is not a visual image, but a feeling that physical things are changing inside the body. For example, patients can sense when the hands are beginning to warm, the blood pressure is going down, the muscles are relaxing, and the brain is alert.

Imagine having voluntary control over your autonomic reflexes. A few decades ago physicians would have dismissed the idea as crazy. Now, informed physicians use and prescribe biofeedback daily to patients with disorders ranging from high blood pressure to urinary incontinence to stress-related disorders.

Neurofeedback, the Next Step Up

Neurofeedback is a sophisticated form of biofeedback that has been demonstrated to be highly effective in treating dozens of physical and psychological disorders. It has also been used for individuals who want to perform at peak efficiency. This is usually called "peak performance training."

Early in the history of neurofeedback, it was used successfully to help individuals with uncontrollable epilepsy. Barry Sterman and colleagues at the Sepulveda, California, Veterans Administration Medical Center conducted their groundbreaking research.[1-5] There are many people who have seizure after seizure with little help from medication. By giving the patients feedback on their EEG rhythms, the patients were able to change the rhythms, thereby bringing the seizure activity under control.

Following closely on that work, Joel Lubar and his associates found EEG biofeedback to be a successful treatment for attention-deficit disorder and hyperactivity.[6-7] EEG biofeedback's effectiveness was also demonstrated by Tansy and Bruen.[8] From there, the modality has demonstrated efficiency with disorders from alcoholism to depression, anxiety to migraines.

Neurofeedback is not a cure-all, end-all treatment. It is, however, an exciting treatment that offers hope to some of the hopeless by teaching them to regulate their own inside-the-skin events. The field is growing and changing rapidly, offering hope to larger and larger populations as research in neurofeedback continues in many universities and private settings.

Significant among the expanding fields of application is performance training. There is a growing interest in peak performance, so many practitioners of neurofeedback offer peak performance training. Many governmental and industrial clients have their management teams go through neurofeedback training because it sharpens the brain, improves creativity, and enhances critical thinking. Japanese companies send management personnel to the United States for neurofeedback training because staying competitive is important and they know neurofeedback makes sharper, quicker thinkers.

Neurofeedback: Training or Treatment or Both

Most neurofeedback training clinics have their roots in client-centered psychotherapy and self-regulation, so there is a lot of personal attention when a patient receives neurofeedback. The neurofeedback therapist understands that a healthy brain has the ability and versatility to change states of arousal and attention. As each new situation in a person's life demands a specific level of arousal and awareness, the healthy brain can quickly move to the appropriate level of alertness.

By contrast, the unhealthy brain may be underaroused and sluggish or overaroused and anxious. Either way, the dysregulated brain has a diminished ability to respond to specific demands. The immature, injured, or disordered brain lacks the normal elasticity of the healthy brain. Scientifically speaking, there appears to be discontinuity in the brain and nervous system processing or break-downs in the way the brain and nervous system communicate. In other words, the brain is not processing information or repsonding at the right speed. It is either too slow or too fast. Also, the brain is not communicating information correctly to itself, so it is out of sync with itself.

The disordered brain seems to be stuck, or "parked," at the wrong place. It produces brainwaves that are inappropriate for the immediate situation. For example, in most of the childhood disorders we have been discussing, the brain tends to produce more lazy daydreaming-type brainwaves than it does thinking, concentrating-type brainwaves.

Neurofeedback training teaches the person what specific brain-wave states feel like and how to turn those states on voluntarily. Individuals being trained can move their own brains to different physiological states, depending on what the immediate situation requires.

We have been training people for many years to change their physiological state through biofeedback. With the aid of biofeedback machines, we can alter practically any physiological process. Neu-rofeedback is the next step up; we are actually training the central processing system, the brain. Most of the early work in biofeedback focused on the peripheral systems of skin and muscle. Now we can go directly to the brain, hence the new name—neurofeedback.

Neurofeedback makes the brain more flexible, and seems to have a generalizing effect on the whole nervous system. The implications of this are profound. Training the brain to correct its dysregulated state has a positive effect on neurological function-ing as well as on the cardiovascular, gastrointestinal, immune, and endocrine systems. Self-regulation not only enhances the brain's ability to improve cognitive/intellectual functioning, but it also aids the body in healing itself.

Self-healing is what biofeedback is all about. It brings what used to be termed involuntary processes under voluntary control. Self-regulation is exciting because it gives patients some control over their own health and well-being. They are no longer at the mercy of a dysregulated brain and no longer completely dependent on the pharmaceutical industry to provide them with the "magic pill."

Changing Inside Out

A neurofeedback machine monitors the electrical activity produced by the brain, and the neurotherapist (neurofeedback professional) can correlate this activity with human behavior. The brain's electrical activity is measured in cycles per second, or hertz. A neurotherapist can examine the activity of a single frequency or a group of frequencies together, called a frequency band. By comparing behavior with the brainwave frequency, conclusions can be drawn about the relationship between the two. As a result of research in this area, we have been able to determine different behavioral states and how they relate to rhythmic activity of the brain. In other words, we know what state of consciousness a person is in when the brain is producing a dominance of a single frequency or frequency band.

By using feedback instruments, the therapist can feed back information to patients on their level of consciousness at any given moment. Patients can subjectively evaluate what that conscious state feels like and, with practice, can begin to reproduce that level of consciousness voluntarily. It takes training time, but patients gradually learn to move the brain out of "park," giving it the power and flexibility to meet life tasks. Once trained, patients developed a level of sophistication in identifying the desired state; they no longer need the neurofeedback equipment to accomplish the task at hand. They are now self-regulating.

Once trained, patients no longer need the neurofeedback equipment to relax, feel calmer, concentrate better, or be more focused.

Therefore the student shows fewer and fewer symptoms of any disorder they have been dealing with. The businessman is much more efficient on the job; the migraine sufferer can dramatically reduce the frequency, duration, and intensity of her headaches. Neurofeedback teaches the fine and profound art of self-mastery. It can make any person less dependent on medical personnel, drugs, machines, or medical technology. It produces strong self-reliance, independence, and self-esteem, and provides patients with some control over their physical and mental states of health.

The Neurofeedback Learning Process

All biofeedback, including neurofeedback, is a learning process. It involves physical learning and mental skills. It is a process of learning how to change your body by listening to its functioning. When you can control your own mental state, you have real power. Neurofeedback is like any other learning process: The more you learn through practice, the more confidence you develop. So we suppose you could say that a side effect of neurofeedback is greater self-confidence.

Neurofeedback is not complicated. In our office practice, children of four, five, and six years learn to change their brainwave patterns. A number of neurotherapists have trained infants; a parent holds the infant during the session. Anyone except the very mentally deficient can learn self-regulation, so neurofeedback is not just for the elite. It is for all humans who want self-control and self-determination. Although patients cannot explain what they have learned and how they have learned it, they know they have changed.

For example, in temperature training, we have many patients who can quickly learn to increase a hand temperature of seventy-two degrees to ninety-five degrees. They know they can do it, but they cannot tell you how they do it because the learning is at a subconscious level.

In neurofeedback, the brain learns what it needs to do to accomplish the task. You want it, you tell the brain to do it, and it does it, leaving you never knowing exactly what you've learned.

Truly, if there is any magic left in the world, it is the magic inside each of us.

Some biofeedback processes, like hand temperature training, may only take a few training sessions to achieve. The more complex the system, the longer training takes. Brainwave training takes longer than temperature training because you are dealing with a more complex system. In brainwave biofeedback, the patient learns the "feel" of a particular brainwave. The more training patients have, the more easily they perfect the skill of producing a particular rhythmic state in the brain. Learning to modify a brainwave state in the direction of a desired mental state is a "discovery" process, a process of gaining more and more control over your thoughts, feelings, and behavior.

Global Dysregulation

We have talked about clusters of disorders, but now we want to delve deeper into why people have multiple symptoms that seem to emerge at the same time. Because of the wide variety of disorders that have been helped with neurofeedback, the idea of a global dysregulation effect emerged. This is a simple concept that means that if the brain is dysregulated, it can have a global, or body-wide, effect. Seldom does a patient present to a health professional with a single symptom, and the symptoms usually involve more than one body system.

For example, patients may present with the chief complaint of depression, but after a thorough intake evaluation, they acknowledge trouble sleeping, poor attention span, irritable-bowel-type problems, low-back pain, sugar cravings, weight gain, alcohol use, irritability, and chronic anxiety. So the symptoms are not just in one system; they tend to be global, or body-wide. Once neurofeedback treatment begins, symptoms from several systems begin to respond, and the response generally has lasting benefits.

It appears that once the brain becomes dysregulated, it can have a global effect on the body. After all, the rhythmic activity of the brain affects all functional systems of the body, and this rhythmic activity is central to all systems. Therefore, regulating the central rhythmic activity of the brain improves body-wide functioning. It appears that neurofeedback not only affects such problems as attention and concentration, but also has a systemic effect. When we treat people for ADHD with neurofeedback, other systems begin to improve because the brainwaves become regulated. For example, in treating ADHD, not only does attention improve, but oppositional behavior, sleep, irritability, depression, anxiety, antisocial behavior, tics, and many other problems also improve.

To give you an unusual example, several years ago we were treating a ten-year-old for ADHD. During the treatment period, he started having visual problems. His mother took him to his ophthalmologist who told her, and us, that after years of following this child's visual problems, the child's "lazy eye" had suddenly gotten much better. We all concluded that focusing on the neurofeedback monitor must have helped train the eye to focus more normally.

Early on, we noticed that while treating women for depression, anxiety, or other disorders, their PMS or menopausal symptoms improved dramatically. At first we thought it was just a coincidence, but it happened again and again. We now realize that if you regulate the brain, you affect all systems, even the endocrine system.

Neurofeedback has the ability to reduce or correct global dysregulation. The future implications of this are profound. Neurofeedback training could preclude taking multiple medications for multiple problems, or seeing several different specialists, each treating a different problem. Neurofeedback treats problems at the core—the brain—and when the functioning of the brain improves, it produces global body-wide changes.

16

How Neurofeedback Works

When you make claims that a particular treatment is highly effective for a number of different diagnoses, professionals and laypersons alike tend to become suspicious. And we think they should. Snake-oil salesmen have long pervaded the arena of medical treatment. How many times have we all heard that this pill or that herb will heal, give us more energy, give us greater sexual prowess, or help us lose weight? Most products with broadly based claims just do not hold up under close inspection. They may help with one thing or reduce one symptom, but they seldom meet our expectations. When they don't, our optimism turns sour.

Brainwave Researchers Take Advantage of Modern Computers

When we first ventured into the field of neurofeedback, we kept waiting for the bottom to fall out. After all, we remembered with vivid disappointment the "alpha craze" in the 1960s and 1970s. The promoters of alpha brainwaves promised that if we could make more alpha brainwaves through meditation, drugs, and primitive neurofeedback machines, we could achieve a life of bliss. In the 1960s, some people were even turning on their TVs and adjusting the picture until it was a snowy fuzz. They sat staring at it because it was supposed to help them produce more alpha waves. Transcendental meditation was the craze, acid was the party drug, and companies made alpha machines. Those who promised nirvana could not deliver on the promise. The machines were too primitive and research too scarce. The alpha phenomena hurt the science of neurofeedback; it did not produce all the promises we were told to expect. In retrospect, there is nothing wrong with meditation, biofeedback, and learning to produce more alpha waves, but there were lots of reasons for the failures: The equipment was not as sophisticated; the science was too new to make such exaggerated claims; and it was too entangled with the metaphysics of the 1960s and 1970s.

Over time, brain science has taken some curious turns. We have vacillated between looking at the brain in small components versus the notion of understanding the brain as a complete functional system. Neurotherapists have always looked at the brain as a functioning system and so, with any disorder, we hoped to see how the systems had failed. For example, when we first started looking at the ADHD phenomenon, we had the intuitive understanding that it was a functional problem and not some minute component. As we discussed earlier, this idea is reflected in the terminology of "minimal brain dysfunction."

Brain scientists are still in conflict. Many scientists are attempting to understand the brain from a molecular level and that is a positive thing to do. They break the brain down into the smallest bits, rather than seeing it as a whole. In treating the disorders we are discussing, we want to understand the brain as an entire functional system.

Often our patients come in with normal CT scans, normal EEGs, and/or normal MRIs, but functionally they are a mess. So, structurally, and perhaps molecularly, they appear normal, but it is their routine brain function that seems disturbed. We frequently describe patients' disorders to them by giving this example: "You are like a car with faulty timing. Your brain is okay—it just needs a tune-up."

By examining the brain at a molecular level, the issues of gross motor, gross thought, and gross emotional behavior are not the primary focuses. Most of our patients are not concerned with their molecules, but they are concerned about balance and strength, quality and quantity of thought, and being overwhelmed by their emotions. Neurotherapists are not concerned on a daily basis with the trillions of molecules that make up the brain; we are concerned with the global functioning of that system we call the brain and nervous system. This has translated into practical therapeutic treatments for clusters of disorders.

For example, accompanying depression, the person may also have tiredness, loss of interest, irritability, loss of sleep, and/or a decreased sense of humor. This cluster of symptoms all relate to the same problem. Global symptoms may reflect problems from several systems. Therefore a practical therapeutic approach focuses on a treatment such as neurofeedback that not only has a positive effect on a cluster of symptoms, but also on global dysregualtion.

Think for a minute about that brain inside your skull. Your brain is a large, complex, self-organizing system. Occasionally, the functioning of that system becomes dysregulated. As we explained earlier, it is likely a result of genetics or some type of injury. When the brain is dysregulated for a period of time without restoration of its normal functioning, it interprets the new functioning as normal. That dysregulation produces a cluster of unwanted symptoms.

To use an example from the area of dependence, if you smoke cigarettes long enough, the body begins to act as though cigarettes are as necessary to you as oxygen, water, or food. Therefore, if you try to quit smoking, your body rebels, making you uncomfortable and quitting very difficult. Brainwaves are much the same. If a brain received a head injury during birth, that injury may cause the brain to produce the wrong brainwave for any given task. After a long enough time, the brain doesn't try to correct the dysfunction because it thinks the current waves are normal.

Neurofeedback works by challenging the brain to make different waves. It is this challenging of the brain that seems to awaken the brain's self-regulating mechanism. We nudge the brain's firing patterns in the direction of a healthier balance. A process then begins to take place that appears to be the brain teaching itself to normalize. Because the brain is trying to maintain a balance, we push and it pushes back, resisting a rapid change in one direction or another. This is why progress is not rapid with neurofeedback. This slow learning process ensures that the brain does not rush to a new firing pattern that could be in 'a more dysfunctional, opposite direction. The fact is, we can change any functional system of the body, including the brain and nervous system, if we give it appropriate feedback and enough time.

It took the newer, faster, more compact computers to make neurofeedback a practical therapeutic treatment that could be made available to the general public. If you are going to give the brain information about its own rhythmic activity, and give it fast enough for it to recognize and change the pattern, it has to be real-time fast (not delayed information). It has only been in the past decade or so that we could even begin to formulate treatment protocols and to experiment on what types of disorders would respond positively to the training. We don't apologize for being a new science, but we still eagerly await the next research paper or treatment protocol for some disorder with which we have not previously worked.

Neurofeedback offers hope to so many people who feel hopeless because it is able to provide the brain with information about its own rhythmic activity. It assists in regulating not only the dysrhythmic activity of emotional problems such as depression and anxiety, but also the dysrhythmic activity of physical and neurological disorders such as autism, epilepsy, migraines, head injury, stroke, and PMS.[1-2]

The brain communicates to all systems, including itself, through electrical activity. As odd as it may sound, it appears that the brain has generators that produce the brainwave activity, which are actually low-frequency electrical rhythms. It is this electrical activity that gives the information about what and how to do everything. This low-frequency rhythmic activity is central to life and the second-to-second functioning of every organ system in the body. If this rhythmic activity becomes dysregulated, it leads to dysfunction.

We could end up sleeping rather than reading, anxious rather than calm, dull rather than alert.

We know now that the brain responds to many forms of intervention, including classical and operant conditioning, which we discuss later. Neurofeedback directly affects the brain, so its impact is on the central processes of the entire person. Since the brain is intimately involved with every organ and system in the body, neurofeedback affects us at the core. You cannot change the brain without it having some effect on every functioning system. Because neurofeedback directly affects the brain, it has the opportunity to elicit a faster, more comprehensive, longer-lasting resolution to functional problems.

Adjusting Our Own Brain Rhythms

To be more specific about how neurofeedback works, the brain controls our physiological state of arousal. This is done by the rhythmic activity of the brain, expressed through brainwaves. If brainwaves become dysregulated for whatever reason, they may not return to a healthy functional state after the event has passed.

Earlier we discussed the notion that the brain may assume dysfunctional rhythmic activity to be normal and work to maintain it. When the brain is producing a steady state, regardless of the activity level, we say it is "parked," to use a term coined by brain researcher Dr. Michael Tansy. For example, if the brain is consistently showing a dominance of seven hertz, regardless of the human's functional activity, we say the brain is parked at seven hertz.

There are certain brainwaves that are characteristically seen as a result of a specific event. For example, when there is a blow to the head or a seizure, the brain will emit a high burst of a single brainwave or a band of brainwaves. These are referred to as spikes. In closed head injuries, we may see spikes in the very low delta range (one to four hertz). In epilepsy, we see high spikes in the area of seven hertz. When there is trauma to the brain, these injuries usually show up on conventional imaging, such as MRIs or CT scans. We can see the inappropriate burst and also determine the focal point.

In other types of problems, such as ADHD and depression, we do not generally see spikes, but we see single brainwave frequencies or frequency bands that are inappropriately dominant. For example, if sleep waves are dominant when you are trying to read, they are inappropriate. We have seen ADHD children exhibit large inappropriate spiking. In such cases, we suspect these children have suffered some type of closed head injury: a fall, a sharp bang or hit, or some other trauma.

Dominance is a key term to remember when thinking about appropriate and inappropriate functioning. Brains produce all of the various brainwaves all of the time, but depending on our level of arousal, a single brainwave or a band of several brainwaves will be higher than others. That wave or band of waves will be the dominant wave or frequency band. To function at peak efficiency, we want the dominant wave to reflect the activity we are engaged in at the time. For example, if we are sleeping, we want slow "sleep" brainwaves; if we are doing a complicated math problem, we want the faster, "alerting" brainwaves to be dominant.

Children and adults who have attentional disorders demonstrate a dominance of low-frequency waves. In fact, both epileptics and children with ADHD show a dominance of slower EEG waves and a deficit of faster-frequency waves.[3] If a person is asleep, it is appropriate to have a dominance of slow waves. But if the person is producing excessive slow waves in math class, there is a problem. This person appears to be in a fog, short-term memory is compromised, and either lethargy or hyperactivity is common.

A multitude of symptoms may be present when we see a dominance of low-frequency waves. If the brainwave states are not normalized, all other areas of the patient's life may be affected. If the rhythmic activity is normalized, normal functioning is restored. The normalization of the brain generally produces the following positive changes: improved executive functioning, restful sleep, improved memory, improved concentration, reduced hyperactivity, and elimination of depression and anxiety.

To better understand how brainwaves are related to functioning, let's look at brainwaves in generalities. Think of brainwaves on a continuum from very slow to very frantic; each band of brainwave activity reflects a level of arousal or consciousness. Our behavioral functioning varies according to the dominant frequency on the continuum. What we would like is a highly flexible brain where the brainwaves go up and down according to what we are doing. We definitely do not want the brain to get "parked" at any one frequency.

In deep sleep, we are producing more of the very high-amplitude, low-frequency delta waves, four or fewer cycles per second, so delta is dominant. Moving along the continuum, next we have theta waves. They are slightly lower in amplitude, and there is an increase in frequency. We will see four to eight cycles per second. In other words, they are not quite as "loud," but there are more of them. Theta is characterized by a drowsy, partial awareness or an unconscious state nearing sleep.

The next frequency band on our continuum is alpha. These brainwaves are lower in amplitude than theta, and, again, there are more of them. Their frequency increases and we see eight to twelve cycles per second. Alpha is characterized by a relaxed, focused awareness, somewhat like in meditation or yoga.

Next, we find a low beta identified and named sensorimotor rhythm (SMR) by the brain scientist Barry Sterman, PhD.[4] Dr. Sterman first observed this process in physically relaxed cats. SMR is from twelve to fifteen hertz followed by the beta frequency band, which is a higher-frequency band from fifteen to eighteen hertz. Beta is characterized by low amplitude, higher frequency. It is very focused, but busier, and not as relaxed as the rhythm of alpha.

Last, we have a low-amplitude, very high-frequency band labeled high beta or gamma. This high beta wave is characterized by an excited, super focused, anxious, fearful, or angry mental state, and ranges from more than nineteen hertz to forty hertz and beyond.

If the brain moves toward the slower frequency brainwaves, a person becomes less aroused, until they finally achieve sleep or an unconscious state. If the brain moves to higher and higher frequencies, the person becomes increasingly more aroused until they are finally out of control due to excitation. Some people are able to sustain a state of super focus in the higher frequencies. There is some controversy about the exact labeling of such terms as alpha and theta, and about the exact frequencies that should be included in the bands, but we will leave such issues to academia. It is important, however (and generally agreed upon), that the lower the frequency, the more lethargic we become, and the higher the frequency, the more agitated we become.

You can easily see how brainwaves affect our state of arousal. If we are underaroused, we don't function at full capacity because we are dull, lazy, or sleepy. It is okay to sleep in the low waves, but we don't want to be parked there all the time. It is okay to become excited over something, but no one would want to stay there. The normally functioning brain is very flexible, and can move easily up or down the frequency range, depending on the level of arousal needed for the task at hand. Unfortunately, most people with dys-regulation disorders are parked in the lower frequencies.

In the case of ADHD, it is surprising to most parents to find out that their wild, hyperactive child is actually in a state of underarousal. The child is using hyper movement to wake up and stay focused in his surroundings. Otherwise, the child is in a dull, lethargic state. Hyper movement then becomes a very functional behavior for keep-ing the brain awake. There are other children, primarily females, who do not use the hyper movement. When these children do not use movement, they tend to be dull, listless, and often irritable.

Another consequence of the slow rhythmic activity is sleep disturbance. A large number of individuals with dysregulation dis-orders suffer from sleep problems. These may be delayed-onset insomnia, frequent awakening, early awakening, and/or restless sleep. This list could include restless-leg syndrome, bed-wetting, encopresis (fecal incontinence), nightmares, and other nocturnal problems. It is not uncommon for people with dysregulation disor-ders to report that their bed is torn apart every morning.

From a practical standpoint, it is hard to sleep at night if the brain has been semi-asleep all day. As practitioners, we often end up training the brain to wake up so that it will be able to sleep later.

When we treat any dysregulation disorder with neurofeedback, we see dramatic improvement in the other symptoms that manifest as a result of too much low-frequency brainwave activity. Low-frequency brainwave activity is directly or indirectly responsible for a host of problems. While neurofeedback cannot fix everything, it can improve dysfunctional rhythmic activity, which can alleviate many different symptoms. A treatment such as stimulant medications may make the child alert, but it frequently causes collateral damage and makes other symptoms worse.

Take the case of Ritalin. Parents often report school grades improve when the child is on the medication, but sleep is awful, irritability more prevalent, and tic behavior much worse. In contrast to stimulant medications, neurofeedback treats the patient's central processing mechanism, the brain. It doesn't merely chase one symptom with one drug and another symptom with a second or third drug. Neurofeedback treats the cause and not the symptoms, which is why it is the preferred treatment for many people.

One technique to determine if the brain is functioning within "normal" parameters is to look at the ratio between the low frequencies and the mid-range frequencies. We generally compare the ratio of theta averages to beta averages, measured with electrodes placed at different locations on the head.

To do this, neurotherapists use what is known as the international ten-twenty system of electrode placement. This system indicates the exact placement sites of the sensors. Research protocol and clinical treatments are standardized by placing the electrode sensors at specific head sites. Correct sensor placement is critical to success, so neurotherapists take great care to place the sensors at specific locations on the head. To train the wrong area prolongs or increases the existence of the dysregulation.

The theta-to-beta ratio in adults generally ranges from one-to-one to one-and-a-half-to-one. With younger children, the ratio is somewhat higher, but we still want a ratio near that range. Frequently, patients with dysregulation disorders have excessive ratios, often two-, three-, and four-to-one. In the case of severe injury, the ratio can climb much higher. The job of neurotherapists is to train down the high ratio.

When treating patients with these high ratios, we do not always see the ratios change dramatically, but there is always some change somewhere in the brainwave patterns. It is surprising to see how a little change in brainwave activity can make a huge change in behavior. If we don't see anything else, there is almost always a reduction in amplitudes. Not every dysregulation disorder looks the same. In anxiety disorders, we may see excessive high-frequency waves. They may even have a V-type pattern, with elevated low-frequency and elevated high-frequency waves and the nice mid-range frequencies in the basement. The objective, in this case, would be to train up the mid-range waves and reduce the high amplitudes of the waves on the ends of the continuum.

Operant Conditioning, the Secret to Training

The process of training the brain to make appropriate adjustments in rhythmic firing is as simple, in theory, as the way Dr. Ivan Pavlov conditioned his dogs to salivate at the sound of a bell. Dr. Pavlov's training paradigm is known as classical conditioning. Operant conditioning is about rewarding behavior that approximates a desired behavior. In education, we give an A to students who more closely approximate the learning behavior we want to see; we give Bs to those who are close, but not quite as close; and we give Fs to those who miss the mark.

An example of operant conditioning is if we wanted a child to play in the sandbox, we rewarded the child every time she went to the sandbox and ignored her when she played elsewhere. Soon she would play in the sandbox because it is the most rewarding place to be. Giving Fido a treat when he sits for us is also operant conditioning.

Brainwave training works the same way. If the brain's dominant frequency is low frequency, we reward the trainee with points or a tone each time he makes the more desirable, higher-frequency brainwaves. Unfortunately, this is not as direct and as quick as training Fido to sit because the brain is "parked." It takes time to nudge it back to a more functional, flexible position.

With neurofeedback, we eavesdrop on complex inside-the-brain events, run the information through a computer, and feed back the information through the eyes, ears, and/or skin of the trainee. Each time trainees improve their brainwaves, we reward them. If the brainwaves stay the same, there is no reward. The most stubborn child will eventually get involved in the "game."

One of our standard training screens is a "video game" in which the patient directs a large dot along a path, eating smaller dots. If the brain is functioning better, the big dot eats more of the small dots faster, and the patient scores more points. There are a variety of games used to stimulate the brain to wake up, but they are specialized games programmed to reflect EEG functioning. Traditional video games lull the brain into producing the wrong brainwaves. These traditional video games drive the patient deeper into dysregulation. In addition, we are very skeptical of EEG games that can be bought through magazines and such. When dealing with the brain, make sure you seek professional help from qualified individuals with medical-grade equipment.

Balancing the Brain

Figure 16.1 illustrates how the brainwaves normalized and the ratio balance was improved in the case of Otis, an eleven-year-old with ADHD. The figure shows Otis's progress at his twenty-second neurofeedback session. During the first treatment, the theta-beta ratio was in the range of eight-to-one. This means that Otis was making eight times more slow sleep waves than the faster alert waves. By the time Otis completed twenty-two training sessions, his beta ratio was in the range of 4.6-to-one. Otis required many more sessions to normalize the dysregulation, but there were dramatic behavioral improvements at session number twenty-two.

You will note in this figure that, in treatment sessions one and two, the ratio looks better, due to what psychologist label "the novelty effect." Otis is experiencing something new and exciting, so he is more awake. After a couple of sessions, however, the task

Figure 16.1. Neurofeedback Summary Chart

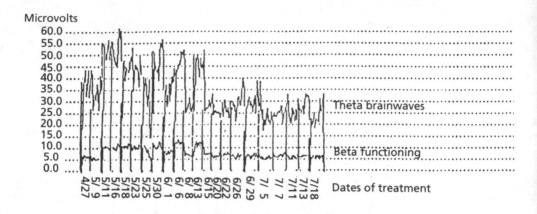

The numbers in the left-hand column are microvolts of electrical activity recorded from the brain. The top horizontal line that starts at approximately forty microvolts and wanders up and down, ending the twenty-second session at approximately twenty-three microvolts, is Otis's theta (4–8 Hz) brainwaves. The lower, less jagged line that starts at five microvolts is his beta (15–18 Hz) brainwaves. At session one, Otis's theta-to-beta ratio was slightly over eight-to-one. By the end of his twenty-second session, that ratio had dropped to slightly over 4.6-to-one and declining. The bottom line reflects the dates of training.

becomes boring, as it usually does for ADHD patients. For them, everything new and wonderful soon becomes old and boring.

For Otis, the twenty-two sessions improved his concentration, raised his school grades, and helped him feel "happier," as described by a parent. Otis made significant improvements, as do most patients who are treated with neurofeedback. It took a total of forty training sessions before we discontinued Otis's treatment, and one year later his mother reported he was doing "great."

The proof that we can do this with neurofeedback has been established for more than two decades. It has just taken a long time to get this sophisticated treatment to the general public, and it has taken us some time to understand what we were seeing.

Neurofeedback has now come of age and can be used therapeutically to help individuals with all types of dysregulation disorders.

It is quite possible that, some day, the use of medications for dysregulation disorders will be a thing of the past. At some point in the future, patients will have easy access to neurofeedback for a wide variety of disorders. In the meantime, practitioners are becoming proficient at correcting disorders of brainwave dysregulation and the number of patients seeking this treatment is growing rapidly. Why give any medication if patients and clients can self-correct a problem with neurofeedback training?

17

A Typical Neurofeedback Session

Neurotherapy sessions are relatively similar, and usually last approximately thirty to forty-five minutes. Sessions begin, continue, and end in the same way unless there are unusual circumstances. What is different from one session to the next is the individualized feedback protocol. The feedback protocol is based on the specific symptom patterns of the individual being treated. Patients present with different clusters of symptoms, so one individual may receive a completely different neurotherapy training protocol from another.

We tailor treatment for patients to their particular symptoms. Our goal is to retrain brainwaves to overcome less useful or "bad" brainwave firing patterns. Not all people with a specific disorder present in the same way. In addition, they may respond differently as training progresses. Neurotherapists vary the training based on the individual needs of the patient or client. Therefore, the therapist may change not only the specific brainwave bands to be trained, but also the location of the electrode placement on the skull. For example, when we train the same site on two individuals, it may make one person anxious while it calms the other. Individuals respond differently to the training and their response plays a major role in guiding the course of treatment. Neurotherapists must rely on good information reporting from patients and their families, and they also need to be keen observers themselves. Unfortunately, many people are "shut down" and have little or no awareness of how they really feel.

To give you an idea of how the neurotherapy session works, we will take you through a typical session. Our example will be Newman, a twelve-year-old in the seventh grade. His mother reported that he had had behavioral problems since "day one." He was tested by the school system and by independent psychologists several times, and this testing revealed a very bright young man with an IQ in the above-average to superior range. The testing also revealed high variability in his performance. In addition, he was sullen and defiant. One minute he could concentrate and the next minute he is off in his own world. As a matter of fact, his mother kept repeating, "Newman lives in his own little world."

The intake interview consists of an extensive medical and psychological history and review of all aspects of the patient's life. We interview the patient as well as any family members available, usually parents. When we did Newman's intake interview, it revealed that his symptoms ranged from moderate to severe and that there were a lot of them. Newman had moderate attentional problems and was hyperactive. In addition, he had a moderate level of tic behavior, which included throat clearing, sniffing, hiccups, head tossing, blinking, lip licking, and coughing.

Newman had many other symptoms including anxiety, depression, fearfulness at times, difficulty getting along with just about everybody, being difficult to manage, having temper outbursts, and accepting no responsibility for any of his behavior. Additional symptoms included poor school performance, not obeying rules, low self-esteem, tearfulness, social withdrawal, oppositional behavior, lying, taking things and denying it, fighting, and destruction of other people's property. Newman could have been diagnosed with a number of disorders, including but not limited to depression, ADHD, oppositional defiant disorder, and Tourette's syndrome. What was clear is that he had a dysregulation disorder.

Oppositional defiant disorder is defined by a persistent and pervasive pattern of negative, defiant, disobedient, and hostile behavior, particularly toward authority figures. Tourette's syndrome is characterized by persistent motor and vocal tics, such as Newman's sniffing, head tossing, lip licking, and coughing.

Because it is impossible to work on all problems at once, we prioritized which symptoms to treat first. We decided to concentrate on the tic behavior first, knowing that protocol would also have an overall calming effect on global dysregulation. The tics were a major concern for Newman's mother, but as is typical for someone with his symptom patterns, Newman denied he had any tics. As for the head tossing, he said he was just getting the hair out of his eyes. When his hair was cut short, however, the head tossing continued.

We usually see some improvement after four or five training sessions. Once the primary symptom starts to resolve, we begin to see other symptoms in the cluster improve. Protocols are monitored and changed as needed. Occasionally, we find that as one symptom improves another symptom may appear to get worse. That is because a dominant symptom will frequently hide other symptoms. Some disorders require only one protocol while other disorders require a number of protocol changes. This means that we place the EEG sensors in different locations on the head and vary the brainwave frequency to be trained. Changing the sensors allows us to train a different part of the brain at different frequencies.

When Newman came in with his mother for his tenth neurofeedback session, he arrived on time. They had been late for all prior treatments. We observed that he was more relaxed and quieter in the waiting room. His tic behavior was still apparent, but the frequency was diminished by half. When we greeted Newman and his mother, we asked them how things were. "Fine," he replied. We recognized by now that Newman only spoke when spoken to, and he used the fewest possible words to respond to us, unless he was angry—then he was very verbal. Things were always "fine" and "good," or "okay" or "no problem" with Newman, regardless of how difficult things actually were at home, at school, or with friends.

Newman's mother handed us the training report, a short form that is filled out after each neurotherapy session. Because neurotherapy is such a powerful tool, the patient often feels differently or behaves differently after each session. The training report helps us determine whether we are using the correct training protocol on the correct location on the head. Looking at the training report helps us see if we're on the right path and if we are alleviating symptoms, keeping them the same, or making them worse.

One of the benefits of neurotherapy is the rapid information you get from a training session, unlike drug therapy where you may have to wait days or weeks. This is not a therapy that uses the "Let's see how you're doing in six months" philosophy. We want to know how the patient felt and behaved within the next day after each therapy session.

Practically every neurotherapist has some type of training report. To fill out the training report, the patient or family member simply observes any behavioral or mood changes that occur after the training session and checks the corresponding change on the form. Our training report is a simple A-B form: (A) the symptom got worse, (B) the symptom improved. For example, (A) sleep was worse, (B) sleep was better.

The information from Newman's training report form indicated that he was generally calmer, there was a reduction in his disruptive behavior, and there had been no angry outbursts. So we felt it was appropriate to make no protocol changes. If the training report information or information obtained from Newman's mother had given us different information, we might have altered the protocol.

While still in the waiting room, we engaged Newman and his mother in general conversation. In this way, we were able to provide important modeling to Newman as to how to talk appropriately with his mother and other adults. It was also important to demonstrate to his mother how to talk to Newman. Communications is usually a problem with children and adults who suffer from dysregulation disorders. We always work on communication skills with every patient because it is so important in developing good life habits. We generally do the modeling without telling the patient or family what we are actually doing. Occasionally, a parent wants a conference to discuss new events or how to handle a particular situation, so we try to allow time for them before proceeding with the neurotherapy training.

Newman was escorted to a neurotherapy room where he was able to discuss with us anything he wished without his mother being present. In Newman's case, he wished to discuss very little. Some of our youngsters are very verbal and often insightful, which can be extremely helpful in their treatment. We have learned a lot about children by listening carefully to so many of them. The secret, however, is to really listen; children know if you are listening or just pretending to listen.

Because Newman had great problems with trust, he was always very guarded and defensive. He did not trust us, his parents, or the world. We had to be particularly careful about how we made suggestions to him. He generally viewed every suggestion as a criticism. His responses were very predictable. First he withdrew even more, and then he might start crying and deny any wrongdoing. Some days, he would go into a violent temper outburst, kicking and throwing. We handled Newman calmly and carefully, always reassuring him that things would get better.

Our neurotherapy rooms are specifically designed for biofeedback. They are approximately eleven-by-nine feet and well insulated for soundproofing. They offer individual privacy and comfort. At one end of the room is a large desk-type surface that holds the neurofeedback equipment—two computers and monitors, one that the patient watches and one for the therapist that shows the patient's EEG brainwave activity.

The patient sits in a large comfortable recliner on wheels. Everything is designed to be adjustable for maximum comfort. Newman wanted to recline the chair to full extension, and we wanted him sitting up. It's too easy to fall asleep when the chair is fully reclined. We always had to negotiate a compromise, which was usually for him to elevate the footrest but not lean back. Once Newman was seated and the chair was adjusted, we programmed the neurofeedback computer for the placement of the sensors on his head as well as the frequencies to be trained. The sensors are like little stethoscopes, listening to brainwaves and feeding this information into the biofeedback system. The reference sensor clip and ground sensor clip usually go on the earlobes; these provide no feedback but are necessary for a good signal.

The earlobes are used as a ground because there is little or no brainwave activity coming through the ears. The ears are prepared by gently rubbing the earlobes with a preparation solution on a small gauze pad. The prep solution cleans the surface of the skin of any body oils or other material so as to not impede conduction. We always try to get the best contact possible between the skin and the sensors. A conductive paste is then placed in a little cup on the ear clips. The conductive paste helps transfer any electrical signal from the brain to the biofeedback system. Once the ear clips are in place, generally one sensor is placed on the head.

The individualized protocol directs us to a specific head location. Once the correct site is located, it is prepared the same way as the ears. The site is rubbed gently with the preparation solution to clean the area. The conductive paste is placed in the small sensor cup, and the sensor is pressed onto the selected location on the scalp. The conductive paste holds the sensors to the scalp. We then place a one-inch-square clean gauze patch over the sensor to help hold everything in place. Now we are ready for the neurotherapy session.

Before starting the biofeedback, we spend a few minutes relaxing and focusing the patient. Our instructions are usually simple and consistent. We want patients to put aside everything that is not in the room with them, to focus their attention on the monitor, and to sit back and relax. They are usually instructed to take a few deep breaths, and the biofeedback session is then started.

At first we watch them closely to make sure they are not chewing gum, singing, talking, or playing with something because this type of movement distorts the feedback. Once the trainee is quiet and focused on the monitor and the audio feedback, we begin adjusting the feedback to a certain level of reward. We generally want the trainee to be rewarded about 70 percent of the time. Rewards come in the form of beeps, a score on the monitor, and/or some other visual cue to indicate the level of performance.

So if the task on the monitor is to have a big dot gobble smaller dots, we want it to do so about 70 percent of the time. If the task is to keep a ball going higher in the air, we want it to go higher 70 percent of the time. People generally learn a biofeedback task best if they succeed approximately 70 percent of the time. If they succeed at a higher rate, they lose interest and are not as motivated to succeed. If they succeed at a lower rate, they can become frustrated and give up. The reward schedule is adjusted, of course, to the needs of the trainee. Some people, for example, with head injuries, have a lower frustration tolerance and so we make it easier.

It only takes a few minutes to make the hookup and there is no discomfort at all. In fact, it is usually pleasurable. Once Newman was hooked up, he played a video game with his brain. If his brain generated the desired brainwaves, the game went well, and he had a high score on the game. He monitored his own progress by the audio beeps produced by the video game: the more beeps, the higher the score. The volume of the beeps can be adjusted to suit the individual needs of the patient. If the patient gets bored, loses attention, or gets distracted, the game goes poorly and the patient scores low.

Newman was like most of the young people we work with; at first, neurofeedback was fun and exciting, then after a few sessions, it became boring. The trick is to keep working with them until they work through the boredom. Boredom is an essential feature of the dysregulation disorders. Children often get in trouble at school or home because of boredom. So when they complain of boredom, we acknowledge their complaint but encourage and reinforce their effort to keep working. Our instructions to every trainee are always simple: Sit quietly, focus on the game screen, and relax. We usually say one word, such as "focus" or "attend," if we observe that a trainee is nodding off or not paying attention.

If we need to give more lengthy instructions, we stop the training until the new instructions are understood.

During the neurofeedback session, the lighting is usually dimmed so the most prominent feature in the room is the monitor. This helps the patient maintain focus. In Newman's case, after the initial excitement wore off, he became bored and had a tendency to drop off to sleep after about fifteen minutes. To avoid this problem, the lights were brightened, the sound was turned up, and we had more interaction with him. We moved the therapist's stool closer to him, encouraged him more, and verbally reinforced his efforts.

Sometimes if the trainee is very talkative, we move just outside the room in order to keep him focused on the task at hand. Sometimes our staying in the room is a distraction. There are some people who would talk through the entire session and no training would be accomplished. The point here is that good neurotherapy requires good observation. If trainees need the therapist to help keep them focused, the therapist is there. If they need to be left alone, the therapist leaves the room or sits quietly in the background. Once the neurofeedback session starts, the neurotherapist becomes only a part of the protocol.

The most important relationship is the trainee's relationship with the feedback. If the therapist plays too big a role in the process, the learning does not transfer outside the training room. In the case of Newman, we usually remained in the room, but only to keep him awake and focused on the task.

On this particular day, once Newman was engaged in the therapy, he was left alone in the training room so we could have a brief conference with his mother. She was a very concerned mother who had had to deal with a lot of family difficulty. Our conferences with her were often just to let her talk about her fears and frustrations and to reassure her. On this day, we made specific suggestions for parenting. If we do leave the neurofeedback room for a brief conference, we always return quickly to the room. When we returned on this day, Newman was doing well and was excited about a high score.

We developed a grading system for the children based on

four criteria. If the trainee scores better on one criterion than was scored during the last training session, he gets to go to a "number one" prize box, which contains little toys. If he scores better on the second, third, or fourth criteria, he gets to go to the number two, three, or four toy box. Each box contains a toy of a different level of quality. The number four box contains some nice, though inexpensive, toys. Today Newman felt sure he would score a four, and this kept him focused and alert. We instituted the graded toy boxes as an added incentive to the children. We have even had adults go to the toy boxes for key chains or other items.

Because of Newman's many varying symptoms, we designed his protocol to include changing the sensor placement halfway through the session to bring more balance to his brainwaves. Fifteen minutes into the session, we interrupted the training and moved a sensor from the left side of his head to the right side of his head. This break was not only a balancing protocol, but it also helped keep Newman more awake and alert.

When the training session time was up, we turned the lights completely bright and discontinued the training. We removed the sensors from Newman's head and ears and cleaned the paste from those areas with alcohol. The computer gives us a complete report of how Newman's brain functioned during the training, and this information was printed out and saved to a disk. We evaluated how well he had done on the four criteria. In this particular session, Newman advanced on three of the four criteria and remained the same on the fourth. Because of his extra effort, we gave him a four. This was exciting and encouraging for him.

While removing the sensors and cleaning the sites, we asked Newman a number of questions about how he was feeling, how he felt the session went, and how easy it was to concentrate. The response was typical of Newman: "It was okay," he felt "fine," and "no problem." Initially in the treatment of Newman, it was somewhat frustrating. We knew he was struggling, but we could not get him to open up. Fortunately, he finally began to trust us and to talk a little about how he was feeling. A few times, he even filled out the treatment report form without his mother's input.

Once the session was completed and Newman had been debriefed, we took him out to rejoin his mother. We reviewed the session with her and gave her a treatment report form to return to us at the next session. Newman got his toy from the number four box, his mother checked out at the front desk and made Newman's next appointment, and they left the office. After the training session was complete and Newman and his mother had left the clinic, the staff discussed his progress and shared their observations.

Almost all treatment sessions go the same way. They may vary slightly due to specific problems, but the overall program is relatively standard. Some patients require as few as twenty training sessions, most require about forty, and there are a few rare cases that go over a hundred. The average is forty to fifty, depending on how firmly entrenched the problem is, how dysfunctional the person is, and the difficulty of the home or school environment. In Newman's case, we had to do more than fifty sessions to calm his aggressive behavior. The tics started to disappear after between ten and twenty sessions. When we discontinued treatment, there were no tics, the violent temper outbursts were gone, and there was significant improvement in the remaining symptoms.

Newman remains mildly oppositional, but he is no longer hostile. He and his parents are doing a much better job of communicating with each other and they are optimistic about the future.

Neurotherapy is not magic, but we accomplished in twenty-five or so weeks what could take years to accomplish in traditional talk therapies or might never be accomplished at all. We accomplish some amazing things at a fraction of the cost of traditional therapies. Traditional talk therapy for the same number of treatment sessions generally costs four thousand to six thousand dollars. Neurofeedback for most dysregulation disorders at our office usually costs between two thousand and two thousand five hundred dollars. Newman's course of neurotherapy cost his parents less than a set of braces would have cost, and, like braces, the benefits are usually long lasting.

We have had many young people come back to us and say that they would never have made it through high school, college, or even graduate school had it not been for neurofeedback. We have also seen patients who were headed for serious legal troubles turn their lives around. A forty-five- to fifty-minute visit for a training session two to three times a week for twenty weeks is a small price to pay for improved quality of life. The sessions are quick, noninvasive, affordable, and can even be entertaining. Even Newman thanked us when we finished his training.

18

Nutrition: The Good, the Bad, and the Ugly

Now, this should be easy. How do you eat healthily? Think about it, all you have to do is know some biochemistry, oh, and some gastrointestinal physiology and microbiology. Let's see, did we mention some endocrine physiology as well? Toxicology would sure help, yes, and some physics. Then all you need is to be able to access scientific data suppressed by multinational corporations and learn to detect when government regulatory agencies mandated to protect our health are serving those corporations and not us.

As if parents do not have enough on their shoulders. On top of decisions and concerns about educational, social, health, safety, and security issues for their children, they must negotiate a minefield if they want to get to a place where they know what they want to be feeding their children and putting in their own mouths. They have to know and make decisions about: what water to drink; how to prepare food; what kind of cookware, containers, and wrappings to use; how the food was grown and raised; how the food was processed; and what labels tell us and what they don't.

Why should we add this burden of figuring out how to feed our kids in a healthy manner? Well, remember the thousands of possible expressions by a single gene? That is a big reason. Diet is one of the major factors that determine our gene expression. The path our life takes—our intelligence, our degree of health or illness, how we age—is in no small way directly related to what we eat. Developing fetuses, newborns, infants, and toddlers are the most susceptible to the life-altering effects of diet, first their mothers' and then their own. Our diets determine how at risk we are to our genetic vulnerabilities and how close we come to our genetic potentials.

What we eat determines the quality of our structure and the quality of our structure's functioning. At the cellular level, diet affects everything. Think about the following in terms of brain cells:

- The ability of the cell to produce the chemicals it is designed to produce.

- The amount of energy the cell creates for itself.

- The cell's capacity to remove waste and toxic substances.

- The cell's ability to build a cellular membrane capable of maintaining an optimum environment for its functioning.

- The cell's ability to carry out its function for the organism.

A healthy diet can begin to turn around a condition plaguing a child with autism. It can have significant effects on ADHD, depression, anxiety, and even some learning problems. Diet is one thing that you choose for yourself and your young children—no clinicians, no testing, no medical insurance codes. There may be limitations due to the price of good, clean food. Ironically, food that is not sprayed with expensive chemicals, is not processed, and has no chemical additives is more expensive. But it is worth the sacrifice.[1-2]

An autistic child, in particular, is more likely to have very rigid eating preferences that seem nearly impossible to change, as was true for Sierra (see the chapter on autism). Parents like Shawna, who patiently work at it until they succeed, are our heroes. It is worth the effort and a gift of love to their children.

When changing a child's diet, slow and sneaky works best. We make suggestions here, but first, let's look at some things that can mislead us into making assumptions about what is good to eat.

The Ugly

Let's go backward and start with the Ugly. The food industry, biotechnology companies, and the petrochemical industry play hardball. With pockets that get deeper every year, an army of lawyers, and an army of lobbyists, they have managed to legislate that black is white. For example, the Food and Drug Administration (FDA) has determined that genetically engineered/modified (GM) foods are "considered safe."

Foods that are genetically engineered or modified are plants that have had a specific gene sequence (from a different organism) placed into their DNA. This changes the plant's blueprint. For example, a potato may now secrete a substance that kills certain insects that would otherwise be able to attack the potato plant. That certainly sounds like a good idea.

To come to the conclusion that GM foods are safe, the FDA accepted the industry-funded safety studies, yet ignored the non-industry–funded studies that raised serious questions and concerns about the dangers of GM foods. Ironically, the most damning study was actually industry funded.[3]

Arpad Pusztai, the world's leading expert on plant proteins, called lectins, set out to show, without a doubt, how safe GM foods are, so his study received excellent funding. He carried out his carefully designed study on GM potatoes for years, only to be shocked by what his team found—sick, infertile, dying animals that were fed the GM potatoes. He analyzed the data and concluded that the damage to the animals was not due to the presence of the chemical the potato produced. It was due to the way the gene had been inserted and what it did after insertion, apart from producing the intended chemical. The conclusion was that the process of genetic engineering itself was dangerous. That was a big "oops" for the hardballers.

After some high-level calls between the U.S. and British governments, Pusztai was promptly placed on suspension by the research institute's director, his records were seized, a legal gag order was placed, and his work was then systematically discredited by industry scientists.

What does this have to do with young brains? Due to the hit-or-miss nature of the process, GM foods produce many other unknown chemicals in addition to the one intended. These rogue chemicals serve as allergens and toxins. The increase of GM foods in our diets parallels the rate of growth of many degenerative diseases and life-threatening hypersensitivities. These parallels do not prove anything, but there is scientific evidence that indicates the possibility of serious, even catastrophic consequences of eating these foods.[4] Plainly, GM foods need to be studied more rigorously, and only if those foods are found to be safe beyond a shadow of doubt should they be allowed into the food supply.[5–7] But it is the other way around: They are "thought to be safe" by the FDA so rigorous scrutiny is not mandated. It is a "let's put it out there and see what happens" scenario. The urgency to do it this way is due to the huge profits involved.

Another lesser concern, though not insignificant, is that most GM foods are receiving a gene sequence to become resistant to Monsanto's herbicide, Roundup. Consequently, farmers are spraying approximately a third more Roundup on their crops, which means a third more herbicide residues in the food. Another concern is that, due to technical reasons, an antibiotic-resistant gene is also present in the GM foods we eat. Does that sound smart?

A larger, scarier possibility is that, once introduced, GM foods may be impossible to remove from the food supply. Labeling of GM foods is not mandated, so tracking problems from GM foods, even catastrophic ones, is nearly impossible. There are areas where cross-pollination has already occurred. There is evidence of harm to delicate ecosystem balances, like disappearing honeybees. What will happen if after GM fish are released, it turns out to be regrettable? How can that be fixed? Even the beneficial bacteria in our gut may take up some of the gene sequences, rogue and otherwise, and they can become part of the bacterium's DNA blueprint and produce allergens and toxins, like stealth invaders.

Why do you suppose the scientists and leaders from the European Union banned GM foods? Guess they didn't read Monsanto's nice reports. It could be that it occurred to them that preventing tampering with the world's food supply before rigorous long-term safety testing was completed was more important than lining the pockets of powerful businesses.

There are more uglies out there. The general equation is the same: questionable decisions by federal regulatory agencies + questionable regulations and laws passed = windfall profits.

The Bad

So what foods should we avoid eating or feeding to our children? Genetically modified food, right? We are sorry to say this is next to impossible if you ever eat out, as in the school cafeteria, at McDonald's, or at the five-star restaurant downtown. The new, purportedly healthy, no-trans fat oil that many restaurants are cooking with is a combination of GM canola and GM soy oils. We would never use these oils for cooking even if they were non-GM; GM just puts a couple of exclamation points on them.

By the way, if you want to do something about GM foods at your child's school, you may want to visit the Institute for Responsible Technology website (www.responsibletechnology.org/GMFree/GM-FreeSchools/index.cfm). The institute's director, Jeffery Smith, is another one of our heroes. He is tirelessly educating parents, teachers, and world leaders, and advocating intelligent legislation of GM foods.

There is a long list of foods to avoid when you want to promote health, but there are some foods that are more critical to avoid when your child has ADHD or autism. The brains of all children require high-quality fatty acids for their proper development and function, but the elimination of harmful fats is necessary as well. Bad fats not only produce particularly damaging free radicals when they are metabolized for energy, they also are used in the structure of the cell's membrane. The health of the cell membrane is critical to the functioning of the cell. Most known neurotoxins damage cell membranes.

Chemical additives to food are not required to meet stringent safety requirements. Safety studies are often relatively small and of short duration, and the effects of combinations of chemicals are virtually never studied. Many, like aspartame and monosodium glutamate (MSG) are central nervous system poisons. A child whose brain is under siege does not need synthetic chemicals that foul up its complex mechanisms.[8]

Sugar, in its various forms, wreaks havoc on children. It is not just the sugar highs and sugar lows that can cause behavior disruptions. It is elevated insulin levels as well. Insulin increases inflammatory damage, the last thing the brain of a child with autism or autism risk factors should have to suffer.

All children require a high level of nutritional density in their diets for the proper development and functioning of their central nervous systems. Studies show that school-age children given supplements with even modest levels of vitamins and minerals have increases in IQ, improved school performance, and improved behavior. And that is just with a so-so vitamin-mineral supplement.[9]

Virtually all parents of children with autism will want to work toward a gluten-free/casein-free diet, as it produces such a high rate of improvement. Reducing and eliminating the following foods would be a good place to start. Some foods are easier than others to avoid by simply not choosing them, such as fries; others, as we mentioned with GM, may be much harder to avoid.

GM Foods

- Virtually all canola, soy, corn, cottonseed oil products, and Hawaiian papaya; Quest tobacco; some alfalfa, zucchini, and yellow squash.

- Dozens and dozens of other foods, including animals, have been genetically engineered and are just waiting for a go from the FDA.

- Organic foods are non-GM (we avoid organic canola for other reasons).

- Labels are not required to state whether a product is GM; look for non-GM on the label.

- Ask your waitperson which foods are cooked with olive oil; some are, but most use non–trans fat "vegetable oil."

Commercially Processed Foods

- From crackers and cookies to prepackaged dinners and lunch-meats, these foods are chock-full of sugars and/or chemicals and most have scant nutritional value.

Artificial Sweeteners

- Aspartame (Equal, NutraSweet, diet sodas) is a particularly dangerous neurotoxin, especially for children.

- Sucrulose (Splenda); scientists stumbled on this while trying to make a pesticide; brain, skin and gut problems possible.

- Saccharine (Sweet'n Low) and acesulfame may increase cancer risk.

Sugar

- We all know too much sugar is bad, and for children with problems like ADHD or LD it can be calamitous, not just unhealthy.

- The added sugars in foods are even worse; for one, high-fructose corn syrup, corn syrup, maltodextrin, and modified food starch all are made from GM corn; in addition, these sugars raise glucose levels in the blood much faster than table sugar.

- These and other forms of sugar are in many foods in large amounts but hidden by using multiple sugars so they are farther down the ingredients list on the label.

- Fructose is a good sugar in small amounts, as it occurs naturally in fruit; but large amounts, as when it is added to foods and in products like agave syrup, are not good; fructose is very efficiently converted to fat, raises triglycerides, increases the stickiness of platelets, and increases cross-linking, a process that damages proteins; use a little honey or stevia instead.

Artificial Colors, Artificial Flavors, Flavor Enhancers, and Preservatives

- The majority of children who have these removed from their diets exhibit better attention and improved school performance; see appendix C for a good list from the Feingold Association, website www.feingold.org.

- MSG is another dangerous neurotoxin for children; see appendix B for the pseudonyms on food labels that are used to deceive you.

Soft Drinks

- They are a hideous combination of the five previous categories.

- Many so-called fruit juices are little more than sweetened chemicals.

White Flour and White Rice

- Devoid of nutritional value, then bleached and bromated just to make things worse.

Partially Hydrogenated Fats or Oils

- Trans fats are still around, still damaging cell membranes.

Deep Fat Fried Foods

- Any fat cooked at very high temperatures is going to be unhealthy, way too many dangerous chemicals.

- If you must have the occasional serving of French fries, cook them yourself in coconut oil; restaurants filter and reuse the oils, which concentrates the toxic substances significantly.

The New "No Trans Fat" Butter Substitutes

- They may not have trans fats, but the process to make them the right consistency, called interesterification, appears to produce as bad or worse problems as trans fats, which are very bad.

Margarine

- It is just not a good idea to eat something that is more plastic than it is food, especially something that does not melt at body temperature.

The Good

Healthy eating decisions for children are clear-cut. They need nutrient-dense foods that are as clean as possible, as fresh as possible, and as untampered with as possible.

Children do not require carefully designed diet plans that provide a certain number of calories from this category and a certain number of servings of that one. Simply provide them with good foods, and only good foods.

Several researchers over the last hundred years have painstakingly looked at the diets of extraordinarily healthy and long-lived peoples around the world. These folks were basically disease-free, energetic, and lived long, active lives. Their children were the picture of health: graceful, lean, cheerful, with delightful behavior, no "usual" childhood diseases, and no obesity or tooth decay. They were isolated from industrialized society, so they ate no refined or tampered with foods. Predictably, they systematically began to lose their remarkable degree of health as foods from more developed societies were introduced.[10] White sugar and white flour were usually the first bad foods introduced.

When the researchers compared the compositions of the various diets of those healthy peoples, they found that there was no overall pattern other than that their diets were loaded with nutrient-dense foods. Some ate a very high percentage of fat, and had no heart disease or obesity. Others ate a high percentage of carbohydrates, and were lean and muscular. Protein came from a range of sources, from a variety of mammals and sea creatures to fowl and insects, as well as dairy and/or eggs. No one was counting calories.

Nutrient-dense foods are foods that have a high concentration of vitamins, minerals, fiber, and enzymes. Foods that have the highest concentrations are either raw or fermented, and are grown in rich soils. Since our farmlands have shown evidence of serious soil depletion for more than fifty years, organic foods are the better choice for us.

We should clarify a few things about organic foods. Organic certification only means that certain substances are prohibited from being used, such as synthetic pesticides on plants or feeding GM foods to animals. Certification does not require a farmer to do anything in particular, such as use the soil amendments that an organic gardener might use to create the healthiest of soils. Now that the organic food industry is booming and most of the big organic producers have been bought by the giant food companies, many organic farms are using the more cost-effective methods that pervade commercial farming. Unfortunately, this means more factory farming techniques, such as using varieties of plants that have a longer shelf life, even if they are inferior in nutritional value and taste to other available varieties. Corners are cut that a farmer or gardener who is growing the healthiest food for his or her family would never cut, such as the mentioned soil amendments.

In addition, certain loopholes exist, such as allowing a manufacturer to use nonorganic ingredients if organic ones are not commercially available, or that up to five percent of a product does not have to be organic, and still be labeled organic. And deceiving terms exist. "Free-range" may only mean that a chicken has access to the outdoors during its life, even if the door is on the other side of a large henhouse and out of view; "cage-free" only means it does not live in a cage, so it can live in a large, heavily populated henhouse without an open door.

Then there is the matter of certifying agencies that appear to be gradually increasing the number of allowed additives in organic foods, decisions that appear to be economically favorable to the big dogs in the organic industry. Further, there are questions as to how well certifying agencies monitor the farms and food producers that sell organic products.

And just because a product is labeled "organic" does not mean it is healthy. An organic cake may have fewer toxins, but it can still be void of nutrients, high in sugars, and full of harmful fats—and bad for a child's brain and health.

All this said, we still think our best chance of getting higher-quality food, while decreasing toxins, is with organic food. One organic distributor available in our area that we give an A to is Organic Valley Farms. They actively seek out small farms that maintain the higher organic standards and sustainable agricultural practices.

Nutrient-Dense Foods

Children require generous amounts of good fats, ample protein, nourishing carbohydrates, and plenty of fiber and enzymes for healthy development.[11-12] Reducing fats in children not only compromises the development and functioning of their brains, but also puts the brakes on their major detoxification pathway, the liver-gastrointestinal system. Children do not get fat when they eat good fats; they get fat when they eat empty calories and they get sick when they eat bad fats.

Fats

Good fats should be eaten in good foods, such as the ones we list below.[13] Added fats for cooking should be monounsaturated (olive oil) or saturated (butter or coconut oil). If there is one thing you buy that is organic, it should be fat. Toxins have a high affinity to fat cells, so toxins in plants and animals are concentrated in the fat. Nonorganic butter is almost always in the top five foods with the highest concentration of carcinogens.

Butter is actually a healthy food when eaten in moderation and not overheated. The nutritional dogma for some time has been that saturated fats, such as butter, are bad. That thinking came from studies that always lumped saturated fats with trans fats as a single category. They are not the same.

Saturated fats are necessary in our diet for the proper structure of the membranes of every cell in our bodies, and as we have stated, the health of the membranes in our brains is critical to its proper functioning. Saturated fats comprise half of the lipid molecules in a healthy membrane. In addition, saturated fats are an important fuel for the production of energy, especially by the heart. They are naturally antimicrobial to viruses and fungi.

Coconut oil (organic) is an excellent source of saturated fat. It is highly saturated so is good for cooking, since it produces far fewer damaging free radicals when heated.

We choose not to use canola, organic or otherwise, even though it is a stable, monounsaturated fat. Non-GM canola comes from hybridization of rapeseed. The rapeseed plant is poisonous to humans and animals due to the high number of toxins present. Its oils are used for various industrial purposes, such as lubrication, and can also be used as an insecticide. The hybridization process designed to reduce the toxins eventually produced a plant that had far lower levels of toxins, but by no means reduced them to acceptable levels. Also, we cannot be certain organic canola does not contain GM canola. There have been several instances in which non-GM canola fields were contaminated by GM canola, likely by the wind.

Polyunsaturated fats should only be eaten as they occur naturally in foods, such as fish and bananas. Extracted polysaturates, such as corn, safflower, peanut, sesame, and sunflower oils should be minimally used, and not used at all for cooking. When heated, these fats produce large numbers of damaging free radicals, especially the kind that damage cell membranes. But even unheated, polyunsaturated oils are not as beneficial as those in foods, due to their processing.

The process of extracting oils may use solvents, such as the carcinogen benzene. But even if they are mechanically extracted, they are subjected to numerous manipulations to get them to look and smell a certain way, or to have longer shelf life, including bleaching, degumming, and deodorizing. These practices make the oils unfavorable.

By the way, olive oil is not extracted by solvents, and the cold-pressed extra virgin oil does not require the aforementioned tampering.

Protein

We require protein for the maintenance of every cell in our bodies, and children require additional protein for growth. In term of servings, two to three per day is usually necessary. We begin our discussion of protein with good ol' red meat, loved by some and reviled by others.

Red meat, like saturated fats, has gotten a bad rap. The problem is not the red meat; the problem is what cattle are subjected to that changes a good food into an objectionable one. And it is not just the pesticide and herbicide residues, antibiotics, and hormones that concentrate in the meat. Even organic meat may be undesirable. The problem is that almost all cattle are removed from pastures and taken to feedlots for a minimum of three months of grain feeding before slaughter. This grain finishing, as it is called, is the process that converts a healthy composition of fats in the meat into a terrible composition—healthy fats converted to unhealthy ones just to make the animals fat.[14-16] It is said that the grain finishing produces a higher quality and better tasting meat. It certainly marbles the meat better, but any improvement in taste or texture is doubtful. Participants in double-blind testing with grain-finished and grass-finished meat cannot identify which is which by taste or texture.

Animals that provide table meats are healthy when allowed to graze and forage; grain is an unnatural food for them. Grain fed to beef cattle causes a shift in the conditions in their bowels to one that allows E. coli to flourish.[17] Grass fed animals do not have problems with E. coli. Meat contaminated with E. coli is a serious problem, and it is due to grain feeding. Because of the risks, many school cafeterias serve meat that has been sterilized by irradiation. Irradiation of foods is yet another processing that produces harmful substances in food.

Meat from animals that are not fed grain, but only pastured, are more desirable than even organic meat if the organic meat has been grain fed. Of course, grass-finished meat that has not received a cocktail of chemicals is best. If you are able to obtain such meat, there is no need to attempt to minimize your intake to an occasional serving.

If red meat got a bad rap, liver got a double bad rap. It is thought that since the liver detoxifies, it must have a concentration of toxins. Toxins concentrate in fat, not in the liver. So if you like liver, go ahead and enjoy this food that is as nutrient dense as any. Make sure it is from animals that were properly raised, not from grain-fed and drugged ones.

Fish is another high-quality protein and fat food. But as you no doubt are aware, there are official government recommendations for restricting the consumption of fish due to mercury. The Environmental Protection Agency advises young children, nursing mothers, pregnant women, and women who may become pregnant not to eat shark, swordfish, king mackerel, or tilefish at all. They further advise eating no more than two six-ounce servings a week of shrimp, canned light tuna, salmon, or pollock. In Australia, they include billfish and orange roughy on their list of highest accumulators, and recommend for children only one serving per week of seafood. The United Kingdom adds marlin and Canada adds snake mackerel to the list of undesirables, and both countries have similar recommendations as Australia. In Japan, where seafood consumption is approximately four times that of the United States, the list of highest mercury levels includes sea mammals we do not eat here, whale and dolphin. Their concern for adverse health effects is only for pregnant women, but there are no specific recommendations other than avoiding the seafood with the higher amounts of mercury.

Studies on the effects of mercury from fish on children are conflicting. Large studies done on children in the Seychelles Islands[18] and another in the Faroe Islands,[19] where fish consumption and mercury levels are high, found no evidence of harm. But another study done in Boston found that mothers who had high mercury levels from fish consumption during pregnancy had children with lower IQ scores by 7.5 points, but mothers who ate more than two servings of fish per week during pregnancy, but had low mercury levels, had children who had higher IQ scores by four points.[20]

An explanation is that the islanders may not have the same degree of exposure to other toxins that the children in Boston do. Higher amounts of mercury may overwhelm a child's brain that is already dealing with a host of other neurotoxins. Do the children on those islands live in and breathe the same chemical soup that we do? Until we have more definitive information, we advise avoiding the high mercury fish mentioned, and add seafood with moderately high levels to the list to minimize: Gulf Coast oysters, albacore, bluefin and yellowfin tuna, halibut, mahi mahi, sea bass, largemouth bass, pike, and walleye. Sadly, this list will grow as tons of mercury pour into the environment from coal burning, chlorine plants, PVC production, and the scrapping of electronic switches in cars and computers. For now, stick more to the lower mercury seafood choices: flounder, Alaskan salmon, haddock, shrimp, Atlantic blue crab, crawfish, scallop, ocean perch, anchovies, freshwater trout, whitefish, and shad. Avoid farm-raised fish due to their low-quality diets and increased levels of antibiotics and petrochemicals in their tissues.

Eggs are also a high-quality protein and fat food. The yolks in particular are excellent for the developing brains of babies; you can introduce yolks as a first food at four months of age (egg whites at one year old). Even if you do not do it for yourself, feed your children pasture-fed organic eggs. The proteins in eggs are of high value and readily assimilated.

Because of the fats in the yolks, eggs are best when cooked without breaking the yolk sac: boiling, poaching, baking. If you must scramble eggs, do not overcook them. Avoid scrambled eggs at a buffet.

Dairy products are another source of high-quality proteins, but a number of people have problems when they eat dairy. Some are lactose intolerant; others have difficulty with the casein content. A large percentage of children with autism improve when they avoid both casein and gluten. But for those who do not have these problems, dairy can be another high-quality protein and fat. But obtaining healthy milk products is no easy task.

The best milk products are fermented and from raw, organic milk.[21] That's the kicker, raw milk. Almost half of the states prohibit the sale of raw milk. Pasteurization heats milk and denatures its highly beneficial enzymes. Ultra-pasteurization uses even higher heat, 280 degrees instead of 145 degrees. When an enzyme is denatured, it is not simply inactive; it no longer promotes life's processes. Foods contain enzymes that break down their nutrients for absorption and utilization by our bodies. This is why raw foods are so health promoting. It is not surprising, then, that many people have problems with pasteurized milk with its array of nutrients without the enzymes to digest them.

Homogenizing of milk does us no favors either. It disperses the fat into droplets that bypass the usual digestive processes and enter the bloodstream very rapidly. Not only does this bypassing of the liver take away the opportunity for removal of toxins in the milk fat, the droplets are just the size that are readily taken up by artery walls. Nonfat milk avoids this problem, but children must then have other foods to get the beneficial fats. Sometimes this is difficult in a recently weaned child who is a picky eater but who drinks milk.

Raw milk from healthy cows, predominantly grass not grain fed, is very safe. Cows are easily checked for *E. coli* and other diseases and can be certified as safe. The fear that bovine tuberculosis was causing human tuberculosis kicked off the pasteurization craze even after it was found not to be the cause. But by then, pasteurization had proven useful for handling and shipping purposes, that is, less careful handling and longer distance shipping, which increase profits.

Raw milk not only has viable enzymes, it also has beneficial bacteria to support bowel health, as well as lactoferrin and immunoglobulins (antibodies) to reduce viruses and harmful bacteria. These, plus the protein, carbohydrate, fat, vitamin, and mineral content, make raw milk a complete and balanced food.

If you live in a state that prohibits the sale of raw milk, you can obtain it by buying a share of a cow, and paying the farmer a fee for raising and milking your cow. As an owner, you are entitled to use your own milk as you see fit. The Amish farm in our area that has set up such a program delivers the milk to their cow's owners at the Farmer's Market in town, to make it easier than driving out to their farm. For their protection, it is labeled "for animal use only."

Powdered protein can be a source of high-quality proteins but can also be a source of toxicity as well. Milk fats and egg yolks should not be powdered or their fats become rancid and harmful. Non-instant powdered skim milk and egg whites are okay. Powdered whey has a small amount of fat. If you use it, take plenty of antioxidants. Some 1 percent and 2 percent milk has powdered milk added; check with the manufacturer if you use these reduced fat products. Our friends at Organic Valley Farms do it right.

An excellent source of protein, suitable for vegetarians too, is nutritional yeast. It has high-quality proteins, like a steak, and a high concentration of B vitamins. The flaked form is easier to use as it readily dissolves in liquids. It is has something of a nutty taste that most children do not object to. Keep it in a dark container. If you buy it from the bulk section instead of packaged, the bulk container should be lined with foil to prevent light from reducing the B vitamins. Vitamin B12 is particularly light sensitive, so this is even more important for vegetarians.

The following will be controversial. We do not endorse the use of most soy products.[22-24] It is not just the heavily sprayed GM soy, but even organic soy. Soybeans have toxins, and cooking does not remove all of them. The remaining toxins interfere with thyroid functioning, protein digestion (only 55 percent of the protein in soy gets digested), and the absorption of minerals. Processed soy is worse, such as soy protein isolates; it has not received the FDA's rating of GRAS (generally recognized as safe).

Soy is called a phytoestrogen. Phytoestrogens attach to estrogen receptors but have no estrogenic activity. Soy phytoestrogens, however, do have some estrogenic activity, which may in and of itself be detrimental to children. But with the escalating amounts of xenoestrogens, which we discuss in the chapter on toxicity, any added estrogenic activity from foods is unacceptable.

Soy infant formula should be avoided at all costs. It has fifty to eighty times the amount of manganese in human or cow's milk, and infants' livers do not have the ability to metabolize the excess manganese for the first several months of life. The manganese toxicity that occurs increases the risk of autism, ADHD, and learning disabilities. Parents who are considering giving their children soy should read *The Whole Soy Story*, by Kaayla Daniel, PhD. She has analyzed the available medical literature on soy, and her findings are an eye-opener.

Fermentation of soy, however, does remove the toxins in soy. So fermented organic soy products are acceptable: miso, natto, and tempeh. Most tofu is not fermented, just cooked and mashed; it is only acceptable if fermented.

We believe that the misperception by so many people that soy is a health food is because of the powerful soy industry's clever marketing to the health food industry. Most studies that make soy look like a health food are flawed; the better scientific studies indicate otherwise. The notions we have about soy are often incorrect, for example, that Asians eat large amounts of soy. The average intake of soy per person in China, Japan, and Thailand is less than a quarter of a cup per day. It is used mainly as a condiment.

Carbohydrates

Carbohydrates include all fruits, vegetables, and grains. These contain sugars that our bodies convert to glucose, the major energy molecule for most of the cells in our bodies, and in particular, in our brains. Glucose also stimulates the production of proteins. It is stored in the form of triglycerides in fat cells.

In addition to sugars, healthy carbohydrates contain a concentration of vitamins, minerals, fiber, and enzymes. Undesirable carbohydrates have a high concentration of sugars that cause a rapid rise of glucose in our bloodstreams, and a low concentration of the other nutrients. An example of these carbohydrates is white flour products: bread, cereal, pasta cookies, crackers, pastries, bagels, and pretzels.

Scientists determine the speed at which carbohydrates increase blood glucose levels individually for each food, and the foods are then ranked by number in the glycemic index. The higher the number of a food, the more rapidly it elevates blood glucose levels. High levels of glucose damage cells, so our bodies respond swiftly to prevent that. When glucose levels are rising rapidly, we secrete insulin to bring levels down quickly. Even though high glycemic index foods may be otherwise nutritious, they are nonetheless detrimental to health if eaten frequently.[25-26] They should be placed in the same category as desserts: to be enjoyed from time to time, not frequently.

The elevated insulin levels that these foods cause turn out to be the last thing our children need. A high insulin level not only makes us fat and elevates blood pressure, but it also significantly increases inflammatory activity, the very type of inflammatory activity that toxins trigger.

Certainly, many processed foods are loaded with sugars that increase glucose and insulin levels. But there are a number of otherwise nutritious foods that also elevate glucose rapidly. These foods have a higher concentration of amylose-amylopectin. An amylose-amylopectin carbohydrate is a compacted and highly branched chain of glucose molecules. We digest amylose-amylopectin with lightning speed, starting with the saliva in our mouths. When we eat high amylose-amylopectin foods, we are essentially swallowing lots of glucose. Lots.

We are not happy to report the foods that are high in amylose-amylopectin; you're not gonna like it. They include all the grains, yes, even whole grains, and vegetables that grow underground: potatoes, beets, carrots, even peanuts (they are not really nuts, but hard legumes). Now, carrots and peanuts do not have as high a density of sugars as the others, so eating a few carrots or a handful of peanuts is fine, but carrot soup, cooked carrots, or handfuls of peanuts can be a problem. Basically, when you eat bread, cereal, pasta, rice, or potatoes, the effect on your glucose level is similar to having dessert. The irony is that most people who come to our clinic are preferentially trying to eat more of these foods because of the mistaken idea that, since they are low fat, they are desirable. In reality, adults would do well to limit high amylose-amylopectin foods to one serving per day.

Children handle grains and potatoes with fewer problems than adults, so limiting their intake is not as necessary unless the child is overweight. The problem we see is that the more grain-based foods children eat, the less likely they are to eat a wide range of fruits and vegetables, and this is a major drawback. Try to limit grains and potatoes, and stick to whole grains, and organic as possible.

Juices can also be a problem for children. Certainly, avoid any "juice" drink that is not unsweetened 100 percent juice. But even those juices do not provide the density of nutrients that fruits do. They are tasty and children generally like them, but they can reduce a child's appetite or restrict it. It is a different story if you have a juicer, such as a VitaMix, in which you toss the entire fruit in to be juiced. It is also a different story if juice is the vehicle by which you are delivering nutrients, such as a vitamin-mineral powder, nutritional yeast, or antifungal medication, to a child with autism.

Fermented foods are super foods. They are highly nutritious and are beneficial to the intestinal tract by providing an abundance of enzymes and beneficial bacteria that promote favorable bowel conditions and a healthy balance of organisms. Every country has their traditional fermented foods since fruits, vegetables, grains, fish, meat, and milk can be fermented. Yogurt, sauerkraut, kefir, and kimchi are readily available, though the store-bought kimchi may be too hot for a child. Make sure the yogurt is not sweetened; add fruit if your child does not care for the taste of plain yogurt. Also, be certain the sauerkraut was fermented, not just made with citric acid. It can be fun to ferment foods with your children, plus they learn a little chemistry. And you can make kimchi to suit the hotness preferences of your family.

Yogurt is in particular an excellent food to introduce early or to work patiently into the diet of an older child who has not developed a taste for it. Many parents use it as the vehicle for major supplementation or to disguise medications.

Fiber

Most parents we talk to are surprised at the importance we place on fiber for their children. The assumption appears to be that it is more for older adults, for proper bowel functioning. Fiber is not only for elimination. In adults, good fiber intake lowers the rates of colon cancer, heart disease, adult onset diabetes, and diverticular disease. It facilitates weight control as well. The reason children need optimum fiber intake is the importance of gastrointestinal health for the functioning of the brain and immune system.[27] These three organ systems share hormones, chemicals, and control systems to the extent that they could be viewed as a single organ system. You cannot have a healthy immune system or have optimum brain functioning if your bowel is not healthy. For example, children who are given extra fiber have fewer ear infections.

There are two kinds of fiber: insoluble and soluble. Insoluble fiber has a good mechanical action on the bowel that promotes the movement of materials through the bowel at the optimum rate, while soluble fiber causes absorption of water for properly formed stools.

Soluble fiber has an additional role that is critical. It is made up of sugars that we cannot absorb, so they remain in the bowel; it is these sugars that feed the beneficial bacteria in our bowels. The importance of these bacteria on health cannot be overstated.

We have two to four pounds of bacteria in our bowels, and the number of organisms is larger than the number of cells that make up our body. Estimates vary depending on the methods used, but there appear to be in the neighborhood of ten trillion cells and tens of trillions of organisms, and more than five hundred thousand different species. Different types of bacteria take up residence in different parts of the bowel; most are found in the large intestine. Acidophilus, which most people have heard of, lives in the small intestine. Approximately 50 percent of a stool is bacteria. We need to take in plenty of soluble fiber to feed this important little universe.

Beneficial bacteria produce nutrients that we cannot get elsewhere, enzymes for digestion, and enzymes for the immune system. They also detoxify, not only toxic substances, but also common substances in food that would otherwise be toxic if the bacteria did not convert them to a harmless form. Since the bowel is the site where most things enter our bloodstream, the lining cells of the bowel contain a significant percentage of our immune system.

In addition to the beneficial bacteria, many other types of organisms live in our bowels,. When we are healthy, there is a great predominance of the beneficial bacteria and small numbers of other, undesirable organisms. The most prevalent undesirable is yeast, which is a fungus. The undesirable organisms are harmless when in small numbers, but in increased numbers are harmful. They have the opportunity to proliferate whenever the beneficial bacteria are reduced or when the immune system is compromised. We discuss this more fully in the chapter on toxins.

Diet plays a major role in the composition of the organisms that inhabit our bowel; high-soluble fiber intake feeds the beneficial bacteria, while, foods high in sugar feed the undesirable organisms. Fruits and vegetable have the highest amounts of soluble fiber; grains have predominantly insoluble fiber.

Additional fiber can be added to assure that more optimal amounts are being ingested. They do not have much of a taste, so can be added to water or juice, or sprinkled in moist foods. Two of the better fibers are ground flax and acacia. Due to the volatile fats in flax, we prefer to grind seed each time. If you buy ground flax, it should be vacuum sealed and in the freezer. FitSmart sells two fiber products that are acceptable to most children, and good for you too, Dad.

Enzymes

Enzymes are the stuff of life. They drive life's very processes, the biochemical activities of every cell in the body. They are the catalysts that make life possible by both reducing the energy required for a chemical reaction and increasing the speed of the reaction by several orders of magnitude. Tens of thousands of different enzymes are needed since each one has a unique task. Many genetic diseases, some that are devastating, are due to the absence or deficiency of a single enzyme.

Many people take a vitamin-mineral supplement, but most do not think of enzymes in the same way. Yet a major role of vitamins and minerals in the body is to serve as coenzymes. Many enzymes in the body require coenzymes to become active and without them will have no activity at all. Other nutrients also serve as coenzymes; CoQ10 and glutathione, two powerful nutrients, increase important enzyme activity.[28]

Immune function, detoxification, and healing require vast enzyme activities, so for children to maintain health or to recover from illness, parents must consider how to help provide optimum enzyme activity in their children. Raw and fermented foods are excellent sources of enzymes, but since we cook food, supplementation of enzymes is essential.

There two general categories of enzymes, digestive and metabolic, and both are important. Digestive enzymes include different sets of enzymes to digest proteins, fats, and carbohydrates. Specific enzymes, lactase and DDP-IV, can be added to help those children who have problems with lactose and gluten.

A major reason to add digestive enzymes is because we cook our food, which denatures the enzymes in the food. The more digestive enzymes we must make to digest cooked food, the fewer metabolic enzymes we are able to make. With fewer metabolic enzymes, energy production, detoxification, and immune function all suffer.

Metabolic enzyme activity can be supported by taking enzymes in the protein-digesting category. These must be taken on an empty stomach to be absorbed—a half hour before or two hours after meals—or they will do no more than help digest proteins. Once absorbed into the tissues, they have a wide array of anti-inflammatory activity and improved immune function in healing, detoxification, and antimicrobial activity.

Foods for Health

- Fruits—a variety of fresh, preferably organic

- Vegetables—a wide variety of fresh, preferably organic; raw and fermented are best

- Meat—grass-fed and grass-finished, on unsprayed fields

- Seafood—lower mercury varieties

- Dairy—organic, raw is best; fermented dairy

- Eggs—organic, pasture raised

- Nuts—raw, soaked, and dried

- Seeds—raw, soaked, and dried; sprouted; try hempseeds, too

Babies can begin eating these foods by one year of age.

We close this chapter with a clarification. If you think our grandchildren eat only the ways we have recommended, let us disabuse you. Although our own children take nutrition as seriously as we do, this is a world of birthday parties, soccer snacks, sleepovers, and pizza parties; there are financial realities as well. This chapter is intended to provide information, to help parents do what they can. Any introduction of healthy foods and removal of any detrimental ones will benefit your child.

19

Toxicity

I hope we shall crush in its birth the aristocracy of our moneyed corporations, which dare already to challenge our government to a trial of strength and bid defiance to the laws of our country.

—Thomas Jefferson, 1812

We are Virginians, so please indulge our unabashed admiration of Mr. Jefferson. What he is warning is that corporations wield enormous power. It is a power that influences government, even the greatest government that was ever created. Why bring this up in a book about how we can help our children? It is so that we are not lulled into a complacency that our governmental agencies are necessarily protecting citizens adequately in all areas. Over time, regulatory agencies, mandated to protect the public interest, become increasingly influenced by the businesses they regulate. We did not think this up. Montesquieu wrote about this a long time ago, and later, Karl Marx. Modern economic theorists call it "regulatory capture."[1]

The reality for us today is that the Food and Drug Administration (FDA), the Environmental Protection Agency (EPA), the Federal Trade Commission (FTC), and other agencies are to different degrees captured. Big business influences government in ways that are good for business. Although this has always been true, the concentration of money and power in multinational corporations is unprecedented, as is the degree of corporate misrepresentation and concealment.

Parents are now obliged to consider that government recommendations regarding health, disease prevention, and safety are a blend of science and financial interest. Official safety standards that are determined by agencies can make or break a business, or sometimes be the difference between making a profit and windfall profits. This is true of genetically modified (GM) foods, of allowable levels of mercury or dioxins, of approved additives, of vaccination schedules, and levels of safe electromagnetic field exposure. We believe that parents, especially parents of children with autism, ADHD, and the rest, need to inform themselves and decide for themselves.

First, we believe that GM foods present a danger to health that may well become catastrophic; it is quite possible that we are seeing the tip of the iceberg.[2] Though it is difficult to avoid these foods, it may be worth the effort to do so, at least until we know more.

We also believe that we have been deceived about the safety of pesticides. What are pesticides, anyway? They are poisons that kill various forms of life by disrupting their biological processes, processes that are common to many life forms including humans. Many pesticides disrupt hormones, for example; others harm the immune system.[3] The safety studies on pesticides in no way demonstrate the realistic potential harm.[4-5] Each chemical is studied separately with no attention at all to combinations of exposures. Consider the body burden study initiated by the Environmental Working Group in 2004. In the study on infant exposure, they identified 287 chemicals in the umbilical cord blood of ten babies at birth. The average number for the ten was 200. The chemicals included numerous pesticides as well as other chemicals we discuss later. Of the 287 chemicals present in these babies at birth, 217 are neurotoxins, 208 cause developmental defects in animals, and 180 are carcinogens.

Eating organic food does not solve the problem; it only reduces it. Pesticides occur in groundwater, as has been well documented for fifty years. Men in parts of the Midwest with higher pesticide exposure from drinking water have lower sperm counts. What is happening to their sons?

In addition to eating and drinking pesticides, we absorb them through our skin and inhale them. The concentration of pesticides and other chemicals is usually higher in household dust than in food or water. Each year, household dust is produced in the range of twenty-five to thirty pounds per thousand square feet of living space. So children have the greatest exposure by simply being closer to the floor, not to mention crawling, and chewing and sucking on things they find on the floor. They are also more vulnerable because their surface area is relatively large compared to their size. Their respiratory, absorption, and metabolic rates are greater. Their immune systems are not fully developed until their early teens. Growing tissues have accelerated rates of the accumulation of toxins. Large EPA studies on chemical body burden show that children have twice the amounts of many pesticides, industrial chemicals, and other pollutants as adults. Is it any wonder that our children are the canaries in the coal mine?

Pesticides are not our only serious pollutant.[6] We are awash in a petrochemical soup; the EPA estimates there are close to one hundred thousand commercial chemicals. And with less stringent requirements for evidence of safety than for pesticides, we do not really know where we stand with these chemicals until a problem surfaces. Usually, more rigorous studies are done only after there is evidence of harm, along the lines of innocent until proven guilty. That is good for the justice system but not for the guardians of our health and environment.

A large category of chemicals of great concern is the xenoestrogens. These are synthetic chemicals that mimic the activity of estrogen in the body. No one knows how many of these chemicals there are since companies are not required to determine if their product is a xenoestrogen before introducing it into the environment. Some of the known xenoestrogens are in pesticides, plastic bottles, baby bottles, plastic food wraps, microwave containers, food can linings, paints, detergents, fragrances, sunscreen, detergents, bubble bath, shampoo, flame retardants in clothing and baby mattresses, and plastic toys. Even if laws are passed to remove ubiquitous xeno-estrogens such as bisphenol-A or phthalates from toys and baby bottles, children are by no means safe from the risks.

Studies show xenoestrogen exposure increases risks of brain, immune system, and reproductive system defects. Breast and pros-tate cancers are implicated, as are low sperm counts, and early puberty in girls.[7] Children exposed in utero have lower IQs, mem-ory deficits, behavioral problems, and motor deficits.[8-10]

Not all toxic petrochemicals are xenoestrogens. Perfluorinated chemical exposure is widespread as it is in nonstick cookware, stain-resistant materials, Gore-Tex clothing, some shampoos, and dental flosses. Scotchgard removed perfluorinated chemicals from its stain-resistant products, so furniture or rugs treated before then contain the chemical. Perfluorinated chemicals, like most xeno-estrogens, have a long life inside the body and in the environment. The EPA has deemed as safe the chemical substituted in Scotch-gard based on studies supplied by its maker, 3M. We have not been able to access those studies. It may be like banning DDT and intro-ducing dioxin. Perfluorinated chemicals caused birth defects and cancer in animals and plant workers had increased birth defects. The EPA fined DuPont $16.5 million dollars for keeping its little secret for eighteen years—a slap on the wrist for a company with a market capitalization of close to forty billion dollars at the time.[11]

Brominated flame retardants are another class of pervasive, damaging man-made chemicals. They are in clothing, mattresses, furniture, carpeting, car upholstery, and electronic equipment of all types. They contribute to cancer rates, damage immune and thyroid function, and are neurotoxic.[12-13]

Another large category of toxic substances is metals. These include lead, mercury, cadmium, arsenic, nickel, and aluminum.

To these, we add the nonmetal elements fluoride, chlorine, and bromine. For years, the Agency for Toxic Substances and Disease Registry, a federal agency, has listed arsenic, lead, and mercury as the top three substances on its priority list of hazardous substances. Cadmium is in the top ten.

Most arsenic exposure comes from pressure-treated wood, which is used in playground structures, picnic tables, and decks. Children get more than we do because of their hand-to-mouth behaviors, ingesting soil and dust. Arsenic is also in groundwater, citrus fruits, cotton, and chicken feed. Arsenic can damage multiple organ systems and is a carcinogen, and children exposed have lower IQs.[14]

Lead is everywhere, less in the atmosphere over cities than when gasoline was leaded (replaced by hydrocarbons and methanol, which provide different risks), but still everywhere, with billions of pounds used in manufacturing yearly. Again, dust and soil are significant routes of entry for children. No safe blood levels have been identified, and just a millionth of a gram of lead in half a cup of blood causes learning disabilities.[15-17]

Mercury, too, is in the atmosphere, soils, and water, and also in many products, including vaccinations, fluorescent and energy-efficient lights, electronic switches and relays, and thermostats. Not long ago, it was used as a fungicide in interior water-based paint. You do not have to have amalgam fillings in your teeth or eat fish to get your share of it. Of course, if you do have amalgam fillings, you are likely to have two to three times the amount in your brain as folks who do not have "silver" fillings. But still, with mercury, a small amount in the wrong places in the body can wreak havoc while larger amounts in less critical places do not.

Mercury likes brain tissue, and it likes it a lot, especially the major regulatory centers: the hypothalamus and the pituitary gland. The thyroid gland is another favorite. The time it takes to eliminate mercury from the body is only several months, but animal studies correspond to clinical experience and suggest that mercury in the central nervous system is sequestered, like lead in bones, and takes years to be eliminated.

Mercury is highly neurotoxic, suppresses immune system function, yet triggers damaging autoimmune activity, and inhibits hormone activity. It disrupts critical enzyme activity, disturbs cell membrane permeability, dislocates genetic signaling, and inhibits the repair of DNA.[18-20]

Aluminum—from cookware, antacids, buffered aspirin, and antiperspirants—is a neurotoxin known to induce dementia. A special concern for children is that it increases the permeability of the blood-brain barrier, which allows other harmful substances access to their brains. Cadmium, from first- and secondhand cigarette smoke and residues on food, suppresses immune function, and is toxic to the brain and liver.

The nonmetals in the halide class of elements—fluoride, chlorine, and bromine—present a different set of concerns. Though there is agreement that toxic metals should be avoided, there is debate as to how much exposure should be allowed. These elements are considered beneficial, and conventional medicine endorses them: fluoride to resist dental decay, chlorine as a disinfectant, and bromine in medicinals. We believe there is credible evidence that these should be avoided.[21-27] While taking in small amounts may well be beneficial, it is increasingly difficult to keep intake small due to their abundant presence in the environment from manufacturing and industry.

A problem that these elements cause is suppression of thyroid function—not the hypothyroidism with which physicians are familiar and that can be detected by blood tests, but a more subtle condition that is only picked up clinically. Persistently low body temperature is a key indicator and other signs include dry skin, low energy, easy weight gain, cold intolerance, constipation, elevated cholesterol, low vital signs, joint or muscle pain, cold hands or feet, and brittle fingernails.

These nonmetal elements interfere with thyroid function because they are in the same class of elements as iodine, that is, the halides. Thyroid hormones have either three or four iodine molecules. Fluoride, chlorine, and bromine are smaller than iodine, so can readily displace it from the hormone, which inactivates the hormone.

Fluoride and chlorine have their own serious toxicity risks. And it should be noted that while fluoridated water was being credited with the reduction in tooth decay in the United States, European countries that chose not to fluoridate their water due to the risks had parallel reductions in tooth decay, due to significant improvements in nutrition and hygiene, which were similar to improvements occurring in the United States at about the same time. Fluoride's touted effectiveness in decreasing tooth decay may well have been due, in part, to better nutrition and hygiene. So regarding fluoride, we choose to err on the side of caution for children: more flossing, less fluoride.

Chlorine is tough to avoid if you have tap water. Unless you use a filter, you will likely absorb more chlorine from your shower by inhalation than by drinking and cooking the rest of the day. Olympic swimmers demand that chlorine and bromine not be used for water sanitization; ozone and UV sanitizers are safe alternatives. There are bath balls available that may be swished in your child's bathwater to remove chlorine and filters for shower heads.

The toxins discussed here are some of the more prevalent and are of growing concern. There are many more types of petrochemicals and other toxic metals and elements that are increasing in the environment. The question, then, is what can a parent do to help minimize the damaging effects from these poisons?

Avoidance

Clearly, the first priority is avoidance. For this, we consider the ingestion of food and water, the inhalation of vapors and dust, and the skin absorption from clothing and household products. Consider avoiding, as much as possible:

- GM food

- Food sprayed with pesticides; food with chemical additives—colors, flavors, preservatives, flavor enhancers, artificial sweeteners

- Bleached, bromated flour products

- Unfiltered tap water

- Plastic water bottles with a recycling symbol of #3, #6, or #7 (do not refill #1)

- Plastic baby bottles and liners with bisphenol-A (check product websites; if they do not say they are bisphenol-A free, assume it is present)

- Toys, sippy cups, pacifiers, nipples, teethers not labeled as phthalate-free or PVC-free

- Plastic containers not labeled as phthalate-free

- Styrofoam containers

- Household products with solvents, chlorine, dyes, fragrances, phenols, talc, and virtually all chemicals that have difficult-to-pronounce names with hyphens, numbers, and letters

- Fabric softeners, aerosols, disinfectants, chemical room fresheners, antiperspirants

- Teflon, Gore-Tex

- Textiles with fire retardants

- Aluminum cookware

- Amalgam ("silver") fillings, stainless steel (nickel) crowns

Of course, any such efforts need to be realistic in terms of time, life circumstances, and financial situation. Do what can be done, what works, and by all means, do it without fretting over what you are not able to do. Any small, systematic avoidance of potentially toxic substances is worthwhile.

Use a fruit and vegetable rinse, read labels, phase in less-tampered-with foods, find natural care products for your baby, get an alum deodorant (a nontoxic crystal with antibacterial properties) for your teen, do not use high heat with Teflon, avoid acidy foods (tomato sauce) in aluminum, and do not allow any more silver fillings. Get a water filter, and if you live near farmland or factories, an air filter as well. If you invest in anything that is free of fire retardants, let it be your child's mattress and pajamas.

Removal

Our bodies are detoxification machines, but in a world of increasing toxic substances, we cannot sit idly by and expect these machines to continue to function flawlessly. We must provide effective support. Also, this is where genetics can play a significant role; some children are much less able to handle certain kinds of toxins. But, thankfully, for those children, it is the same as it is for the rest of us: Vigorous, intelligent nutritional support can do wonders.

Detoxifying a child whose brain is overwhelmed with toxins is like dealing with a traffic accident on the highway, where small accidents cause smaller backups of traffic and big ones cause larger backups. Toxins are like the backed-up cars. There should be a constant flow of traffic, just as toxins that enter our bodies should be promptly processed and excreted. When there is a traffic jam of toxins, we see changes in the way brains normally function.

Like clearing a highway accident, detoxifying our bodies necessitates the systematic removal of obstacles to the flow. Sometimes a traffic jam only requires a tow truck; sometimes it requires two helicopters and a dozen emergency medical response teams to treat injuries or a Hazmat crew to clean up a spill.

When we detoxify, two reactions can occur, and it is important to be aware of these. The first is a healing reaction in which symptoms temporarily worsen before a person improves. This appears to be due to a mobilization of backed-up toxins that reenter the system. It is most evident in an energy medicine treatment such as homeopathy. In homeopathy, the drops that are taken are so diluted that no physiological reaction is possible. Yet it is not at all uncommon for someone receiving such drops to experience a transient worsening. As though when energy regains its natural flow through the meridians, it is able to break up accumulations of the toxic obstacles to energy flow.

The second reaction is experienced the same as a healing reaction by someone who is detoxifying, but it has a different mechanism. It is called a Herxheimer reaction or a die-off reaction. Certain organisms, such as yeast or *Borrelia* (causes Lyme disease), release toxins and these toxins are released from the dying and decomposing bodies of the organisms, which increases the number of toxins in the host's system. It also appears that fragments of the organisms trigger the immune system in the same manner that allergens do.

Both of these reactions can be from mild to severe, and modifying the detoxification treatment being used may be necessary. Usually, after a healing reaction or die-off reaction, a person feels much better or a child's behavior suddenly improves. Often, the length of time of feeling worse is an hour or two (longer for Lyme). It is common for these ups and downs to go on for weeks in someone who is significantly toxic. If that is occurring, be patient and continue. The occurrence of the good episodes is an excellent prognostic indicator.

Neither of these detoxification reactions has to occur to get an excellent outcome. There are some people who are so toxic that a temporary increase from treatment does not seem like any more than just another bad day.

The first and most important factor for optimal detoxification, and one that does not cause the reactions noted, is diet. We cannot emphasize this enough. If parents could magically introduce an entirely healthy diet for a child who is struggling with a disruptive process such as autism, they would be amazed at the improvements they would begin to see. But for many parents, it would take nothing short of a miracle to introduce such a diet quickly. Speed is not necessary. Any improvements made will be rewarded in one way or another, and will likely lead to being able to make further improvements.

Especially for children with autism, an optimum diet might be different than it is for others, but a healthy diet is central for all. Some only need nutrient-dense foods; others require it to be gluten- and casein-free as well, or at least until they have recovered.

In terms of the restrictions diets, parents do not need to see a professional to be able to make intelligent decisions as to what dietary strategies to employ. With diet interventions, try it, and if it works, stick with it; if it does not, no need to continue it. The information in *Autism: Effective Biomedical Treatments,* by Pangborn and Baker, which we mentioned in the chapter on autism, is a valuable resource for the parent of any child considering dietary interventions. In addition, the Autism Research Institute (www.autism.com/treatable/index.htm) is another resource for the parent of any child who is struggling, diagnosed with autism or not.

Nutritional supplementation does not replace a healthy diet. If you put a mixture of gasoline and water into a Lamborghini, then add a can of a performance-enhancing fuel additive, how well will it run? Now, supplementation can help patch a few holes in a diet that is not as good as it can be, but when added to a good diet, it can make the difference between having learned to live with a problem and getting to the point where the problem fades into the distance.

We believe that *everyone* should take a daily combination of supplements that provides a foundation for promoting healthy processes. Then other nutrients can be added to target enhancement of a specific organ system or a specific physiological process that needs assistance. Reducing illness and improving healthy processes in the body with nutrition is supported by a large database of scientific studies. The reason that most physicians are unaware of this, and are likely to disparage the notion, is that the studies are small compared to the large, costly studies the drug companies conduct, studies many physicians and others assume must be done before drawing conclusions. Certainly, the FDA requires these large studies before granting approval, but that does not mean that a physician using evidence-based medicine principles would hesitate to use nutritional supplements based on the body of information available for nutrients, especially when realizing the benefit-to-risk ratios that are documented. The reason nutrients are not subjected to the same type of large studies is not because there is a lack of abundant evidence of their effectiveness and safety for many conditions; it is solely because they are not patentable. Drug companies spend hundreds of millions of dollars per drug to get patented drugs FDA approved because, by owning exclusive rights to the product, they stand to make excellent profits. Who would spend hundreds of millions of dollars if they would not retain those exclusive rights for a nutrient studied, since anyone is free to produce the nutrient and sell it? It is a simple business reality that has nothing at all to do with the effectiveness of nutrients compared to the effectiveness of drugs.

The foundation nutrients include a high-quality vitamin-mineral supplement and essential fatty acids, specifically omega-3 fatty acids. The vitamin-mineral supplement should hit certain benchmarks for each nutrient; for older adolescents and adults, this takes six (average-sized) tablets or capsules daily. Children's essential fatty acid supplementation should be DHA and EPA, which are omega-3 derivatives. Early on, children do not effectively convert omega-3s to these derivatives, and even later, some children still do it ineffectively. These fats are crucial for brain development and other systems, such as the immune system.

Based on extensive medical research over the last several years, it is a mistake not to include extra vitamin D on your must-take list. The immune-enhancing ability of this simple substance is nothing short of staggering. Spend an hour or two on www.vitamindcouncil .org and it will open your eyes. John Cannell, MD, and his staff have compiled, organized, and summarized a huge body of important medical literature that, if its information is integrated, will lead to fewer cancers, fewer infections, less mental illness, and even more hope for parents of autistic children. Daily vitamin D doses of 1,000 IU for children under one, 1,500 IU for children one to four years, and 2,000 IU for children four to ten years of age are desirable. Over ten years, use the adult recommendation of 5,000 IU of vitamin D. The form of vitamin D should be D3, not D2.

When all the vitamins, minerals, and essential fatty acids are well supplemented, the results can be remarkable.[28] If that is all a parent is able to do, it is substantial in and of itself. And it does not make sense to us, before providing the foundation nutrients, to try this nutrient or that one because they are touted to help. After the foundation nutrients, it is a different story; this nutrient or that one may accelerate improvement.

Other nutrients we have found to be particularly good are CoQ10, glutathione and its precursor N-acetylcysteine, extra vitamin C, extra vitamin B12, extra magnesium, extra zinc, taurine, and alpha-lipoic acid; in autism, extra B6 is a must. Nutrients like SAMe, TMG (trimethyl glycine), and DMG (dimethyl glycine) can target detoxification processes. Children who are identified or suspected of having problems with detoxification often have deficiencies with some of the processes involved in detoxification, sulfation, methylation, or creatine formation.

Some children with autism may appear to worsen on some of the nutrients that support detoxification. This situation requires a clinician who either knows how to identify the problem with laboratory testing or how to figure it out clinically, because once the deficiency is corrected, the nutrient can often be reintroduced.

For example, if a child is not handling well the sulfur-containing nutrients (particularly glutathione or N-acetycystine), which are critical for detoxification, we administer methyl vitamin B12 shots, decrease mercury, and make sure yeast in the bowel is not excessive. Then we retry the nutrient to see if it is now tolerable. The reason we do not go straight to laboratory testing is because it is expensive.

Metals removal can be accelerated by increasing glutathione levels (N-acetylcysteine, magnesium, methyl B12, vitamin C) and the use of TTFD, a fat-soluble form of vitamin B1, and topical glutathione. Also, DMSA, the medication for reducing mercury and some of the other toxic metals, is available over the counter in 25 mg and 100 mg capsules. A dose we have found useful and tolerable is 3 mg/lb. For children who have problems with sulfur, it is best to wait until the corrective nutrients have been introduced and it is clear they are handling sulfur without problems.

The gastrointestinal tract must be in good working order for detoxification to proceed. One bowel movement per day is the minimum. We discuss supporting the gastrointestinal tract later.

Sweating helps eliminate metals and petrochemicals. A sauna can be a great detoxification option for an older child or adolescent. A far-infrared heater in a sauna can significantly lower the temperature needed to work up a good sweat so is more tolerable to someone who has problems with the higher heat in regular saunas, 120 to 130 degrees compared to 190 to 200 degrees. Either way, drink water before, during, and after, and take towels with you to wipe down from time to time; toxins can be reabsorbed if the sweat dries.

We include our discussion of vaccinations in this chapter to underline the need to think carefully about what vaccination schedule you will use for your child because of the risks of toxicity.[29–32] You must decide which of the vaccines you believe are necessary and at what age your child will receive them. Does it matter if your daughter gets the mumps and misses a week of school or if your son gets rubella for a few days? Whatever you decide, there are some guidelines to take seriously.

Children should not be vaccinated if they are sick (even the sniffles), if they are not fully recovered from a recent illness, or if it appears they might be coming down with something. Children with seasonal allergies should not receive vaccines during allergy season. Those who have an adverse reaction to a vaccine should not receive that vaccine again until they are years older and in perfect health.

Spacing the shots out and not giving combinations not only makes it less likely that a child will have a serious reaction, it also improves the likelihood of actually becoming immunized. A vaccination does not confer immunity unless the immune system is able to respond in a proper manner. Though reasonably functional by two years of age, the immune systems of children are not fully developed until they are teens. Another concern in children under two years is that the vaccinations themselves suppress immunity for a month or more. Also, children's brains are particularly susceptible to injury from their own immune response to vaccinations until they are around two years old.

Though a good case can be made for several of the recommended vaccinations, a few are highly questionable. A hepatitis B vaccine on the first day of life is simply ludicrous, unless the child's mother is hepatitis B positive. The use of live viruses in vaccines for babies—measles, chickenpox, polio (the Salk polio vaccine is a dead virus)—is also questionable.

A yearly flu shot (containing mercury) for all children six months and older is another questionable recommendation; it does not even base the need for a shot on whether a child has an underlying condition that places that child at particular risk if he or she does get the flu. Also, the flu shot is a roll of the dice. A flu virus in Asia is identified six months or so before flu season and a vaccine is prepared, so it may or it may not be the flu that ends up spreading in the United States. Even if it is the virus that comes to the United States, it has months during which it can mutate enough for the vaccination to be useless.

Thought should be given to when a child will need protection. We want all of our girls to be immunized for rubella, also called German measles, since it causes serious medical defects in babies if their mothers are infected during their pregnancies. But why give the vaccination to a baby instead of waiting a few years until her immune system is much more likely to respond appropriately?

There are numerous websites packed with information that take a hard stand on one side or the other of this highly controversial issue. The National Vaccine Information Center (www.909shot .com) is one that does a good job of presenting information to take into consideration.

One of the most common medical conditions we see in children and adults does not exist, according to conventional medicine. It is a bowel dysbiosis, that is, an imbalance of the organisms that inhabit the bowel.[33] Some people call it candida, for *Candida albicans*, a highly prevalent yeast in our bodies; others call it yeast, or yeast-related illness. As we stated in the chapter on nutrition, a healthy balance of organisms in the bowel is of uppermost importance for the health of the bowel, brain, and immune system.

Frequent use of antibiotics is the most common cause of dysbiosis, but the use of immune-suppressing drugs like prednisone can also contribute. It is not uncommon to learn that a child's antibiotic regimens started after receiving vaccinations. Vaccinations cause immune suppression on many levels of activity, and make a child, or adult, more susceptible to infection for longer than a month.

There are many children with autism who have had only a single course of antibiotics or none at all. We believe there is sufficient evidence to implicate the MMR (measles, mumps, rubella) vaccine and/or mercury. The measles vaccine in the MMR is a live attenuated virus that is thought to have only slight virulence. But when it is administered to a child with an immature immune system, and the vaccination itself suppresses immune function, the measles virus can cause a chronic, subclinical, inflammatory condition in the bowel. This is not to say there is a measles infection in the bowel, but rather an abnormal inflammatory condition caused by the virus. It leads to dysbiosis and hyperpermeability of the bowel wall (leaky gut), which allows more toxins to enter the bloodstream, as well as proteins that should be broken down before absorption. This can lead to food intolerances and allergies. Mercury appears to have a similar ability to damage the intestinal lining.

When there is a significant dysbiosis, pathogenic organisms are able to proliferate. The most prevalent of these is yeast, a fungus that produces toxins. The toxins are absorbed into the bloodstream from the bowel, and can stress any organ or tissue. More than ninety yeast toxins have been identified, and more than sixty can also serve as allergens. The result is an overburdened and overstimulated immune system. If a child has allergies or asthma, the condition always worsens when a dysbiosis is present, sometimes severely. The brain in particular is the target of many yeast toxins. When these toxins increase, older adolescents and adults complain of overwhelming mental and physical fatigue, and many have headaches, insomnia, depression, or anxiety. Children with elevated yeast toxins exhibit symptoms in their behavior, which can manifest as defiance, rage, anxiety, depression, hyperactivity, learning problems, and even full-blown autism.

We have seen cases of severe autism completely resolve with nothing more than treatment of dysbiosis caused by antibiotics following vaccinations. Recall, conventional medicine does not recognize this condition so will never look for it or consider it. A child who had such a recovery had been to the Mayo Clinic and Johns Hopkins for evaluation and treatment prior to coming to our clinic. Those are two of the best hospitals in the world. They did not miss it because of lack of thorough, thoughtful evaluations by savvy clinicians; antibiotic-induced dysbiosis is simply not something to think of in the conventional medical approach. When a clinician knows about dysbiosis, however, it stands out and begs for attention when it is present in a patient. We are indebted to our mentor, Elmer Cranton, MD, who taught us about this disorder and how to treat it, as well as about multiple other areas involving health and nutrition and, especially, how to evaluate data.

The strategy for treatment of a dysbiosis is to reduce the pathogenic organisms with antifungal medication, promote the proliferation of the beneficial bacteria with diet and nutrients, and maintain an optimum balance until the conditions in the bowel return to those that favor a healthy balance of organisms. This usually takes two months, sometimes longer. As you read our protocol, if it seems like a lot to do, keep in mind that it has ended a hell for many children and adults, and returned them to a life they or their parents thought was lost forever.

The antifungals we use are Nystatin and Amphotericin B.[34] Neither of these is absorbed from the gastrointestinal tract. This is especially important for Amphotericin B, because in intravenous form, there is a high risk of liver damage. None goes to the liver when taken orally; these are safe enough to give to toddlers.[35] U.S. conventional medicine may not recognize this disorder, but other countries do.

Technically, the antifungals have no side effects, but with die-off reactions, which are likely, it does not appear that way. Most children exhibit a worsening of behaviors for a period of time, followed by improved behaviors. Other children, especially those with autism, have an occasional meltdown. These type of reactions should be quickly treated with activated charcoal; recovery usually begins in twenty to thirty minutes. Normally, we do not give activated charcoal, a potent binder, with food, medications, or nutrients, but this situation is the exception.

Most physicians who treat autism with biomedical treatments learn of the usefulness of the antifungal treatments for this condition, but in our opinion, most are not aware of the need for longer and more aggressive treatment regimens in most cases, like the treatment regimen that Dr. Cranton developed. We are happy to consult with any physicians who would like to hear of our extensive experience treating this condition.

Increasing the beneficial bacteria is the other leg of treatment. A high-quality probiotic helps seed the bowel with healthy organisms. The bacteria in these must be the types that live in the small and in the large bowels, and the numbers should be in the billions. The tablets or capsules should weather their trip through the stomach to avoid stomach acid. The better products are from companies that state how many viable organisms are estimated to be present at the time of consumption, not just how many there were at the time of production.

The beneficial bacteria should be fed with a healthy diet and with additional soluble fiber. As we stated earlier, FitSmart makes fibers that can be easily worked into children's diets. Avoid products like Metamucil, which is sweetened with sugar or aspartame.

Sugar and foods that turn quickly to glucose need to be discontinued to stop feeding the pathogenic organisms. Casein and gluten should be avoided the first month of treatment, even if there are no sensitivities to them, because they are hard on an overburdened immune system.

Just because some children have problems with casein does not mean it is undesirable. Not only is it present in otherwise nutritious foods, it also appears to improve regeneration of damaged nerve cells. So children who do not have sensitivity to casein, or those with a mild sensitivity who do okay when taking enzymes with the casein, are likely to benefit from including it in their diets.

Children with a dysbiosis who complain of abdominal pain or

exhibit tenderness often benefit from a form of licorice, deglycyr-rhizinated licorice, by chewing a tablet or two fifteen minutes prior to meals. Licorice has a number of benefits, and the one most use-ful for a dysbiosis is that it promotes the growth and maintenance of the cells that line the gastrointestinal tract, the ones that become damaged in dysbiosis. We use this with success in adolescents and adults with gastritis, heartburn, colitis, or irritable bowel—any inflammatory condition in the bowel.

A supplement that all parents should know of and have on hand in the refrigerator is *Saccharomyces boulardii*. *S. boulardii* is a bene-ficial yeast obtained from the lychee nut or mangosteen fruit. It not only appears to improve significantly the conditions in the bowel that favor an optimal balance of organisms, it also apparently kills the harmful yeasts. We say this because it appears to cause die-off reactions, and if activated charcoal is given, they subside in the same time frame as when antifungal medication is given.

Two highly useful things about *S. boulardii* are that it is available over the counter, so a parent can initiate a treatment of dysbiosis with this and the aforementioned nutrients. Keep in mind, how-ever, some children, including many autistic children, still require the dysbiosis protocol we describe. The other nice thing about *S. boulardii* is that it can, and likely should, be taken if antibiotic med-ications are necessary, along with probiotics, fermented foods, and fiber, to avoid the development of a dysbiosis.[36]

A more recent illness we now must be alert to is a variant of Lyme disease. Lyme had been thought to be strictly a deer tick–borne illness, endemic to certain areas of the United States, and one that was readily diagnosed and treated. For the past years, however, there appears to be a more virulent form of Lyme that can be transmitted by human-to-human contact and can present with predominant neurological[37–38] or autoimmune features, rather than connective tissue pain. Conventional medicine continues to hold to the earlier precept, so a negative diagnosis from a conventional doctor does not, by any means, rule it out. Many patients with this form of Lyme are being diagnosed with conditions such as multiple sclerosis, rheumatoid arthritis, dementia, and amyotrophic lateral sclerosis (Lou Gehrig's disease). There are a number of laboratory tests that can help, but it is a condition that is diagnosed clinically and confirmed by response to treatment. A Lyme-literate doctor is essential.

More children, especially those with autism, are being found to have this form of Lyme, and are improving with treatment. The main treatment, unfortunately, is a long regimen of alternating antibiotics and antiparasitics to kill the *Borrelia* bacterium in its different forms and the coinfections that are commonly present: *Babesia, Erlichia,* and/or *Bartonella.* These patients need antifungal treatment after the Lyme treatment unless they are aggressive with the precautionary measures for avoiding dysbiosis when taking antibiotics mentioned earlier. Fortunately, there are two herb-based treatments that have success in some patients. There are dozens of not-for-profit sites that are packed with information.

Yet another ever-present concern is electromagnetic fields (EMFs).[39-40] Though there is debate as to how much damage EMF sources such as power lines and radar cause, two sources of EMF present a clear danger to our children: cell phones and cordless phones.

EMF in the microwave frequency penetrates the brain, especially deep in children with their thinner skulls and smaller heads, and their growing brains place them at much greater risk. Do not be reassured by many industry-sponsored studies that show no damage. They often focus on the heat generation from these waves, find little heat production, and declare safety. The waves have been demonstrated to damage without significant heat production. Researchers in this field are describing the risks from EMF and the process of discovering those risks as similar to those of smoking cigarettes in the twentieth century: assurances of safety, suppressed information by the industry, and the emergence of medical problems. The fear is that what lung cancer was to the twentieth century, brain cancer will be to the twenty-first. And for our children, it is not just about a risk of cancer in the future, but the impairments in learning today that we are concerned about.

Do not allow young children to use cell phones. Provide air-tube headsets for older children or encourage the use of the speaker phone. If a phone has a wired headset, attach a ferrite bead to the wire.

Cordless phones in the home are another matter. The base station emits more EMF than a cell phone and does so even when you are not using the phone. The EMF is significant as far as reception is good, so the only safe thing to do is unplug the base station and use landline phones. A good site for safety products is www.lessemf.com/cellphon.html.

This chapter may strike a heavy note to the uninitiated, but many parents find that once they are underway in reducing their children's exposure to various health risks, it is surprisingly energizing. Any small steps taken are gratifying; there is a sense of regaining some control. And often, via Internet or groups of like-minded parents, they realize that there are people and organizations that are tirelessly working to make our planet safer and healthier. They provide invaluable information, organize legal action, and stand up against Goliath. Several parents have found a calling and become dedicated to helping other parents and children. It is the work of love to care for others, and that makes all the difference.

20

The Box in the Room: How Television May Play a Role in Unwanted Behavior

That enigmatic box that sits in virtually every living room (and many bedrooms) in America may play a significant role in dysregulation disorders.

Televisions have found their way into our bedrooms, kitchens, and even bathrooms. With so many of them, you would think we should know more about how they affect us, but we know surprisingly little about how television affects us psychologically or biochemically. Does it, for example, affect our endocrine systems, our neuromuscular or sensory systems, and even our central nervous systems?

This lack of information stems from the fact that research money goes into learning how to keep us watching more television and buying more TVs and more of the products advertised on TV. Precious little has been spent on understanding how television affects us physically, intellectually, and socially.

The research that has been done, however, is unnerving. We can say with reasonable confidence that excessive television viewing, particularly in young children, causes neurological damage. TV watching causes the brain to slow down, producing a constant pattern of low-frequency brainwaves consistent with dysregulation behavior. This low-frequency theta (4–8 Hz) reduces the brain's capacity for higher thought processes. Excessive television viewing by small children causes the brain to miss some of the early development stage, resulting in less-than-adequate brain functioning. The brain becomes limited in creative ability as well as higher levels of abstract thinking.

Television lulls the brain into a dull, barely conscious state resembling hypnosis. Television viewing may be one of the culprits in dysregulation disorders. Children's attentional problems are made worse by television viewing and video games. Television viewing gets in the way of the brain developing the plasticity or flexibility necessary for a successful adult life.

Television viewing affects intelligence and attention and it worsens certain disorders, such as ADHD. We also believe that it contributes to a loss of creative ability.

In this chapter, we explore how TV contributes to other problems, such as violence and aggression, physical underdevelopment, personality changes, visual and language problems, and underdevelopment of social skills.

Since the beginning of time, parents and families have been the models for children's behavior, but all of that began to change when television catapulted sight and sound into our living space. It first happened in the United States, spreading throughout the industrialized nations. Now television reaches every nook and cranny of the planet.

Television is not the only medium contributing to the behavioral problems we see in neurofeedback clinics. The proliferation of video rentals and the now-booming industry of video games are having a profound effect on young brains. Our children are flooded with violence, sex, social stereotypes, and, most significant, brain-numbing programming.

In 1939, a *New York Times* writer characterized the future of television in the following statement: "The problem with television is that the people must sit and keep their eyes glued to a screen: the average American family hasn't time for it. Therefore the showmen are convinced that . . . television will never be a serious competitor of broadcasting." This is one prediction that not only overrated our ability to discriminate good leisure time from bad, but also underestimated the habituating influence of television.

Broadcasting until then had been the exclusive dominion of radio—a wonderful medium that gave us news, information, music, and stories that were illuminated and played out in our minds. You could listen to radio and continue to work, as the vivid pictures danced in your head, involving almost all of the higher functions of the brain. Little did the *Times* writer realize how wrong his prediction could be.

In the course of our medical practices, we have seen what we believe to be the negative results of television played out in the everyday lives of our patients. Nowhere is it more observable than in the children we treat for attentional and behavioral problems. Scarcely a day goes by without TV wrestling, or some other violent act as seen on TV, being acted out in our waiting room.

Recently, we were taken aback when we encountered a family dealing with a relationship dispute. The family consisted of elderly parents and six adult children, four male and two female. The oldest child was a fifty-four-year-old male and the youngest a forty-year-old male. All of the children except the youngest were thin, highly motivated, and attentive. The youngest male was obese, unmotivated, and had a very short attention span. He was so different that we concluded he had been adopted.

When we questioned the two older children regarding whether he had been adopted, the oldest answered, "No, he's not adopted; he's just different. We call him the TV baby. We grew up on a farm and did not get a TV until he was born. The rest of us never got interested in TV, but that's all he did. So we call him the TV baby. We think that's why he's the way he is."

If this is, in fact, the case, then parents and professionals must respond to the looming crisis. It stands to reason that children who grow up receiving a significant amount of their social input from television are bound to be different from children getting these social instructions from family and friends.

Television, for all its potential, is likely to be very harmful, particularly to young viewers. There are eight major areas of concern of which parents and professionals need to be mindful. The areas that offer the most potential for harm from TV watching are:

- Cognitive and attentional problems

- Neurological damage

- Violence and aggressiveness

- Physical underdevelopment

- Gullibility

- Passive-dependent behavior

- Visual and language problems

- Social problems

Let's address each one of these separately.

Cognitive and Attentional Problems: If a child spends more time in front of a television than he does in a classroom, it stands to reason that his intelligence level will be less than that of the child who reads rather than watching TV. Even if he is watching PBS, television viewing causes neurological changes that reduce arousal levels. Television has replaced reading for fun; many young people only read when they are forced to. We contend that the more exposure to television children get, the lower the arousal level and the more difficult it is to read. Reading encourages the brain to build better internal connections and operate at a higher level, whereas television allows the brain to operate at the lowest level of functioning.

Efficient learning takes place when the brain is in a state of active alertness, not when the brain is in a semi-foggy state. When the brain is producing alert brainwaves in the beta range, it is open and receptive to information. It can integrate bits of information into a whole picture. In the slower brainwave states, the brain is less alert, less awake.

When children sit in front of a television, their brains begin to slow down, moving toward the slower, less alert brainwaves. Reasoning, logic, and higher thought processes are reduced in the lower frequencies. These frequencies approximate a state of sleepiness or hypnosis in which you appear dazed and follow the instructions of the hypnotist. This is why children and even adults often appear in a daze when they sit in front of a television. They are in what is known as "ocular lock," or dazed staring.

This is also why it is difficult to get their attention; they are hypnotically locked onto the TV. One study indicated that children who watch TV six hours or more a day are more likely to have lower IQs than children who watch two hours or less.[1] Children who come from lower socioeconomic homes tend to be more at risk because of longer exposure to television viewing.

The child with ADHD cannot sustain attention in most normal situations, but television or video games lock him in. Yet there is a paradoxical effect here: The television grabs his attention, and then lulls him deeper into a low state of arousal. This child, who cannot pay attention to begin with, is now transfixed and it becomes very difficult to break his focus on the TV screen.

Neurological Damage: As dangerous as the possible impact of television content is to children, the neurological damage may be far worse than anyone expects. Television viewing may be causing a significant form of brain damage because of the way the brain reacts to it. The ancient art of storytelling carried on by parents and family, then by radio, had a profound impact on the way our brains formed and built neural connections. Television viewing, as opposed to storytelling, causes the brain to function very differently.

Research indicates that our brains operate by activating small clusters of neurons or brain cells. They, in turn, interact with other clusters of brain cells known as neural fields.[2] A single brain cell is connected to an average of ten thousand other neurons, and clusters of these neurons are organized into fields of neurons containing approximately a million brain cells each.[3] Brain cells communicate with one another through the use of chemical messengers called neurotransmitters. The brain is an amazing network of single brain cells communicating with other single cells in clusters of brain cells interacting with other clusters; entire neural fields talk and interact with other neural fields.

When the brain is involved in low-level activity, not requiring a lot of thought, it only requires a single field of neurons to be activated. This is exactly what happens in television viewing. It requires a very low level of brain activity. When complex thought is engaged during a behavior like problem solving or seeing a story in the mind, many neural fields are interacting with each other. The brain is a buzz of activity when this happens. Efficient brains are capable of speeding up for problem solving or slowing down for relaxation. When brains are busily engaged in problem solving or creative activity, all kinds of information is being passed back and forth between neurons and neural fields. To summarize this idea, TV requires only single-field firing to get all the information, whereas complex thought requires multiple-field firing.

Violence and Aggressiveness: Violence and aggressiveness are the most researched area of potential harm from television. Television has a great capacity for manipulating our emotions. We can watch TV and feel sad, excited, frightened, or happy. Small children have difficulty distinguishing reality from fantasy, and when exposed to certain scenes on TV, they may feel frightened or threatened. When our emotions are directly linked to fear, our expressions may come out as an explosive reaction, or we may go underground into sadness. This could eventually lead to depression. Our brain stems and central nervous systems react to scenes on TV, video games, and in movies; in younger children, the reaction may be violent, giving rise to aggressive tendencies. If children learn by what adults model, then what are they learning when they watch violence on TV and video games?

Research on violence in the media and its effects on our children has been accumulating for the past thirty years. There is scarcely a health professional who does not accept the idea that violence in the media encourages violence in our children and society at large. Perhaps the most convincing argument for limiting these violent programs came in July 2000. The American Medical Association,

American Psychological Association, American Academy of Pediatrics, and the Academy of Child and Adolescent Psychiatry joined together to issue a statement to Washington lawmakers. These professional organizations urged legislators to take action curbing violent programming in television, music, video games, and movies. These organizations declared, "Its effects are measurable and long-lasting. Moreover, prolonged viewing of media violence can lead to emotional desensitization toward violence in real life." The most powerful condemnation in the communication stated, "The conclusion of the public health community based on thirty years of research is that viewing entertainment violence can lead to increases in aggressive attitudes, values, and behaviors, particularly in children."

The only way that children will learn to deal with conflict and emotion appropriately is to have good models. If we want our children to deal with their feelings in healthy ways, we must demonstrate healthy ways over and over until good patterns are formed. If a child has a propensity toward aggressiveness and impulsivity, neurotherapy can alter the course of that predisposition.

Physical Underdevelopment: Another area of concern is the physical development of our children. Childhood obesity has reached epidemic proportions in our society. It is not uncommon to read medical reports attesting to the presence of coronary artery disease in a growing number of young children. The FDA has now approved the use of cholesterol-lowering drugs in children as young as eight years old. So why is this happening?

It is logical to assume that if you spend more time in front of the television than you do outside and in classroom activity, it will take its toll on your physical well-being. In addition to the sedentary lifestyle of TV viewing and video game playing, there is the propensity to snack while viewing. Though it is hard to snack while doing it, we must now include message texting.

It seems that the "age of play" is over and has been replaced by the "age of TV, video gaming, and texting." Kids are no longer building forts, riding broomstick horses, and sword fighting with sticks. They are riding the couch and circling the refrigerator. Inactivity is the daily routine. Parents of yesterday could not get their children to interrupt their play long enough to come in the house for supper. Parents of today cannot get them to go outside. Children are becoming like the elderly; their lifestyles do not include exercise and activity.

Gullibility: Television seems like a cheap baby-sitter, but the price we are paying may be horrendous. Small children do not have a well-developed ability to distinguish reality from fantasy; they accept everything uncritically. This makes them easy prey for marketers who want to sell everything imaginable to children.

Saturday morning cartoons are neatly spliced with product commercials designed to stimulate childhood desires. Small children are unable to realize that commercials are designed to sell products and these products do not necessarily perform the way they do on TV. Instead, children see commercials as entertainment, a wish fulfillment, showing something that, if they had it, they could have fun. Children do not realize that commercials are not the whole truth. They are completely accepting of whatever they see.

Passive-Dependent Behavior: Not only does television create a sedentary lifestyle, but it also fosters a state of passivity by actually changing the way brainwaves fire. Younger children are more vulnerable to being lulled into passivity, because their brains are more susceptible to change. Viewing television is an easy activity, requiring no physical or mental effort—just sit passively and be lulled into a hypnotic state. If the program loses its interest for you, hit the remote and go to another mindless channel.

We contend that this passive attitude dramatically reduces sustained attention. A natural consequence of having the television provide every part of the story, without the brain having to work, is that children develop a low frustration tolerance. They give up too easily if they have to work on something that requires sustained effort. Learning is an active process that involves effort, often trial and retrial. It requires that one push through frustration, failure, and boredom. If we are trained to hit the remote when we are bored, we lose that necessary mechanism to try again. The truth is we are only bored when we cannot pay attention.

Our children are losing their creative geniuses because TV is the prime source of their adventure. For many children, their after-school activity involves hitting the remote, walking to the refrigerator, or facing a video game or text screen. They are deprived of real-world activities and appropriate human emotional expressions. Jane Healy, in her excellent book, *Endangered Minds,* refers to these children as "touched starved."[4] If left with TV and video screens alone, they are also physically starved, intellectually starved, creatively starved, emotionally starved, and nutritionally starved. They can develop a number of unwanted characteristics, such as passivity and unmotivated or undirected behavior.

Visual and Language Problems: There is very little research in this area, but it appears there is a negative relationship between watching TV and visual and language problems. From a logical perspective, it makes sense that long hours of watching TV would impair visual development. To understand this, we need to explain a few facts about the eye. The eye contains two types of light receptors: rods and cones. Rods outnumber cones 95 percent to 5 percent. Cones are concentrated in the central part of the eye and require bright light. They come into play for such two-dimensional activities as reading, television, or looking at a computer screen. Visual development requires taking in the whole world, not an excess of two-dimensional patterns. Therefore, we have another important reason to limit the exposure of small children to television, video games, and computer screens. Not only are their brains developing, but also their ocular systems. The human eye needs sufficient interaction with the natural world in order to maintain its perceptual ability.

Language is an expressive skill that is enhanced by speaking and listening to other individuals speak. Without language, humans would not have developed abstract, categorical thinking.[5] So language fosters intellectual growth. Language poorly understood and poorly spoken reflects on the intelligence of an individual. The problem with television is that language is spoken too quickly. Children often pick up words and phrases that make them sound more intelligent, but they lack the ability to integrate these words or phrases into proper context. Language development takes time; children need to play with words, roll them around in their heads, and put them in an integrated context. Neurofeedback enhances neural connections, making visual and language arts skills more accessible.

Social Problems: Socialization occurs through social contact and good social modeling. When a child spends more time watching TV and playing video games than going to school, the social influence of these activities is strong. Since television and video games do not accurately reflect our society, the influence may be an undesirable one. The same is true for Internet communication and message texting. Anything that inhibits social interaction with real, live humans can have a detrimental effect on socialization. We fully agree that e-mail makes life simpler, but again, everything in moderation.

Children need appropriate gender role identification and good adult role models. Perhaps one of the reasons males exhibit hyper-activity approximately four times more often than females is the gender role portrayed on TV and video games. Look how often our male role models on TV are fighting, shooting, and risk-taking, and their activity in video games goes off the chart. We think these mediums play a major role in dysregulation disorders where risk is involved. If children see high adventure on television, they are likely to imitate the behavior. Professional wrestling on TV has become a favorite show for many young people. Though it is staged, not all children realize this. Violent behavior, mistreatment of women, disrespect for authority, and drug and alcohol abuse are portrayed daily on TV and video. A favorite expression in our office is that no child ever got changed by a lecture; they get changed by example. Neurofeedback can reverse the negative effects of TV and video games by correcting dysregulation.

The Importance of Developing the Brain's Functions

Brainwave activity is an important measure of the transmission of information. Brainwave activity relates to the vibrational quality of the neurons. For example, a sleepy brain is vibrating more slowly than a brain that is problem solving. A brain that is afraid or experiencing a panic attack is vibrating much more quickly than a brain that is listening to a story or reading a book. The efficient brain speeds up or slows down its vibrations to match the task at hand. Dysregulation disorders lack the flexibility to move to the desired frequency.

For higher thought processes like problem-solving or creative projects, it is important that our minds form images. This is why storytelling and family conversations are important. They allow, and even encourage, the brain to make images. Television gives both the stimulus and the response, so our brains do not need to make them. When young children are exposed to television, they do not learn to make the mental images the way non–TV viewers do.

Television makes brainwork too easy. It gives us everything we need and, therefore, we do not develop fully. It is for this reason that television lulls the mind into low-frequency or low-vibrational states. Even the most exciting television programs require so little brainwork that watching eventually leads the mind to a dull state of thinking. Television is like the hypnotist, talking and doing all the work until the patient is eventually lulled into a hypnotic state.

In higher thinking processes, neural fields are firing and inter-acting with each other with lightning speed. The brain adjusts to television quickly because it does all the work. The brain very quickly stops all of that intricate communicating with itself; it slows down, and the activity of TV watching can be handled by a single field of neurons.[6] As we have discussed before, this is called single-field firing.

While we confess that we do not know what the critical period is for brain development (because no one is willing to fund research of this nature), we do offer several suggestions:

- Only selected supervised television viewing and no video game playing until after age five.

- The television is never to be watched without a parent present until after age eight.

- Limit television viewing for any child to one hour a day up to age twelve, and two hours a day (and that is probably too much) up to ninety-nine years of age. The exception is special programs and events that can be enjoyed by the entire family.

- Let television and video gaming be a privilege and a treat, not a right.

- Carefully govern the viewing of any violent and socially questionable programming.

- Do not be afraid to cut a show off in the middle if it is noneducational or becomes violent or socially questionable.

- Stick to PBS programming until the child is nine or ten. That avoids commercial messages directed at children. Just because a program is a cartoon doesn't mean it has any educational value.

21

More about Aggression and Dysregulation

If you take any child with a dysregulated brain—who is depressed or anxious, who cannot sit still, who is impulsive, who makes poor decisions, and who cannot see the consequences of his or her behavior—you have a recipe for trouble. Then, if you add the wrong crowd or the wrong environment, inadequate parental guidance, and alcohol or drugs, you have a disaster.

In the previous chapter, we discussed the relationship of television to slow brainwave patterns and developmental issues; but that is not the complete picture. There is a relationship between violence and aggression, alcohol and drugs, and dysregulation disorders that goes beyond the effects of television. The relationship between aggression and dysregulation disorders is often direct and observable; other times, it is subtle and difficult to see. We have seen the relationships in our clinical work so often that we intuitively look for early symptoms that indicate future behavioral problems such as oppositional defiant disorder or conduct disorder. If we see oppositional behavior or conduct disorder, we look for signs of brain dysregulation. If we see any of these disorders, we are on the alert for substance abuse problems.

All of these disorders are likely to have undesirable companions because they have the probability of brainwave dysregulation at their core. The one bright spot in an otherwise gloomy picture is that neurofeedback has been shown to be an effective treatment for all of them.

Individuals with violent and aggressive tendencies, drug and alcohol abuse problems, and ADHD live dysregulated lives. The more serious problems that we discuss in this chapter may start out as ADHD. Over time, however, problems such as alcohol abuse and antisocial behavior become so prominent that other problems get overlooked or seem insignificant by comparison. It is significant that the dysregulation seen in ADHD-type symptoms may be our first observable clue that serious problems are to follow if the dysregulation is not corrected.

Dysregulation and Violence

Brainwave dysregulation is more than an inability to sit in class and pay attention. Dysregulation disorders include poor impulse control, acting before thinking things through, and unpredictable behavior. They also account for endogenous mood disorders and anxiety. We speculate that a high percentage of aggressive acts are committed by people with dysregulated brains. We also hypothesize that our prisons are filled with inmates with dysregulation disorders.

Neurofeedback is the option that shows the greatest promise in treating violent, aggressive behaviors; it has been demonstrated to be a successful treatment for violent juvenile offenders. The implications of this are profound. Since dysregulation disorders and aggressive behaviors are often companions, to treat one is to address the other. If we can successfully treat these populations quickly and cost-effectively, we have not only helped the individual, but also benefited society at large.

It's easy to sit back and label aggression and violence a direct result of poor parenting, a breakdown of the family, some deep character flaw, or not having prayer in school, but that is too easy. These "easy" solutions are generally based on ideology rather than science. Science has been telling us since the 1940s that violent offenders have brainwave irregularities; perhaps it is time to address the cause of the problem. Besides, the strategies we have tried have done little more than fill our jails and prisons.

We need to be more aware of dysregulation disorders and start early before problems escalate. By correcting dysregulation, we can change the criminal mind. The only way to change the upward trajectory toward societal chaos is to treat what science indicates is the root cause of the problem: a dysregulated brain.

If we corrected the dysregulated firing patterns of the brain, we would end up with a person who is much more resistant to negative influences. The well-regulated brain is not as vulnerable to undesirable social influences and is not as impulsive. We need to stop ignoring solid evidence that implicates the dysregulated brain as the single most important factor in such disorders as ADHD and aggressive behavior.

Dysregulation in Family Relationships

Over the years we have seen too many cases of brainwave dysregulation in families to think this is just a random occurrence. For example, the child with ADHD often has an ADHD family history. To a lesser extent, this is also true of aggressive behavior, depression, and anxiety. During our extensive intake interview, we observe closely to see if there are recognizable symptoms in the parent(s). Family histories frequently reveal that grandparents, uncles, cousins, and other relatives have dealt with the same problems as the child we are seeing. We are convinced that there are genetic components to many dysregulation disorders, including aggressive behavior. When we see a violent parent with a violent child, it is more likely a genetic injury that gets reinforced over time.

Let's look at a single dysregulation disorder. ADHD children are more prone to aggressive behavior than non-ADHD children, but this certainly does not mean that all ADHD children are aggressive and will get into legal trouble. The overwhelming majority of these children will never commit a crime, but the possibility is there to a greater degree than in the non-ADHD person.

Some aggressive behavior is a natural part of childhood development. At some point in his development, practically every child will demonstrate some aggressive behavior. He takes a toy, pushes another child, or sasses the parent. This usually occurs first in the preschool era when children are learning to deal with integrating themselves into society. It usually happens again when they are in their teens and begin to experiment with independence. And it could happen at any point between. Most children grow through these aggressive stages, but some children get "parked" in bad brainwave states and remain there for the rest of their lives if not treated. This is where neurofeedback can help: It nudges the brain out of "park," making it more flexible and adaptable to change.

If a brain is "parked" in low-frequency brainwaves, it lacks the flexibility necessary for normal life functioning. Such skills as sharing, communicating, negotiating, and getting along with others are dependent on being flexible. Children with ADHD, violent tendencies, and oppositional behavior lack flexibility. They lack the ability to deal with daily frustrations and feelings of aggression. How we deal with our feelings of frustration and anger makes the difference in our societal integration. If our brains lack the necessary flexibility to deal with different situations, we are likely to respond inappropriately to those situations. If there is dysregulation when it comes to dealing with impulses of aggression, a person is likely to lash out aggressively because the dysregulated brain lacks the control to deal with impulsivity and hostility.

Parenting a child who has aggressive tendencies is never an easy job. It is very easy to give mixed messages that only end up confusing the child. Teaching the difference between standing up for one's rights and not being aggressive is tricky. Understanding these often subtle differences requires a lot of time, clear explanations, and, above all, good modeling. But if these lessons are not learned early, they become increasingly difficult to teach as a person ages. For that reason, we usually recommend psychotherapy or family therapy to complement the neurofeedback when treating an older child or an adult. By using both modalities, you not only change the dysfunctional brainwaves that preclude effective problem solving, but you can also teach appropriate responses to social situations.

Medication Rebound

Many children who take stimulant medication have a rebound when the medication wears off. Even individuals on the street using "speed" will become more aggressive as the drug is wearing off. The drug rebound is a phenomenon that occurs in late afternoon. The child has been on stimulant medication all day, and when the effects wear off, the child becomes tired, irritable, angry, and difficult to manage. He may even exhibit episodes of rage. We have talked with many parents who were overwhelmed and had no idea what to do with these episodes. We have actually had parents who were afraid of the child and so they reinforced the bad behavior by ignoring it, giving in to the child's demands, or pampering the child. When you reinforce any behavior, there is a stronger likelihood it will be repeated. Imagine the power some children must sense when they see their parents afraid of them. At the very least, the child learns that he can get away with inappropriate behavior. Unfortunately, this behavior tends to escalate over time until you have a late adolescent who is completely out of control.

Neurofeedback can eliminate or decrease the need for stimulant medication, thereby reducing or entirely eliminating medication rebound.

Fix It with Neurofeedback

No matter how loving, kind, and caring the parents are, there are some children who will not respond well to love; these are the cases where love is not enough. If the brain is too dysregulated, it cannot incorporate normal societal rules and behavior. These children will have the tendency to act inappropriately in social situations, be aggressive, and take unusual risks. Often these children take risks that threaten life and limb, with no thought of the consequences. Violent behavior leads to more violent behavior; risky behavior usually leads to more risk. If not treated, this can become a way of life.

The low frustration tolerance of people with dysregulated brains often leads to aggression that gets them into trouble. The children and/or adults with dysregulated brains often feel powerless to change things, so they resort to desperate measures. Frustration leads to aggression. If things do not go their way, they overreact. Brainwave dysregulation can make a person feel unworthy, unwanted, unloved, and overwhelmed. When they become overstimulated by life's ordinary demands, like cornered animals, they fight back.

Individuals with aggressive tendencies are self-defeating; they tend to "shoot themselves in the foot." They can generally hold it together for brief periods, but just when it looks like they are gaining some self-control, they "explode" and are in trouble again. It is not easy seeing yourself as being "alone against the world." So they often fight back as though it is necessary for their very survival.

One of the most remarkable transformations we have seen was filmed by Dr. Moshe Pearl of Melbourne, Australia. Dr. Pearl was treating a boy for violent behavior and a large cluster of other symptoms; the child could have had multiple diagnoses. Dr. Pearl filmed the entire process and we could see the child was initially extremely violent and destructive. He terrorized his family and was in the process of destroying his house. After a complete course of neurofeedback training, he was a completely normal child again. His mother, in her delightful Australian accent, said, "I've got my son back." And indeed she did, thanks to neurofeedback and a skilled therapist.

Add Addictive Substances to Dysregulation . . . Bang!

As if it is not enough to deal with brainwave dysregulation, throw in mind-altering substances such as alcohol and street drugs and the picture can get much darker. This is what happens all too often. As bad as it is, it is understandable; sometimes the only thing that seems to offer relief from the ongoing problems of dysregulation is alcohol and drugs. They calm the racing mind and numb the senses. We have seen many adolescents and adults who have tried to "fix" things with drugs and alcohol, but this only makes things worse.

Significantly more children with ADHD develop problems with drugs and alcohol than do children without ADHD.[1] If you are looking for a place to hide, forget, or escape, and you have impaired decision-making abilities, alcohol or drugs can certainly look or feel like the answer. We feel the same is true for children with any type of impulse control problem, as well as for children and adults with mood disorders and anxiety.

Violence, aggression, and criminal behavior tend to increase when adolescent boys with dysregulation disorders turn to drugs and alcohol. Substances that alter the mind inevitably alter behavior. Shy boys become loud; angry boys act out their anger. These substances give people a false sense of courage. A major reason that these juveniles turn to drugs and alcohol is that these substances seem to offer relief from the chronic feelings of inadequacy and unworthiness. ADHD and other dysregulation disorders are lifelong disorders if not treated. Dealing with brain dysregulation day after day, year after year, wears the person down. They are searching for relief. Drugs and alcohol make them feel a sense of happiness, relaxation, and invulnerability. They think they are ten feet tall and bulletproof. A little drink or smoke can boost their courage and give them a false sense of superiority.

Soon they are addicted and find themselves acting out their impulses. At this point, they have often crossed the line and are in trouble with the law. After they have a few minor brushes with the legal system tucked under their belts, their confidence grows along with their aggressive behavior. When the body is full of alcohol and/or drugs, years of pent-up frustration, anger, and feelings of failure can be unleashed. It's like mixing gasoline and matches.

The telltale signs of aggression are usually there, but families often miss them, choose to ignore them, or forgive them as isolated events. Most people with dysregulation disorders who have aggressive tendencies present with consistent patterns. Often when we are meeting with parents, we can almost see light bulbs going on as we ask certain questions and they begin to see the patterns of aggressive behavior emerge.

Neurofeedback has a proven track record, not only in treating dysregulation disorders, but also in successful treatment of substance-abuse disorders. Move quickly. If you see developing problems, seek out a neurofeedback provider.

Conflict

Conflict is a big issue with many dysregulation disorders—conflict with the world; with teachers, parents, friends, siblings, school peers, coworkers, even the law. Individuals with dysregulation disorders do not manage conflict well. They have poor negotiating and compromising skills, they tend to escalate rather than negotiate, and they are too inflexible. If they are not in direct conflict, they use passive-aggressive techniques such as tears and helplessness. Overreaction is commonplace, and a minor conflict can quickly escalate into a major catastrophe.

Impulsivity is common for individuals with dysregulation disorders; they will impulsively drop out of school or quit their jobs over minor events. They may drop out of school because the principal "is a jerk." It is always someone else's fault. In a best-case scenario, they walk out; in a worst-case scenario, they hurt someone.

Perhaps more tragic than being in conflict with others, these individuals are usually in conflict with themselves. It doesn't usually take too long before dysfunctional behavioral patterns lead them to dislike themselves. They are usually "parked" only a short distance from being out of control; and when they do lose control, the aggression may be directed toward others or toward themselves. Self-aggression takes different forms. You may hear the negative self-talk: "I hate myself," "I'm so stupid," "What is wrong with me?" "I'm going to kill myself." Or you might even see self-hitting or worse.

Sometimes dysregulation causes hyperactivity; their life is at full speed. At other times, it is slowed down and they cannot get moving or accomplish anything. So they can be bouncing from one thing to another or become frozen. They race or are broken down, but whatever it is, it is not dynamic and seldom is it appropriate to the time at hand. High emotions or deep holes are the story of their lives. They seldom experience the usual gradual ups and down most of us have. It usually takes the extremes before they come to the attention of professionals.

How can you not be in conflict with the world when your brain causes you to be disruptive, frenetic, or impulsive? How can you not be angry if your brain makes you feel depressed, sad, or anxious? When things get painful enough, people will usually seek help. Sometimes, however, it has to be painful to others before they intervene and help.

When the dominant brainwaves are low-frequency waves, the brain will often compensate by increasing the high-frequency waves. This causes racing thoughts and the person pays attention to everything at once, so nothing stands out. They end up in a state of perpetual overload. In overload, you feel as though you have no control over anything and can't put the brakes on. These feelings can lead to a state(s) of anger and/or fear toward everything and everybody. Life is no fun when you are in a constant state of irritability, grumpiness, and discontentment.

We have worked with some very difficult cases, not all of which were treated to a satisfactory conclusion. People suffering from dysregulation disorders such as ADHD, oppositional disorders, conduct disorders, and antisocial behavior frequently drop out of treatment before they can be helped. They generally do not think they have a problem—everyone else has the problem. We have also seen parents and spouses give in and allow the patient to drop out if they become too difficult to deal with at home.

For example, it's almost impossible to take an adolescent to treatment twice a week if they are fighting you every step of the way. Over the years, we have seen dropouts from treatment quit school, destroy relationships, get into trouble with the law, go to jail, and even get killed because of their risk-taking behavior. Fortunately, we have seen many more turn their lives around.

We have seen angry, disruptive children become model students, and brawlers become peaceful. We have witnessed chaotic relationships settle down, risk-takers give up dangerous activities, and law-breakers stop getting in trouble. We have also seen families and friends able to stop worrying.

Oppositional Defiant Disorder

The essential features of oppositional defiant disorder (ODD) are, of course, being defiant and/or oppositional. ODD also includes a chronic negative attitude. In the more severe cases, there is overt hostility toward authority, which can eventually lead to trouble with the law. Children with this disorder are usually annoying to others, resent being told to do anything, and, as a matter of fact, usually resent almost everyone. Sometimes these children can be very sweet toward some people and hostile toward others. One minute you want to "whack" them and the next minute you want to hug them. They often show an unrealistic stubbornness, even toward requests that would be fun for them.

Having treated many of these children over the years, we can tell you that they are difficult cases, but it is very rewarding when they start to change. As the brainwaves normalize through neurofeedback, their behaviors modify dramatically. We have had countless cases in which parents were ready to "send him off to military school." Parents get exasperated when they have tried everything and nothing helps. One parent of a fifteen-year-old boy once told us that if they could lie about their son's age, they would send him off to the army. It took twenty-nine weeks of twice weekly training before son and parents started liking each other again.

ODD usually has some companions. Some experts suggest that as many as 50 percent of males with ADHD meet the criteria for ODD. You often see ADHD children with long-standing histories of oppositional, defiant, disobedient, and hostile behavior. We have all seen this type of child: If you say the sky is blue, he will argue it is green. If you say he can go on Saturday, he will insist on going on Friday. These children are almost impossible to please. Oppositional-defiant children are rarely in serious trouble, but they do tend to cause a lot of trouble for others. They get suspended, get sent to the principal's office, fail their classes, and stay perpetually grounded, but they seldom end up in front of a judge. Now, if the behaviors get reinforced, they may get a free ride to the judge later in life.

We see the same types of dysregulated brainwave patterns in ODD that we see in ADHD children. The dominant brainwaves are in the low-frequency range. The primary goal of neurotherapy is to reduce the low-frequency waves and increase the mid-range waves. Not only would we say that neurotherapy corrects the psychological diagnosis of ODD, but it also changes personality. Parents report that they are astounded with some of the changes they see in their children after brainwave training. One third-grader who was in constant trouble with the teacher became the hall monitor after neurofeedback.

Conduct Disorder

Conduct disorder is a more serious disorder. This disorder goes far past the point of being annoying. Children with this disorder demonstrate a flagrant disregard for others and the rights of others. They often show overt aggression toward people, animals, and property. Fortunately, there are fewer conduct disorders than ODD. It is estimated that the rate ranges from 6 percent to 16 percent of males and from 2 percent to 9 percent of females under the age of eighteen years. The disorder is also more prevalent in urban areas than in rural areas. Children with conduct disorders engage in fighting, threatening, cruelty, stealing, lying, fire setting, and cheating. They may even use a weapon to gain what they want. So members of this group often end up in front of a judge.

Unlike the oppositional child, the conduct disorder child is more likely to commit a crime and come to the attention of legal authorities. The person with conduct disorder usually has their first brush with the law in adolescence, then he is "in the system." Subsequent run-ins with the law may become increasingly serious and the criminal sentencing usually becomes stiffer.

Girls who have conduct disorder diagnosis tend to be less violent, although they can be just as self-destructive as their male counterparts. They tend to be impulsive and make poor decisions, and they are not able to predict consequences any better than the boys. Like the boys, they tend to develop poor self-esteem, which leads them to do things they might not ordinarily do. Because they tend to be more promiscuous than other females, they have more unwanted pregnancies. Again, the inability to see consequences plays a major role in acting-out behavior; this is particularly true of children who carry a dual diagnosis of conduct disorder and ADHD.

If the conduct disorder is not resolved before a teenager turns adult, the diagnosis changes to "antisocial personality disorder." We can have a full-blown problem on our hands—an adult with total disregard for the rules and regulations governing society. It's "every man for himself," get what you can get, regardless of how you get it. There is no sympathy or empathy for anyone else. If they are able to take something from someone else, it is that person's fault for being so stupid or weak. Individuals with antisocial characteristics have no feelings of guilt and nothing is ever their fault. The only time they show remorse is when they get caught; then we may see tears and regret, but it is possible we are seeing "crocodile tears." With the antisocial personality, you never know when you are being conned. (For a complete description of the diagnoses we have discussed here, consult the DSM-IV.)

We have treated individuals with both conduct disorder and antisocial personality disorder and they are extremely difficult cases—not because neurofeedback is unlikely to succeed, but because "it is not my fault" and "there is nothing wrong with me." They will usually drop out of treatment at the first opportunity. They will condemn the treatment until they are in trouble again and, at that point, they ask the judge to let them do treatment rather than jail. When we have been able to finish treatment, we have had great success. Personalities do change when you change the brainwaves—depressed individuals brighten up and antisocial personalities develop empathy—but it is a problem keeping them in treatment. The problem with personality disorders is that it is never them, it is always someone else.

The Dysregulated Life

The individual with dysregulation disorders may be more vulnerable to peer pressure. They are hungry for acceptance, and if the only way they can be accepted is to associate with the wrong crowd, so be it. They get acceptance where they can. It becomes much like the child who will gladly accept negative attention over no attention at all. They will exhibit more of the wrong behaviors in response to praise from the group or gang. This can escalate until they cross the line, break the law, and we find them pregnant or in jail.

Individuals with dysregulation make poor decisions in almost every area of their lives. When these individuals carry their problems into adulthood, they have even greater opportunities for failure and more chances to get into trouble. This is because adults have so many more options open to them. If you can't make good decisions when you have limited choices, what will you do when you have an infinite number of choices? The late adolescent and the adult remain challenged with depression, anxiety, impulsivity, poor decision-making, and inability to see the consequences of their actions. If a depressed person could "redo" their suicide, do you think they would do the same thing? The dysregulated life is always one of reacting to the messes one has gotten into.

Brainwave patterns are a significant indicator of behavioral patterns, and there are certain brainwave signature patterns that reflect behavioral problems. Researchers were discussing the relationship of violence to dysfunctional brainwave patterns as early as the 1970s. Investigators at Boston City Hospital identified epileptictype brainwave patterns in individuals prone to violence. You will recall that epileptic-type patterns are seen in ADHD. A 1970 research paper is quoted as saying, "We find that violent-prone persons have a childhood history of hyperactive behavior, multiple fire settings, prolonged enuresis (bed-wetting), cruelty to animals, destructive activities generally out-of-keeping with their peers."[2] The author labeled this behavior syndrome "episode dyscontrol." There are neurotherapists out there who can treat people with these devastating disorders.

Dysregulation Summary

It is increasingly obvious that dysfunctional brainwave patterns correlate with a number of disorders. These dysfunctional patterns are likely to be the product of some type of injury: genetic injury, injury in utero, birth trauma, poor nutrition, heavy metal toxicity, physical trauma, and/or stress injury. There are also the social injuries such as poor parenting, social rejection, and other learned insults. We also know that parental and societal influences can, to some degree, modify the manifestation of these injuries. Even the most wonderful parenting or the best psychotherapy in the world, however, will not eliminate dysfunctional brainwave firing patterns. The dysregulated brain is the root cause of most of the negative behaviors we have discussed. To be specific, the actual cause may have been something like chemical toxicity, but the result was dysregulation. We cannot go back and undue chemical exposure, but we can regulate the dysregulation with neurofeedback.

Electroencephalograph researchers continue to find associations between abnormal brainwave patterns and violence. In a recent article in the *Journal of Neurotherapy,* Dr. James R. Evans and Suzanne Claycomb reported finding quantitative EEG abnormalities in a group of men with histories of violent behaviors.[3] This type of research confirms the clinical findings of neurotherapists everywhere. There is a growing recognition and acceptance that neurotherapy can successfully treat individuals with violent behavior. Within a matter of weeks, neurofeedback can reduce violence and antisocial behavior in patients.

We have successfully treated the types of behaviors discussed here for years. We recognize that dysfunctional brainwave patterns reflect a dysfunctional lifestyle. Left untreated, these problems can become much worse. Dysregulation disorder not only affects the person, but it can also affect the family, the community, and society at large. Living in a household with a person dealing with a dysregulation disorder is like sleeping on a water bed—every time someone moves the whole thing changes shape. Individuals with dysregulation disorders are constantly stirring things up and the dynamics are in a constant state of flux.

Violent and disruptive behaviors can be caused by a bump on the head, a fall, a birth trauma, and many other types of injury if it affects the right spot in the brain. We have seen many patients in our clinic who have unremarkable (no abnormality) conventional imagery such as X rays, CT scans, and MRIs. Yet when we analyze their EEG biofeedback records, we see abnormal brainwave signatures.

One case that stands out involves a young man we will call Charlie, a nineteen-year-old who had been charged with murder. The only head injury we could find in his history was a fall from a ten-foot wall when he was ten years old. This fall resulted in a big bump on his forehead. He was x-rayed and released from the ER with a "he's okay." Charlie's parents noticed subtle changes in his behavior from that time on. He was soon diagnosed with ADHD, and he demonstrated more and more oppositional behavior, which escalated to conduct disorder. Alcohol and drugs became part of his daily life. At home, he was often difficult to manage. He had a few minor scrapes with the law, but nothing serious.

Then one evening while his parents were out, Charlie had friends in. One thing led to another and before long there was a full-blown party going on with lots of drinking and probably drugs. As most often happens at parties of this type, uninvited people showed up. One uninvited "guest" started trouble. There were words, then scuffles. Finally, the stranger passed out.

To get even and to play a bad joke on him, the other boys drove the stranger to an isolated area and put him out, expecting that when he woke up, the joke would be on him and he would be really upset and lost. As it turned out, the joke backfired. The night turned cold, it rained, the ground froze, and the boy died. All three of the boys involved were charged with first-degree murder.

While awaiting trial, a family member saw a TV show on the treatment of violent behavior with EEG biofeedback. The family contacted the doctor on the show and he referred them to our clinic. Charlie's psychological testing indicated strong antisocial tendencies. We immediately began neurofeedback treatment, working in as many treatments as possible in the time we had. At the end of twenty treatment sessions, Charlie was retested. There was a remarkable drop in his antisocial and other pathological scores. He had completely quit drugs and alcohol. He had secured and maintained steady employment, and his family reported he was a different person. There were changes in his brainwave patterns; they were beginning to normalize. We were pleased with his progress and continued to treat him until his trial date.

We went into court armed with EEG records and psychological test results. Many witnesses testified to the personality changes. Defense attorneys were not asking the court to forgive his crime, just that he be placed where he could continue to receive treatment, and that he be given some consideration for the positive changes and the good efforts on his part. Sad to say, he received no consideration and was, in fact, sentenced to a longer term than the other defendants. Charlie was promised leniency if he cooperated with authorities; he did cooperate fully, but it made no difference. Our testimony was not taken into consideration and was, in fact, treated without regard. This type of ruling seems to reflect the legal system's jaded view of any mental health treatment, and particularly of a treatment that reports such a remarkable change. Sentencing day was a sad day for Charlie and a sad day for us. We had all worked so hard to change his dysregulation, and even with success it made no difference in the mind of one judge.

Contrary to the conclusions you might have drawn from media reports about the state of Texas, some Texas institutions have incorporated neurofeedback programs in their criminal justice system. There are those officials who know neurofeedback can successfully treat violent juvenile offenders. Drs. Steve Fahrion and Patricia Norris have implemented another such program in a Kansas prison. Douglas Quirk, PhD, a psychologist at the Ontario Corrections Institute in Canada, used biofeedback to treat violent offenders as early as 1959.

Dr. Eugene Peniston, who developed the now-famous Peniston protocol while working in the Veterans Administration Medical Center in Fort Lyon, Colorado, treated alcoholics with phenomenal success. Dr. Peniston is now training others to treat alcoholics, drug abusers, and people with posttraumatic stress disorder (PTSD) using neurofeedback. The results are startling.

Not all of the violent behavior we have treated has come to us as a result of a patient having a run-in with the law. We once got a call from a tearful mother of a five-year-old boy who had been kicked out of four nursery schools. She was understandably frantic. At that time, we did not see children under the age of seven for EEG biofeedback treatment, but this mother was so desperate and the conduct disorder so severe, we agreed to evaluate the child. After they arrived at the clinic, it was obvious that we were going to be challenged on this one. This boy, we'll call him "Rocky," was a handsome, bright-eyed, blond-haired "terror." He was all over the office and difficult to manage. It took a lot of time, but we were finally able to start his treatment. The mother's chief complaint was his aggression. He had a history of assaulting any child in his path and he needed no reason at all.

Initially, Rocky was very difficult, but the more neurofeedback sessions he had, the easier he was to deal with. By the time we terminated Rocky's treatment, he was regularly hugging us and bringing us gifts he had made or pictures he had drawn. His mother now reports he is the model student, the leader on school field trips. He has become easy to talk to, pleasant to be around, and nonviolent. When Rocky's treatment was terminated, his mother was again in tears, not tears of desperation, but tears of happiness and appreciation.

There are many success stories like Rocky's. There are also successes with sad outcomes like Charlie's. Every neurofeedback practice in the world has similar stories about aggressive behaviors being ameliorated and personalities being changed for the positive. Dysregulation disorders abound and they can manifest in numerous ways. Neurofeedback can address these behaviors quickly and in a cost-effective way.

It goes without saying, as with any new treatment modality, there needs to be much more research in this field. In the meantime, we cannot sit back and wait another five, ten, or fifteen years while more data are gathered. We need to act now. Neurofeedback is already available as a powerful treatment that has demonstrated results superior to anything else available.

Neurofeedback is a revolutionary treatment that can successfully treat children and adults with oppositional and hostile behaviors. In addition, it has been proven to treat alcohol and drug dependence with the best success rate in the literature. Not only does neurofeedback treat the disorders, but it also improves personality characteristics. We must consider the many lives that will be ruined each year if we fail to implement effective treatment programs like neurofeedback.

Pardon us for belaboring the point, but once more, ADHD, oppositional, aggressive, violent, and addictive behaviors have, at their core, dysfunctional brainwave patterns. They are likely companions of each other: If you see one of them, look for others. Even some professionals have the tendency to approach these disorders as mutually exclusive rather than as being in a cluster of disorders with a common origin. Parents and professionals must begin to approach these vexing problems with a treatment modality that can treat the cluster. Neurofeedback may well be the answer we have been looking for.

The Neurofeedback Solution ... Getting Started

For those struggling with dysregulation disorders and for parents of children with dysregulation disorders, there are treatment choices other than medications. As we've demonstrated throughout this book, neurofeedback is a safe, natural treatment for dysregulation disorders, and one that addresses the underlying causes. Treatment with neurofeedback commonly leads to significant and far-ranging improvements in all the symptoms of the cluster. After treatment with neurofeedback, most children and adults dramatically reduce the symptoms that brought them into treatment. In addition, those individuals on medication are usually able to decrease their doses of medication or stop taking drugs altogether.

The fact that neurofeedback is not better known or not yet embraced by all health-care providers does not detract from its ability to improve serious and chronic problems. Not all patients demonstrate dramatic improvement, but the majority of those treated gain significant benefits that extend to school or job, health, relationships, and personal life.

We suggest that in addition to reading about neurofeedback, you arrange to talk with neurofeedback practitioners, with people who have been treated, and with parents of children who were treated more than a year ago. Though such evidence may be considered anecdotal, the genuine enthusiasm you will hear is often an important intangible. This enthusiasm has a distinct character that results from experiencing or witnessing an important, authentic outcome. It is unlike the brief cheerfulness that a placebo provides. We have provided websites that will allow you to find neurofeedback providers in your area.

Be cautious of clinicians who are unfamiliar with neurofeedback yet claim that it has not been proven effective. It is effective and there is research to back up this claim. Though neurofeedback uses rigorous scientific methods as much as possible, it is an evidence-based, outcome-based treatment modality. There is a wealth of evidence and outcome data that supports neurofeedback's safety and effectiveness. Do not blame your doctor if he or she is completely unaware of the documented evidence concerning neurofeedback. No one can keep abreast of everything in the journals. For the most part, it is an overwhelming task for doctors to stay up with all the research that is presented to them. Those of us who have learned about, studied, and practice neurofeedback feel fortunate, as it has more often been by chance encounters that physicians and psychologists became aware of this powerful treatment.

Though this book is intended primarily to introduce you to neurofeedback, another important purpose is to relay our belief that the optimal treatment for dysregulation disorders is not as simple as taking a pill. All treatment for dysregulation disorders should consist of a wider strategy that seeks to improve brain functioning. So we include proper nutrition and freedom from toxic substances in our protocols. The combination will help support optimal brain activity in anyone. Providing good nutrition for their children seems like such an uphill battle for so many of the parents who come to our clinic, so we suggest a gradual change in diet patterns rather than an overnight transition. Let's face it, children like junk food and don't like fresh raw veggies. We build on success and we do it a day at a time.

A careful evaluation of possible toxicity should be considered for anyone with possible exposure to harmful chemicals. There have been occasions when detoxification made the neurofeedback training work much better. Sometimes we have to get the junk out before we can change the brain.

Possible exposures include frequent courses of antibiotics, prednisone, nonsteroidal antiinflammatories, or acid blockers; the presence of silver fillings in the mouth; unwanted chemicals in the water supply; proximity to industrial fumes or engine exhausts; pesticide/herbicide spraying; or mold-resistant paints. The list is actually much longer, but these are among the more common sources.

Neurofeedback, optimal nutrition, heavy metal detoxification, and yeast treatment are only a few of the many safe and effective methods now approaching mainstream medicine. The huge upsurge of interest in and the utilization of alternative forms of treatment for a wide range of diseases is an indication of the benefits many are realizing. The growth of alternative approaches has probably been more the result of heartfelt testimonials to friends and relatives than from the dissemination of the scientific studies that have been done.

Given this, there are two reasons for not waiting for more conclusive findings before considering an alternative treatment. The first is that many natural or unpatentable treatments will likely never be conclusively studied due to the enormous amount of money required to perform such studies. The money spent on large studies is an investment, and like any investment, it is intended to produce profits. This requires that treatments be patentable.

The second reason is that many of the alternative treatments are safe and support healthy, normal body functioning. They are often "good for you," whether or not they help reduce the symptoms. Those of us who have neurofeedback equipment use it routinely on ourselves and our families to promote healthy brain function.

For those of us who use neurofeedback in our clinical practices, there is seldom anything as gratifying as the consistent and dramatic improvements in our patients' lives. Certainly, the most poignant moments for us are when parents, after seeing their children's lives restored, talk about the anguish and heartache they lived with for so many years. Many tell us about having feared that their children would never come close to realizing their potential, and would go on to live lives of disappointment, self-doubt, and loneliness. Often, parents tell us about experiencing a moment that reveals to them in no uncertain terms the extent of the changes that neurofeedback has helped bring about in their child's life.

The father of a seven-year-old boy said simply, solemnly, "Robbie was invited to a birthday party." Although this might seem routine to many parents, for Robbie's father it symbolized that his son's tormented journey was ending and a new life was beginning.

Here's another example. The mother of a fourteen-year-old girl called to describe how, months after her daughter's treatment was completed, she opened the medicine cabinet looking for an eyedropper and found herself face-to-face with three shelves of medications Brandi had taken for years. They were mostly pain medications for her headaches, but there were also stimulants, tranquilizers, and sleeping pills. She told us when she realized that Brandi had not had a pill of any kind in more than six months, she stood in front of that medicine cabinet and wept.

Witnessing the relief and gratitude of the parents of the children we treat is a gift and brings home the realization of what a privilege it is to be able to offer such a hopeful, effective solution to so many people.

Our memories of patients we have treated are rich with snapshots of their successes that they have recounted to us over the years:

- Kerri, a personable teenager, was an aggressive point guard on her high school basketball team, but was suspended from the team due to academic failures. The next season, after intensive neurofeedback treatment over the summer, not only did her grades improve, but she also became a better player. She felt her court vision improved and her coach reported that she was able to remember and execute more complex tactics. She is now in her junior year of college, majoring in law enforcement, with plans to become an FBI agent.

- Shawn is a fifth-grader who would not spend the night at a friend's house or go camping due to his fear of wetting the bed, which occurred with distressing regularity at home. He was treated for ADHD with neurofeedback and has not had a single episode of enuresis in eleven months.

- Bradley is a middle school principal with adult ADHD whose life was dominated by strategies he used to help him remember what he needed to do and where he needed to be. He had Post-It notes everywhere, he was constantly programming his watch to beep to remind him of things, and his computer was loaded with reminder messages. He drank a pot of coffee each day, and was unable to cut his smoking down to less than a pack a day. Though his friends and colleagues found his methods and his breakneck pace amusing, we knew of the anguish he and his wife were experiencing due to the tremendous burden he was under just to get from day to day. His response to neurofeedback was a wonderful demonstration to us of how a well-regulated brain allows a person to access his inborn abilities. Today, Bradley is a relaxed man with a peaceful demeanor. He is a highly organized administrator and, with the spare time and energy that has been freed up, he has begun to pursue two lifelong aspirations: He has taken up the saxophone and is making preliminary plans to run for a local office.

We could go on with stories such as those we have told you in this book—as could other neurofeedback practitioners—but we have provided enough case histories and information to help you in your search for a better, more productive life for you or your child, so we wish you well in your endeavors.

Finding a Provider in Your Area

In a previous book, we offered a listing of neurofeedback providers organized by countries, states, and cities. We found, however, that the field is growing so fast the list was out of date before the book was released. To give you the best opportunity of finding a provider in your area, we list the websites for neurofeedback provider organizations. There are six primary organizations that list providers, teach courses in neurofeedback, sell equipment, and/ or certify practitioners. Understand that most organizations that have provider lists do not guarantee the competency of their members. You will, however, find valuable information on each of these sites.

EEG Spectrum International (www.eegspectrum.com): EEG Spectrum is the largest organization in the world providing neurofeedback courses and they also have the largest provider network in the United States and foreign countries. They have assembled an excellent group of instructors to teach their courses. In addition to teaching neurofeedback, they provide solid equipment and offer consultation to practitioners. Their reputation in the field of neurofeedback is excellent.

EEG Institute (www.eeginfo.com/institute): Two pioneers in the field, Sue and Siegfried Othmer, founded this solid organization. Sue is the primary teacher and her husband, Siegfried, teaches, writes, and does research. They teach, sell equipment, and provide consultation. Their website also offers a listing of providers.

Brian Othmer Foundation (http://brianothmerfoundation .org): Sue and Siegfried Othmer founded this organization, which is dedicated to research, education, and clinical services in neurofeedback. Siegfried is the chief scientist and his wife, Susan, is the clinical director. The organization was founded in response to the difficulties experienced by their late child, who died at age twenty-three after a lifetime of formidable neurological problems. The foundation focuses on reaching the "unreachable child," those who suffer from autistic spectrum disorders, conduct problems, emotional disturbances, brain injuries, developmental delays, and seizure disorders. The foundation also engages in original research in neurofeedback applications.

International Society for Neurofeedback and Research (ISNR) (www.isnr.org): ISNR is a professional membership organization devoted to the study of neurofeedback and the dissemination of information about neurofeedback. It provides a listing of membership on its website.

Association for Applied Psychophysiology and Biofeedback (AAPB) (www.aapb.org): This is a professional organization for all types of biofeedback providers including neurofeedback. AAPB publishes a peer review journal *Applied Psychophysiology and Biofeedback*. Its website provides a listing of biofeedback providers by specialties.

Biofeedback Certification Institute of America (BCIA) (www .bcia.org): See below.

Finding a BCIA Practitioner

The Biofeedback Certification Institute of America (BCIA) became an official and independent certifying corporation in January 1981, from origins in the Association for Applied Psychophysiology and Biofeedback (AAPB). BCIA was founded primarily to provide a standard that health-care professionals of all disciplines, the public, insurance companies, and other official groups could accept as reliable and valid evidence that an individual had attained minimum specified professional competency.

AAPB is the oldest and largest professional association in the field of biofeedback. It signaled its support for higher standards in the field by endorsing BCIA certification or equivalent education, training, and experience as the minimum standard in the field.

BCIA successfully petitioned the American Psychological Association for recognition of biofeedback and applied psychophysiology as a proficiency in professional psychology. This is only the second proficiency recognized by APA. Because of the stature and history of BCIA certification, APA did not choose to launch its own credentialing program.

Certification is the only empirical way to demonstrate that a practitioner has met educational and training requirements, has met competency standards by way of an exam, and agrees to follow ethical guidelines and remain current in the field as it relates to their specific practice. Currently, BCIA maintains three certification programs: General Biofeedback, which includes EMG, GSR, HRV, and thermal biofeedback; Pelvic Muscle Dysfunction Biofeedback to treat incontinence and pelvic pain syndromes; and EEG Biofeedback or Neurofeedback.

We would like to acknowledge the work of the entire staff at BCIA and particularly Judy Crawford, BCIA Director of Certification. They work tirelessly on the part of the general public to ensure that people receive the safest and best possible biofeedback treatments available from qualified therapists. And, personally, we want to recognize Judy for her invaluable help in finishing this book. Thanks, Judy.

For a current list of BCIA-certified professionals in your area, visit the BCIA website (www.bcia.org) and go to "Find a Practitioner." Their slogan is "More than qualified . . . BCIA certified!"

Information Website

There is one other website we want to include. Michael Cohen is the founder of www.aboutneurofeedback.com. This is a website dedicated exclusively to explaining neurofeedback to consumers and professionals. It provides a realistic perspective on choosing a provider, on equipment, and on expectations. Michael is the president and director of training at the Center for Brain Training in Jupiter, Florida, and former director of education at EEG Spectrum International. He and John Finnick of Tahoe Vista, California, and Sue and Siegfried Othmer of the EEG Institute have probably trained more people in neurofeedback than other trainers in the world.

How to Select a Provider

Once you have located providers in your area, how do you know which one to choose? There are several factors to be included in your decision, such as training, length of time in the field, general experience, and, most important, professional background. Let's start with one of the most important factors: licensure.

Licensure

Neurofeedback is a modality, a tool to be used by appropriately licensed/credentialed and trained health-care professionals. Licensure is handled at the state level and all states have some type of licensure structure in place to guarantee the safety of their citizens. It is important to select a licensed practitioner or, at the least, a person who is legally practicing under the supervision of a licensed person. You also want to make sure that the license is in a related mental health field such as psychiatry, psychology, clinical social work, school psychology, nursing, or licensed professional counseling. You would not go to a dentist for heart surgery, so do not go to an unlicensed person for neurotherapy. Licensed individuals must meet state educational and professional standards. Currently, there is no state licensure for biofeedback; it must be done under the rubric of another mental health license. Just a word of caution: Some independent boards claim they offer a license to practice biofeedback. These are not state-approved boards and the license generally has no legitimacy as a state license. Beware of their claims. If you have any questions about the credentials of a neurofeedback provider, check with your state's licensing agency or board.

We once encountered a person who was doing "counseling" in a poorly regulated state. He identified himself as Dr. and, in fact, he did have a doctorate. It turned out, however, that his doctorate was in the field of agriculture. Nowadays you can get a mail-order doctorate, but that does not represent a license to practice, nor does it reflect a level of education or competency in a field of study.

It is possible to acquire some neurofeedback equipment without being licensed; that does not necessarily mean it was a legal acquisition. There have been companies that sold equipment to parents for their own children and, before long, some people were offering services to others. Let us remind you, we are dealing with the brains of young children, and although neurofeedback is a safe and effective treatment modality in the hands of a professional, an untrained person can cause problems such as seizures. Select a person with a good background in mental health and adequate training in neurofeedback.

Training is critical. Going to a course offered over the period of a day is hardly enough training to be turned loose on the public. Now, going to a four-day course is sufficient for a person to get started, but twenty courses are better. When a practitioner is just starting to use neurofeedback, there should be supervision or, at the least, regular consultations with a well-trained practitioner. Don't pick a practitioner who is excited about just getting the equipment and has no one to supervise him. It usually takes several years to be a good neurofeedback provider. Whether it is a heart surgeon or a neurofeedback therapist, it takes time to master a therapy. Don't be afraid to ask questions about training, competency, and supervision.

Certification

Certification is a noble attempt to ensure the safety of the general public. You do not have to be certified to be a neurofeedback provider, but certification guarantees that the provider has at least met minimum educational and experiential standards. BCIA-certified biofeedback and neurofeedback providers undergo rigorous testing before they are certified. When you meet a BCIA-certified provider, you can be comfortable that the provider has a good basic understanding of all the factors that play a role in biofeedback and neurofeedback services.

Home Trainers

One last area of concern is that of home trainers. There are companies that sell what they call "home trainers." These instruments are designed to train a person to make certain brainwaves. In our opinion, this is not a good idea; the brain is no toy and should never be treated by a layperson at home. As strong and resilient as the brain is, it is delicate. We have heard stories of people who trained at home with no background or experience in the field and ended up dysregulating the brain even more. There are also providers who rent home trainers and do long-distance training. We would never recommend this; in our office, we see people before the session and debrief them after the session so that we have an understanding of exactly what occurred in the session. That way if we used a protocol that, for example, set off a headache, we can fix it immediately. Training long distance may have a travel advantage but may also have negative consequences. In our opinion, it is not worth the risk. If a problem is important, invest the time, energy, and money to see a licensed practitioner. We have had to straighten out several problems created by home training. In most cases, it would have been twice as easy and less costly to do it right in the first place. Neurotherapy is a very powerful treatment, but improperly used, it can be powerful in negative ways.

APPENDIX B

Hidden Sources of MSG

This list is taken from Dr. Russell Blaylock's excellent book, *Excitotoxins: The Taste That Kills* (Santa Fe, New Mexico: Health Press, 1997).

Additives containing monosodium glutamate (MSG):

hydrolyzed vegetable protein
hydrolyzed protein
hydrolyzed plant protein
plant protein extract
sodium caseinate

calcium caseinate
yeast extract
textured protein
autolyzed yeast
hydrolyzed oat flour

Additives that frequently contain MSG:

malt extract
malt flavoring
bouillon
broth
stock

flavoring
natural flavoring
natural beef or chicken flavoring
seasoning
spices

The Feingold Association of the United States List of Food Additives

Additives to avoid:

tartrazine (yellow #5)
quinoline yellow
yellow 2G
sunset yellow FCF
cochineal, carminic acid
carmoisine (red)
amaranth (red #2)
ponceau (red #4)
erythrosine (red #3)
red 2G
allura red AC (red #40)
patent blue
indigo carmine (blue)
brilliant blue FCF

black
brown FK
chocolate brown HT
TBHQ (preservative, may also
    be listed as "antioxidant")
BHA (preservative, may also be
    listed as "antioxidant")
BHT (preservative, may also be
    listed as "antioxidant")
sulphites (sulfites)
nitrites
adipic acid (often included in
    "flavoring")
MSG

Additives that do not cause problems for most people:

curcuma or turmeric
riboflavin (vitamin B2)

chlorophyll
caramel

carotene
annatto
betanin
calcium carbonate
titanium dioxide
iron oxide
sorbic acid and sorbates
acetic acid
lactic acid
propionic acid
sodium propionate
calcium propionate
potassium propionate
carbon dioxide
ascorbic acid (vitamin C) and
   salts of ascorbic acid
tocopherols (vitamin E)
lactates (unless lactose
   intolerant)
citric acid
sodium citrate
potassium citrate

calcium citrate
tartaric acid
sodium tartrate
potassium bitartrate (cream of
   tartar)
niacin (vitamin B3)
alginic acid and alginates
carrageenan
carob-bean flour
tamarind-seed flour
guar gum
xanthan gum
sorbitol
mannitol
pectin
gelatin
powdered cellulose
sodium caseinate (avoid if milk
   sensitive)
calcium silicate
stearic acid

Much more information is available through the Feingold Association website at www.feingold.org.

Laboratory Testing for Heavy Metals

We use the King James Medical Laboratory for DMSA challenge testing and for hair analysis screening:

The King James Medical Laboratory, Inc.
24700 Center Ridge Road
Cleveland, Ohio 44145
800-437-1404; fax 440-835-2177
www.kingjamesomegatech-lab.com

Nutritional Recommendations

Vitamins and Minerals

Stephen J. Schoenthaler, MD, has done extensive research on the effects of simple, low-cost vitamin-mineral supplementation on the intelligence, academic performance, and behavior of schoolchildren.

The following is a formulation he used in a study that resulted in an average IQ increase of 3.7 points in a group of approximately 150 schoolchildren for twelve weeks. For those of you familiar with vitamin-mineral supplementation, you will note these amounts are surprisingly modest—none are above the very conservative U.S. Recommended Daily Allowance (RDA).

vitamin A	5000 IU
vitamin B1 (thiamine)	1.7 mg
vitamin B2 (riboflavin)	1.7 mg
vitamin B3 (niacin)	20 mg
vitamin B5 (pantothenate)	10 mg
vitamin B6 (pyridoxine)	2 mg
vitamin B12	6 mcg
vitamin C	60 mg
vitamin D	400 IU

vitamin E	15 IU
vitamin K	50 mcg
biotin	300 mcg
folic acid	400 mcg
calcium	200 mcg
chromium	100 mcg
copper	1 mg
iodine	150 mcg
iron	9 mg
magnesium	80 mg
manganese	2.5 mg
molybdenum	250 mcg
selenium	100 mcg
zinc	15 mg

Although this formulation is generally sufficient, newer RDA guidelines suggest more appropriate amounts for several supplements. By age seven, the B vitamins could be doubled. Vitamin C should be in the 500 to 1,000 mg range. Vitamin D should be 1,000 IU for children under one, 1,500 IU for children one to four, and 2,000 IU for children four to ten. For children ten years and older, use the adult recommendation of 5,000 IU per day. The form of vitamin D should be D3, not D2. An iron supplement of 4 mg per day is sufficient unless the child does not have a reasonably good diet, then give the 9 mg per day. Magnesium should be at least 200 mg per day.

Protein

Peter W. Lemon, PhD, of Kent State University is perhaps the foremost nutritional researcher of protein requirement, especially in athletes. He notes that the current RDA for protein was calculated for sedentary individuals. Athletes commonly require approximately double the RDA. Children and adolescents are obviously more likely to have requirements more similar to athletes than to sedentary adults.

A relatively simple estimate, based on Dr. Lemon's work, is for children to eat at least 0.5 grams of protein per pound of body weight.

Essential Fatty Acids

Fish oils, hempseed oil, krill oil, and flaxseed oil are the best sources for supplementing omega-3 fatty acids. Other sources with omega-3 have too much omega-6 content to improve the ratio between omega-3 and omega-6 fatty acids.

There are numerous products containing fish liver and flaxseed oils. Fish oils may have contaminants or a high percentage of oxidized fats, as well as high concentrations of toxic metals and chemicals. We recommend using fish oils only from companies that certify that their fish oil has been tested and found to contain zero parts per billion of mercury and zero parts per billion of PCBs.

Cod liver oil should be avoided because the amount of vitamin A in it interferes with vitamin D activity.

Children should get at least 500 mg of DHA per day from omega-3 oil.

Glycemic Index

The glycemic index of a food approximates how rapidly that food will be broken down into sugar and absorbed into the bloodstream. The higher the number, the more rapidly that food will increase glucose levels in the blood. A glycemic index above 80 is relatively undesirable. Those below 60 are more desirable for keeping blood glucose and insulin levels in a more favorable range.

maltodextrin	150	white bread	100
dates	146	wheat biscuits	100
glucose	137	cream of wheat	100
russet baked potato	134	shredded wheat	99
puffed rice	132	cornmeal	98
gluten-free wheat bread	129	whole wheat bread	97
corn flakes	119	taco shells	97
microwaved potato	117	croissant	96
pretzels	116	rye crisps	93
vanilla wafers	110	couscous	93
waffles	109	macaroni and cheese	92
doughnuts	108	sucrose (table sugar)	92
french fries	107	beets	91
graham crackers	106	raisins	91
mashed potatoes	104	muffins	88
bagel	103	ice cream	87

pizza	86	grapes	66
white rice	83	lactose	65
honey	83	sweet potatoes	63
pita	82	orange	63
popcorn	79	peach	60
fruit cocktail	79	apple juice	58
brown rice	79	pinto beans	55
spaghetti	78	plum	55
corn	78	tomato soup	54
oat bran	78	pear	53
banana	77	plain yogurt	51
pound cake	77	garbanzo beans	47
kiwi	75	skim milk	46
kidney beans	74	soy milk	43
orange juice	74	milk	39
carrots	70	grapefruit	36
baked beans	69	fructose	32
peas	68	cherries	32

qEEG and Continuous Performance Tests

Quantitative Electroencephalography

The quantitative electroencephalogram (qEEG) measures the electrical activity of the brain via small electrodes placed on the surface of the scalp. The number of electrodes may vary, but the standard is nineteen. These sensors read the tiny voltages produced by brain activity. These signals are amplified and digitally analyzed, then interpreted in a spectral display—color-coded brain maps. The brain maps provide information about the brainwave activity on various sites on the head. The most useful information comes from comparing the brainwave activity of the patient to a large database to see if and how the patient's brainwaves vary from the norm. The computer analysis is able to provide information about all the brainwave bands—delta, theta, alpha, and beta—simultaneously and individually.

The qEEG is able not only to aid significantly in the diagnostic process, but also to inform and guide the decision-making process for neurofeedback treatment. For example, a child with ADHD may show a characteristic increase in slow brainwave activity in the theta range (4–8 Hz) in the frontal areas of the brain. Another child may have a normal qEEG while sitting quietly, but show an

inappropriate increase in theta while performing a math calculation, rather than the expected increase in the faster beta frequencies (12–60+ Hz). A child may reveal an abnormality that is a
relatively less common finding in ADHD, for example, excessive
coherence of alpha (8–12 Hz) on both sides of the brain. A treatment protocol that trains the brain to decrease the coherence can
produce progress that would otherwise be difficult if only the standard protocols were used.

Some clinicians use qEEG on each patient they treat; others
obtain a qEEG on the patient only if there is inadequate progress
with neurofeedback treatment. Both approaches are sound. It
appears that at least 60 percent of patients with ADHD respond
well to the usual neurofeedback protocols without the need for the
more sophisticated evaluation qEEG provides.

Continuous Performance Testing

Many clinicians refer a patient with suspected ADHD to a
licensed psychologist for a full battery of psychological testing.
Traditional psychological testing evaluates a wide range of psychological functions, and it can reveal whether the patient's behavior
is consistent with ADHD. Such testing, however, does not specifically measure attention. Although these tests may be useful for
determining if there is significant depression, anxiety disorder, or
learning disability that may accompany ADHD, their usefulness in
actually making the diagnosis of ADHD is limited.

The psychological testing instrument that specifically measures
attention is the continuous performance test. This computer-based
testing accurately measures attention and assesses multiple components of attention. Specifically testing attention, when considering
a diagnosis of attention-deficit/hyperactivity disorder, is indispens-
able for both diagnosing and later for tracking treatment progress,
if, in fact, ADHD is present.

Continuous performance testing takes between fourteen and
twenty-two minutes to administer, and the computer analysis
is available shortly after the completion of the test. Parameters
measured include the speed of responses, accuracy, and the types

of errors committed. Scores are compared to a large database to determine how the patient's scores compare to a reference group.

The results of continuous performance testing provide information on how a patient's attention compares to a group that is the same age and sex as the patient. Problems with attention are classified as to whether errors are due more to impulsivity or to daydreaming, or to both. Types and quantities of errors and response time can also shed light on the presence of conduct disorder or neurological impairment.

There are four continuous performance test instruments that are worthwhile at this time: Quick Test, the Test of Variables of Attention (TOVA), the Integrated Visual and Auditory Continuous Performance Test (IVA), and Conners' Continuous Performance Test, not to be confused with Conners' Checklist.

Although all four instruments are useful, we prefer the Quick Test or the TOVA. Both are longer, simpler, have excellent timing precision (± 1 msec), and have the largest reference database with which to compare the patient's scores. These features enhance a clinician's ability to pick up subtler evidence of inattention. The length of these tests lend themselves to standardization of data over four quadrants, which gives information about a person's flow of attention, information not available from shorter tests. TOVA is not language based, uses auditory and visual signals in separate tests, and uses midline stimuli, not right-to-left. These features help elucidate information about the function of attention without uncertainty as to whether other functions, such as memory, may be playing a role in the patient's performance on the test.

Endnotes

SPECIAL NOTE: If you are a skeptic, a researcher, or just obsessive-compulsive and would like to see more scientific research on neurofeedback, we suggest that you start with *The Byers Neurotherapy Reference Library,* by Alvah P. Byers, EdD. This book is published by the Association for Applied Psychophysiology and Biofeedback. It is a treasure trove of scientific research about the field.

1. Autism

1. Centers for Disease Control and Prevention, Department of Health and Human Services, www.cdc.gov/ncbddd/autism/faq_prevalence.htm (2009).

2. American Psychiatric Association, *Diagnostic and Statistical Manual of Mental Disorders, 4th Edition* (Washington, DC: American Psychiatric Association, 1994).

3. C. M. Freitag, "The genetics of autistic disorders and its clinical relevance: a review of the literature," *Molecular Psychiatry* 2007;12:2–22.

4. M. L. Bauman, T. L. Kemper, "Neuroanatomic observations of the brain in autism: a review and future directions," *International Journal of Developmental Neuroscience* April/May 2005;23:83–187.

5. L. Croen, et al., "The changing prevalence of autism in California," *Journal of Autism and Developmental Disorders* 2002;32:207–215.

6. E. M. Roberts, et al., "Maternal residence near agricultural pesticide applications and autism spectrum disorders among children in the California Central Valley," *Environmental Health Perspectives* 2007;115:1482–1489.

7. S. Edelson, D. Cantor, "Autism: xenobiotic influences," *Toxicology and Industrial Health* 1998;14:553–563.

8. J. Pangborn, S. M. Baker, *Autism: Effective Biomedical Treatments* (San Diego, CA: Autism Research Institute, 2005).

9. R. Coben, I. Padolsky, "Assessment-guided neurofeedback for autistic spectrum disorder," *Biofeedback* 2007;35:131–135.

10. F. Volkmar, et al., *Handbook of Autism and Pervasive Developmental Disorders, Vol. 1, Diagnosis, Development, Neurobiology, and Behavior* (Hoboken, NJ: Wiley, 2005).

11. J. Mutter, et al., "Mercury and autism: accelerating evidence?" *International Journal of Prenatal and Perinatal Psychology and Medicine* 2005;17:1–2.

12. S. Bernard, "Autism: a novel form of mercury poisoning," *Medical Hypotheses* 2001;56:462–471.

13. I. Sterzl, et al., "Mercury and nickel allergy: risk factors in fatigue and autoimmunity," *Neuroendocrinology Letters* 1999;20:221–228.

14. D. W. Eggleston, "Effect of dental amalgam and nickel alloys on T-lymphocytes," *Journal of Prosthetic Dentistry* 1984;51:617–623.

15. A. Fido, S. Al-Saad, "Toxic trace elements in the hair of children with autism," *Autism* 2005;9:290–298.

16. Y. Shoenfeld, A. Aron-Maor, "Vaccination and autoimmunity—'vaccinosis': a dangerous liaison?" *Journal of Autoimmunity* 2000;14:1–10.

17. A. Vojdani, J. Pangborn, "Binding of infectious agents, toxic chenicals, and dietary peptides to tissue enzymes and lymphocyte receptors and consequent immune response in autism," Laboratory of Comparative Neuroimmunology 2003 Conference, Portland, Oregon.

18. A. Wakefield, et al., "Ileal-lymphoid-nodular hyperplasia, nonspecific colitis, and pervasive developmental disorder in children," *Lancet* 1998;351:637.

19. A. M. Comi, et al., "Familial clustering of autoimmune disorders and evaluation of medical risk factors in autism," *Journal of Child Neurology* 1999;14:388–394.

20. A. Bransfield, et al., "The association between tick-borne infections, Lyme borreliosis and autism spectrum disorders," *Medical Hypotheses* 2008;70:967–974.

21. C. Reiss, et al., "Scientific toxicity assessment of pesticides, drugs, and other chemicals," *Biogenic Amines* 2003;18:41–54.

22. P. J. Rosch, M. S. Marko, eds., *Bioelectric Medicine* (New York: Informa Healthcare, 2004).

23. G. Khurana, "Mobile phones and brain tumors—a public health concern," www.brain-surgery.us (2008).

24. M. Esteller, ed., *Epigenetics in Biology and Medicine* (Boca Raton, FL: CRC Press, 2008).

25. D. J. Friedland, *Evidence-Based Medicine: A Framework for Clinical Practice* (New York: McGraw-Hill Medical, 1998).

26. B. Scolnick, "Effects of electroencephalogram biofeedback with Asperger's syndrome," *International Journal of Rehabilitation Research* 2005;28:159–163.

27. B. Jarusiewicz, "Efficacy of neurofeedback for children in the autistic spectrum: a pilot study." *Journal of Neurotherapy* 2002;6:39–49.

28. A. G. Sichel, et al., "Positive outcome with neurofeedback treatment of a case of mild autism," *Journal of Neurofeedback* 1995;1:60–64.

29. P. G. Swingle, *Biofeedback of the Brain: How Neurotherapy Effectively Treats Depression, ADHD, Autism, and More* (Piscataway, NJ: Rutgers University Press, 2008).

30. R. A. Crane, et al., *Handbook of Neurofeedback: Dynamics and Clinical Applications* (Hawthorne, NJ: Hawthorne Press, 2006).

31. D. Rossignol, et al., "The effects of hyperbaric oxygen therapy on oxidative stress, inflammation, and symptoms in children with autism: an open-label pilot study." *BMC Pediatrics* 2007;7:36.

32. D. Rossignol, "Hyperbaric oxygen therapy might improve certain pathophysiological findings in autism," *Medical Hypotheses* 2007;68:1208–1227.

33. J. Jerabek, W. Pawluk, *Magnetic Therapy in Eastern Europe: A Review of 30 Years of Research* (Rancocas, NJ: William Pawluk, 1998).

34. A. L. Lansky, *Impossible Cure: The Promise of Homeopathy* (Portola Valley, CA: R. L. Ranch Press, 2003).

2. Learning Disabilities

1. Centers for Disease Control and Prevention, "Morbidity and mortality weekly report series," (Washington, DC: Department of Health and Human Services).

2. American Psychiatric Association, *Diagnostic and Statistical Manual of Mental Disorders, 4th Edition* (Washington, DC: American Psychiatric Association, 1994).

3. H. L. Swanson, *Handbook of Learning Disabilities* (New York: Guilford Press, 2003).

4. Individuals with Disabilities Education Improvement Act of 2004, Public Law 108–446 (December 3, 2004), 108th Congress.

5. M. R. Coleman, et al., *Recognition and Response: An Early Intervention for Young Children at Risk for Learning Disabilities* (Chapel Hill, NC: FPG Child Development Institute, 2006).

6. D. Vernon, et al., "The effect of training distinct neurofeedback protocols on aspects of cognitive performance," *International Journal of Psychophysiology* 2003;47:75–85.

7. L. Thompson, M. Thompson, "Neurofeedback combined with training in metacognitive strategies: effectiveness in students with ADD," *Applied Psychophysiology and Biofeedback* 2004;23:243–263.

8. R. A. Crane, et al., *Handbook of Neurofeedback: Dynamics and Clinical Applications* (Hawthorne, NJ: Hawthorne Press, 2006).

9. J. Becerra, et al., "Follow-up study of learning disabled children treated with neurofeedback or placebo," *Clinical EEG and Neuroscience* 2006;37:198–203.

10. T. Fernandez, et al., "EEG and behavioral changes following neurofeedback treatment in learning disabled children," *Clinical Electroencephalography* 2003;34:145-150.

11. J. L. Carter, H. L. Russell, "Changes in verbal performance IQ discrepancy scores after left hemisphere frequency control training: a pilot report," *American Journal of Clinical Biofeedback* 1991;4:66-67.

12. M. Cunningham, P. Murphy, "The effects of bilateral EEG biofeedback on verbal-special and creative skills in learning-disabled male adolescents," *Journal of Learning Disabilities* 1981;14:204-208.

13. K. S. McGrew, et al., "Improvements in interval time tracking and effects on reading achievement," *Psychology in the Schools* 2007;44:849-863.

14. L. Jones, "Improving motor planning and sequencing to improve outcomes in speech and language therapy," 83rd Annual American Speech and Hearing Association Conference, New Orleans, Louisiana.

15. R. Johnson, J. Zaba, "Vision screening of at-risk college students," *Journal of Behavioral Optometry* 1995;6:62-65.

16. R. Johnson, J. Zaba, "Examining the link between vision and literacy," *Journal of Behavioral Optometry* 1994;5:41-43.

17. I. Suchoff, G. Petito, "The efficacy of visual therapy: accommodative disorders and non-strabismic anomalies of binocular vision," *Journal of the American Optometric Association* 1986;57:119-125.

18. H. Irlen, "Scotopic sensitivity/Irlen syndrome—hypothesis and explanation of the syndrome," *Journal of Behavioral Optometry* 1994;5:62-65.

19. H. Irlen, M. J. Lass, "Improving reading problems due to symptoms of scotopic sensitivity syndrome using Irlen lenses and overlays," *Education* 1989;30:1-5.

20. S. M. Edelson, et al., "Auditory integration training: a double-blind study of behavioral, electro-physiological, and audiometric effects in autistic subjects," *American Journal of Audiology* 1999;14:73-81.

21. J. R. Madell, D. E. Rose, "Auditory integration training," *American Journal of Audiology* 1994;3:14-18.

3. The Labyrinth of ADHD

1. American Psychiatric Association, *Diagnostic and Statistical Manual of Mental Disorders, 4th Edition* (Washington, DC: American Psychiatric Association, 1994).

2. J. H. Satterfield, M. E. Dawson, "Electrodermal correlates of hyperactivity in children," *Psychophysiology* 1971;8:191-197.

3. J. H. Satterfield, et al., "EEG aspects in the diagnosis and treatment of minimal brain dysfunction," *Annals of the New York Academy of Sciences* 1973;205:274-282.

4. L. S. Budd, *Active Alerter Newsletter* (St. Paul, MN). (To order: Active Alerter

Subscription, c/o Linda Budd, PhD, 2301 Como Ave., Suite 204, St. Paul, MN 55108.)

4. You Don't Just Outgrow ADHD

1. R. T. Brown, K. A. Borden, "Hyperactivity at adolescence: some misconceptions and new directions," *Journal of Clinical Child Psychology* 1986;15:194–209.
2. R. Gittelman, et al., "Hyperactive boys almost grown up," *Archives of General Psychiatry* 1985;42:937–947.
3. G. Weiss, L. Hechtman, *Hyperactive Children Grow Up* (New York: Guilford Press, 1986).
4. D. Comings, "The genetics of addictive behaviors: the role of childhood behavioral disorders," *Addiction and Recovery* 1991 (November/December).
5. A. I. Alterman, R. E. Tarter, "The transmission of psychological vulnerability: implications for alcoholism etiology," *Journal of Nervous Mental Disorders* 1983;171:147–154.
6. E. G. Peniston, P. J. Kulkosky, "Alpha-theta brainwave training and beta endorphine levels in alcoholics," *Alcoholism: Clinical and Experimental* 1989;13:271–279.
7. E. G. Peniston, P. J. Kulkosky, "Alcoholic personality and alpha-theta brainwave training," *Medical Psychotherapy: An International Journal* 1990;3:37–55.
8. E. G. Peniston, P. J. Kulkosky, "Alpha-theta brainwave neurofeedback therapy for Vietnam veterans with combat-related post-traumatic stress disorder," *Medical Psychotherapy: An International Journal* 1991;4.47–60.
9. D. Miller, K. Blum, *Overload: Attention Deficit Disorder and the Addictive Brain* (Kansas City, MO: Andrews and McMeel, 1997).

5. The Source of the Problem

1. G. F. Still, "Some abnormal psychological conditions in children," *Lancet* 1902;1:1008–1012.
2. M. Rutter, "Syndromes attributed to 'minimal brain dysfunction' in childhood," *American Journal of Psychiatry* 1982;139:21–33.
3. J. S. Miller, "Hyperactive children: a ten-year study," *Pediatrics* 1978;61: 217–222.
4. J. S. Schmitt, "The minimal brain dysfunction myth," *American Journal of Diseases of Children* 1975;129:1313–1318.
5. B. Feingold, *Why Your Child Is Hyperactive* (New York: Random House, 1975).
6. D. Cantwell, *The Hyperactive Child: Diagnosis, Management, Current Research* (New York: Random House, 1975).
7. J. Biederman, et al., "High rate of affective disorders in probands with attention deficit disorders and in their relatives: a controlled family study," *American Journal of Psychiatry* 1987;144:330–333.
8. J. R. Morrison, M. A. Stewart, "A family study of the hyperactive child syndrome," *Biological Psychiatry* 1971;3:189–195.

9. R. Goodman, J. Stevenson, "A twin study of hyperactivity: II. The aetiological role of genes, family relationships, and perinatal adversity," *Journal of Child Psychology and Psychiatry* 1989;30:691–709.

10. D. E. Comings, *Tourette Syndrome and Human Behavior* (Duarte, CA: Hope Press, 1995).

11. L. B. Hohman, "Post-encephalitic behavior in children,*" Johns Hopkins Hospital Bulletin* 1922;33:372–375.

12. C. S. Hartsough, N. M. Lambert, "Medical factors in hyperactive and normal children: prenatal, developmental, and health history findings," *American Journal of Orthopsychiatry* 1985;55:190–210.

13. M. B. Denckla, M. LeMay, C. A. Chapman, "Few CT scan abnormalities found even in neurologically impaired learning disabled children," *Journal of Learning Disabilities* 1985;18:132–135.

14. H. H. Jasper, P. Solomon, C. Bradley, "Electroencephalographic analysis of behavior problems in children," *American Journal of Psychiatry* 1938;95:641–658.

15. C. Bradley, "The behavior of children receiving Benzedrine," *American Journal of Psychiatry* 1937;94:577–585.

16. J. H. Satterfield, M. E. Dawson, "Electrodermal correlates of hyperactivity in children," *Psychophysiology* 1971;8:191–197.

17. H. Satterfield, et al., "EEG aspects in the diagnosis and treatment of minimal brain dysfunction," *Annals of the New York Academy of Sciences* 1973;205:274–282.

18. M. B. Sterman, L. Friar, "Suppression of seizures in an epileptic following sensorimotor EEG feedback training," *Electroencephalograpy and Clinical Neurophysiology* 1972;33:89–95.

19. M. B. Sterman, L. R. MacDonald, R. K. Stone, "Biofeedback training of the sensorimotor EEG rhythm in man: effect on epilepsy," *Epilepsia* 1974;15:395–416.

20. M. B. Sterman, "Effects of sensorimotor EEG feedback training on sleep and clinical manifestations of epilepsy," in J. Beatty, H. Legewie, eds., *Biofeedback and Behavior* (New York: Plenum Press, 1976):167–200.

21. M. B. Sterman, "Sensorimotor EEG operant conditioning and experimental and clinical effects," *Pavlovian Journal of Biological Science* 1977;12:63–92.

22. M. B. Sterman, L. R. MacDonald, "Effects of central cortical EEG feedback training on seizures in poorly controlled epileptics," *Epilepsia* 1978;19:207–222.

23. M. B. Sterman, "EEG biofeedback in the treatment of epilepsy: an overview circa 1980," in L. White, B. Tursky, eds., *Clinical Biofeedback: Efficacy and Mechanisms* (New York: Guilford Press, 1982).

24. J. F. Lubar, M. N. Shouse, "EEG and behavioral changes in a hyperactive child concurrent training of the sensorimotor rhythm: a preliminary report," *Biofeedback and Self-Regulation* 1976;1:293–306.

25. J. O. Lubar, J. F. Lubar, "Electroencephalographic biofeedback of SMR and beta for treatment of attention deficit disorders in a clinical setting," *Biofeedback and Self-Regulation* 1984;9:1–23.

26. J. O. Lubar, "Electroencephalographic biofeedback and neurological applications," in J. V. Basmajian, ed., *Biofeedback: Principles and Practice for Clinicians* (Baltimore, MD: Williams and Wilkins, 1989).

10. Closed Head Injury

1. M. E. Ayers, "A report on a study of the utilization of electroencephalography (neuroanalizer) for the treatment of cerebrovascular lesion syndromes," in L. P. Taylor, M. E. and Tom Ayers, eds., *Electromagnetic Biofeedback Therapy* (Biofeedback and Advanced Therapy Institute, 1981).

2. ———, "Electroencephalographic feedback and head trauma," in *Head and Neck Trauma: The Latest Information and Perspectives on Patients with Less Than Optimum Recovery* (Los Angeles: UCLA Neuropsychiatric Institute, 1983). (Contact Margaret Ayers, 427 N. Canon Dr., Suite 209, Beverly Hills, CA 90210.)

3. ——— "Electroencephalographic neurofeedback and closed head injury of 250 individuals," paper presented at the National Head Injury Conference, 1987. (Contact Margaret Ayers, 427 N. Canon Dr., Suite 209, Beverly Hills, CA 90210.)

4. ———, "A controlled study of EEG neurofeedback training and clinical psychotherapy for right hemispheric closed head injury," paper presented at the National Head Injury Foundation Conference, 1991.

5. ———, "A controlled study of EEG neurofeedback training and clinical psychotherapy for right hemisphere closed head injury [Abstract]," *Proceedings of the Association for Applied Psychophysiology and Biofeedback* 1993:19–20.

6. ———, "EEG neurofeedback to bring individuals out of level two coma [Abstract]," *Proceedings of the 26th Annual Meeting of the Association for Applied Psychophysiology and Biofeedback* 1995:9–10.

11. Addictions

1. E. G. Peniston, P. J. Kulkosky, "Alpha-theta brainwave training and beta endorphine levels in alcoholics," *Alcoholism: Clinical and Experimental* 1989;13:271–279.

2. ———, "Alcoholic personality and alpha-theta brainwave training," *Medical Psychotherapy: An International Journal* 1990;3:37–55.

3. ———, "Alpha-theta brainwave neurofeedback therapy for Vietnam veterans with combat-related post-traumatic stress disorder," *Medical Psychotherapy: An International Journal* 1991;4:47–60.

14. Medications

1. J. F. Rosenbaum, et al., *Handbook of Psychiatric Drug Therapy* (Philadelphia, PA: Lippincott Williams & Wilkins, 2005).

2. G. Jackson, *Rethinking Psychiatric Drugs* (Bloomington, IN: AuthorHouse, 2005).

3. P. Haddad, et al., eds. *Adverse Syndromes and Psychiatric Drugs: A Clinical Guide* (New York: Oxford University Press, 2004).

4. B. Starfield, "Is US health really the best in the world?" *Journal of the American Medical Association* 2000;284:483–485.

5. H. Melander, et al., "Evidence b(i)ased medicine—selective reporting from studies sponsored by pharmaceutical industry: Review of studies in new drug applications," *British Medical Journal* 2003;326:1171–1173.

6. R. Smith, "Medical journals are an extension of the marketing arm of pharmaceutical companies," *Public Library of Science Medicine* 2005;2:e138.

7. V. M. Montori, et al., "Randomized trials stopped early for benefit: a systematic review," *Journal of the American Medical Association* 2005;294:2203–2209.

8. J. Lenzer, "Whistleblower removed from job for talking to the press," *British Medical Journal* 2004;328:1153.

9. B. Djulbegovic, et al., "The uncertainty principle and industry-sponsored research," *Lancet* 2000;356:635–638.

10. L. S. Friedman, E. D. Richter, "Excessive and disproportionate advertising in peer-reviewed journals," *International Journal of Occupational and Environmental Health* 2006;12:59–64.

11. J. Lexchin, D. W. Light, "Commercial influence and the content of medical journals," *British Journal of Medicine* 2006;332:1444–1447.

12. C. B. Phillips, "Medicine goes to school: teachers as sickness brokers for ADHD," *Public Library of Science Medicine* 2006;3:e182.

13. P. M. Kidd, "Attention deficit/hyperactivity disorder (ADHD) in children: rationale for its integrative management," *Alternative Medicine Review* 2000;5:5.

14. C. C. Pfeiffer, et al., "Stimulant effect of 2-dimethylaminoethanol—possible precursor of brain acetylcholine," *Science* 1957;126:610–611.

15. D. Healy, "Did regulators fail over selective serotonin reuptake inhibitors?" *British Medical Journal* 2006;333:92–95.

16. D. Healy, C. Whitaker, "Antidepressants and suicide: risk-benefit conundrums," *Journal of Psychiatry and Neuroscience* 2003; 28:331–337.

17. J. F. Lipinski, et al., "Open trial of S-adenosylmethionine for treatment of depression," *American Journal of Psychiatry* 1984;141:448–450.

18. K. M. Bell, et al., "S-adenosylmethionine treatment of depression: a controlled clinical trial," *American Journal of Psychiatry* 1988;145:1110–1114.

19. J. Levine, et al., "Double-blind, controlled trial of inositol treatment of depression," *American Journal of Psychiatry* 1995;152:792–794.

20. J. Levine, et al., "Follow-up and relapse analysis of an inositol study of depression," *Israel Journal of Psychiatry and Related Sciences* 1995;32:14–21.

15. The Healing Power of Neurofeedback

1. M. B. Sterman, L. Friar, "Suppression of seizures in an epileptic following sensorimotor EEG feedback training," *Electroencephalography Clinical Neurophysiology* 1972;33:89–95.
2. M. B. Sterman, L. R. MacDonald, R. K. Stone, "Biofeedback training of the sensorimotor EEG rhythm in man: effect on epilepsy," *Epilepsia* 1975;15:395–416.
3. M. B. Sterman, "Effects of sensorimotor EEG feedback training on sleep and clinical manifestations of epilepsy," in J. Beatty, H. Kegewie, eds., *Biofeedback and Behavior* (New York: Plenum Press, 1976): 167–200.
4. M. B. Sterman, L. R. MacDonald, "Effects of central cortical EEG feedback training on incidence of poorly controlled seizures," *Epilepsia* 1978;19:207–222.
5. M. B. Sterman, M. N. Shouse, "Sensorimotor mechanisms underlying a possible common pathology in epilepsy and associated sleep disturbances," in M. B. Sterman, M. N. Shouse, and P. Passouant, eds., *Sleep and Epilepsy* (New York: Academic Press, 1982); "EEG biofeedback in the treatment of epilepsy: an overview circa 1980," in L. White, B. Tursky, eds., *Clinical Biofeedback: Efficacy and Mechanism* (New York: Guilford Press, 1982).
6. J. F. Lubar, M. N. Shouse, "EEG and behavioral changes in a hyperactive child concurrent training of the sensorimotor rhythm (SMR): a preliminary report," *Biofeedback and Self-Regulation* 1976;1:293–306.
7. J. O. Lubar, J. F. Lubar, "Electroencephalographic biofeedback of SMR and beta for treatment of attention deficit disorders in a clinical setting," *Biofeedback and Self-Regulation* 1984;2:1–23.
8. M. A. Tansey, R. L. Bruner, "EMG and EEG biofeedback training in the treatment of a 10-year-old hyperactive boy with a developmental reading disorder," *Biofeedback and Self-Regulation* 1983;8:25–37.

16. How Neurofeedback Works

1. S. Othmer, S. Othmer, *EEG Biofeedback Training for Hyperactivity, Attention Deficit Disorder, Specific Learning Disabilities, and Other Disorders* (Encino, CA: EEG Spectrum, 1998).
2. M. B. Sterman, "Physiological origins and functional correlates of EEG rhythmic activities: implications for self-regulation," *Biofeedback and Self-Regulation* 1996;21:3–33.
3. C. A. Mann, et al., "Quantitative analysis of EEG in boys with attention-deficit/hyperactivity disorder: controlled study with clinical implications," *Pediatric Neurology* 1992;8:30–36.
4. M. B. Sterman, "Power spectral analysis of EEG characteristics during sleep in epileptics," *Epilepsia* 1981;22:95–106.

18. Nutrition

1. J. Breakey, "The role of diet and behaviour in childhood," *Journal of Paediatrics and Child Health* 2008;33:190–194.

2. S. Edelkind, *Behavior, Learning and Health* (New York: Feingold Association of the United States, 2007).

3. J. M. Smith, *Seeds of Deception* (Fort Collins, CO: Chelsea Green, 2005).

4. G. E. Seralini, et al., "New analysis of a rat feeding study with a genetically modified maize reveals signs of hepatorenal toxicity," *Archives of Environmental Contamination and Toxicology* 2007;52:596–602.

5. M. W. Ho, et al., "GM food nightmare unfolding in the regulatory sham," *Microbial Ecology in Health and Disease* 2007;19:66–77.

6. A. Pusztai, "The need for rigorous risk assessment," *Chemistry & Industry* 2000;8:280.

7. J. L. Domingo, "Health risks of genetically modified foods: many opinions but few data," *Science* 2000;288:1748–1749.

8. R. L. Blaylock, *Excitotoxins: The Taste That Kills* (Santa Fe: Health Press, 1997).

9. S. J. Schoenthaler, et al., "The effect of vitamin-mineral supplementation on the intelligence of American schoolchildren: a randomized, double-blind placebo-controlled trial," *Journal of Alternative and Complementary Medicine* 2000;6:19–29.

10. W. A. Price, *Nutrition and Physical Degeneration* (Lemon Grove, CA: Price Pottenger Nutrition, 2008).

11. S. Fallon, *Nourishing Traditions: The Cookbook That Challenges Politically Correct Nutrition and the Diet Dictocrats* (Winona Lake, IN: New Trends, 1999).

12. R. Bernardini, *The Truth About Children's Health: The Comprehensive Guide to Understanding, Preventing, and Reversing Disease* (London: Pri Pub, 2003).

13. M. G. Enig, *Know Your Fats: The Complete Primer for Understanding the Nutrition of Fats, Oils, and Cholesterol* (Silver Spring, MD: Bethesda Press 2000).

14. J. D. Wood, et al., "Manipulating meat quality and composition," *Proceedings of the Nutrition Society* 1999;58:363–370.

15. P. French, et al., "Fatty acid composition, including conjugated linoleic acid, of intramuscular fat from steers offered grazed grass, grass silage, or concentrate-based diets," *Journal of Animal Science* 2000;78:2849–2855.

16. Y. Mercier, et al., "Lipid and protein oxidation in vitro, and antioxidant potential in meat from Charolais cows finished on pasture or mixed diet," *Meat Science* 2004;66:467–473.

17. J. B. Russell, et al., "Potential effect of cattle diets on the transmission of pathogenic Escherichia coli to humans," *Microbes and Infection* 2000:2:45–53.

18. G. J. Myers, et al., "Prenatal methylmercury exposure from ocean fish consumption in the Seychelles child development study," *Lancet* 2003;361: 1686–1692.

19. P. W. Davidson, et al., "Effects of prenatal and postnatal methylmercury

exposure from fish consumption on neurodevelopment," *Journal of the American Medical Association* 1998;280:701–707.

20. E. Oken, et al., "Maternal fish consumption, hair mercury, and infant cognition in a U.S. cohort," *Environmental Health Perspectives* 2005;113:1376–1380.

21. R. Schmidt, *The Untold Story of Milk: Green Pastures, Contented Cows, and Raw Dairy Products* (Winona Lake, IN: New Trends, 2003).

22. C. Sirtori, "Dubious benefits and potential risk of soy phyto-oestrogens," *Lancet* 2000;355:849–849.

23. J. Iegel-Itzkovich, "Health committee warns of potential dangers of soya," *British Medical Journal* 2000;331:254.

24. Editorial, "Phytoestrogens and soy foods in infants and children: caution is needed," *Archives de Pédiatre* 2006;13:235–237.

25. D. S. Ludwig, "The glycemic index: physiological mechanisms relating to obesity, diabetes, and cardiovascular disease," *Journal of the American Medical Association* 2002;287:2414–2423.

26. D. S. Ludwig, et al., "High glycemic index foods, overeating and obesity," *Pediatrics* 1999;103:26.

27. M. A. Eastwood, "The physiological effect of dietary fiber: an update," *Annual Review of Nutrition* 1992;12:19–35.

28. E. Howell, *Enzyme Nutrition* (New York: Avery, 1995).

19. Toxicity

1. F. Boehm, "Regulatory capture revisited—lessons from economics of corruption," 2007 Working Paper, Research Center in Political Economy, Bogota, Columbia.

2. J. M. Smith, *Seeds of Deception* (Fort Collins, CO: Chelsea Green, 2005).

3. F. A. Barile, *Clinical Toxicology* (New York: Informa Healthcare, 2003).

4. E. M. Roberts, et al., "Maternal residence near agricultural pesticide applications and autism spectrum disorders among children in the California Central Valley," *Environmental Health Perspectives* 2007;115:1482–1489.

5. E. A. Guillette, et al., "An anthropological approach to the evaluation of preschool children exposed to pesticides in Mexico," *Environmental Health Perspectives* 1998;106:347–353.

6. S. Edelson, D. Cantor, "Autism: xenobiotic influences," *Toxicology and Industrial Health* 1998;14:553–563.

7. D. L. Berkson, *Hormone Deception* (New York: McGraw-Hill, 2001).

8. S. Patandin, et al., "Effects of environmental exposure to polychlorinated biphenyls and dioxins on cognitive abilities in Dutch children at 42 months of age," *Journal of Pediatrics* 1999;134:33–41.

9. J. L. Jacobson, S. W. Jacobson, "Effects of in utero exposure to PCBs and related contaminants on cognitive functioning in young children," *Journal of Pediatrics* 1990;116:38–45.

10. J. L. Jacobson, S. W. Jacobson, "Intellectual impairment in children exposed

to polychlorinated biphenyls in utero," *New England Journal of Medicine* 1996;335:783–789.

11. News release, www.epa.gov, December 14, 2005.

12. T. Zhou, et al., "Developmental exposure to brominated diphenyl ethers results in thyroid hormone disruption," *Toxicological Sciences* 2002;66:105–116.

13. P. Eriksson, et al., "Brominated flame retardants: a novel class of developmental neurotoxicants in our environment," *Environmental Health Perspectives* 2001;109:903–908.

14. Agency for Toxic Substances and Disease Registry, *Toxicological Profile for Arsenic* (Atlanta, GA: Environmental Protection Agency, 2007).

15. Agency for Toxic Substances and Disease Registry, *Toxicological Profile for Lead* (Atlanta, GA: Environmental Protection Agency, 2007).

16. B. P. Lanphear, et al., "Cognitive deficits associated with blood lead concentrations < 10 microg/dL in US children and adolescents," *Public Health Reports* 2000;115:521–529.

17. H. L. Needleman, et al., "Bone lead levels and delinquent behavior," *Journal of the American Medical Association* 1996;275:363–369.

18. Agency for Toxic Substances and Disease Registry, *Toxicological Profile for Mercury* (Atlanta, GA: Environmental Protection Agency, 2007).

19. M. Pichichero, et al., Mercury concentrations and metabolism in infants receiving vaccines containing thimerosal: a descriptive study. *Lancet* 2002;360:1737–1741.

20. Agency for Toxic Substances and Disease Registry, *Toxicological Profile for Aluminum* (Atlanta, GA: Environmental Protection Agency, 2007).

21. J. A. Ewing, W. J. Grant, "The bromide hazard," *Southern Medical Journal* 1965;58:148–152.

22. F. X. R. van Lecuwen, et al., "The effect of sodium bromide on thyroid function," *Toxicology* 1988;S12:93–97.

23. L. B. Zhao, et al., "Effect of a high fluoride water supply on children's intelligence," *Fluoride* 1996;29:190–192.

24. X. S. Li, et al., "Effect of fluoride exposure on intelligence in children," *Fluoride* 1995;28:189–192.

25. D. Fagin, "Second thoughts about fluoride," *Scientific American* 2008 (January):74–81.

26. L. H. R. Brett, "Fluoridation and child dental health in New Zealand—an update," *Fluoride* 1998;31:219–220.

27. P. Aldhous, "An industry-friendly science policy," *Science* 1994;265:596–598.

28. J. V. Wright, A. Gaby, *Natural Medicine, Optimal Wellness: The Patient's Guide to Health and Healing* (Ridgefield, CT: Vital Health, 2006).

29. S. Havarinasab, et al., "Immunosuppressive and autoimmune effects of thimerosal in mice," *Toxicology and Applied Pharmacology* 2005;204:109–121.

30. M. Tishler, Y. Shoenfeld, "Vaccination may be associated with autoimmune disease," *Israel Medical Association Journal* 2004;6:430–432.

31. O. C. Martin, et al., "Hepatitis B immunization induces higher antibody and memory Th2 responses in newborns than adults," *Vaccine* 2004;22:511–519.

32. M. Geier, et al., "Endotoxins in commercial vaccines," *Applied Environmental Microbiology* 1978;36:445–449.

33. W. G. Crook, "Pediatricians, antibiotics, and office practice," *Pediatrics* 1985;76:139–140.

34. W. G. Crook, "A controlled trial of Nystatin for the candidiasis hypersensitivity syndrome," *New England Journal of Medicine* 1991;324:1592–1594.

35. M. Z. Zait, et al., "Oral Amphotericin-b in the treatment of ulcerative intestinal diseases," *Digestive Diseases and Science* 1970;15:993–1002.

36. L. V. McFarland, P. Bernasconi, "*Saccharomyces boulardii:* a review of an innovative biotherapeutic agent," *Microbial Ecology in Health and Disease* 1993;6:157–171.

37. B. A. Fallon, et al., "A randomized, placebo-controlled trial of repeated IV antibiotic therapy for Lyme encephalopathy," *Neurology* 2008;70:992–1003.

38. B. A. Fallon, J. A. Nields, "Lyme disease: a neuropsychiatric illness," *American Journal of Psychiatry* 1994;151:1571–1583.

39. T. A. Litovitz, et al., "Effects of coherence time of the applied magnetic field on ornithine decarboxylase activity," *Biochemical and Biophysical Research Communications* 1991;178:862–865.

40. L. Hardell, et al., "Long-term use of cellular phones and brain tumours: increased risk associated with use for greater than 10 years," *Occupational and Environmental Medicine* 2007;64:626–632.

20. The Box in the Room

1. K. Moody, *Growing up on Television* (New York: Times Books, 1980)

2. J. C. Pierce, *Evolution's End* (New York: HarperCollins, 1992).

3. K. A. Buzzell, "The neurophysiology of television viewing: a preliminary report," Unpublished research paper, 1987 (obtainable through Dr. Keith Buzzell, 14 Portland Street, Fryeborg, ME, 04037).

4. J. M. Healy, *Endangered Minds* (New York: Touchstone, 1990).

5. A. Luria, *Language and Cognition* (New York: Wiley, 1982).

6. K. A. Buzzell, "The neurophysiology of television viewing: a preliminary report," Unpublished research paper, 1987 (obtainable through Dr. Keith Buzzell, 14 Portland Street, Fryeborg, ME, 04037).

21. More about Aggression and Dysregulation

1. G. E. Barnes, "The alcohol personality: a reanalysis of the literature," *Journal of Studies on Alcohol* 1979;40:7.

2. A. Rosenthal, "Violence is predictable," *Today's Health* 1970;45:56–57, 71–72.

3. J. R. Evans, S. Claycomb, "Abnormal qEEG patterns associated with dissociation and violence," *Journal of Neurotherapy* 1999;3:21–27.

Glossary

ADHD: Attention-deficit/hyperactivity disorder.

Amplitude: Scope or range; width of range of a quality. Usually of a wave or vibration, measured from the extreme to median positions. Half of a wavelength.

APGAR score: A numerical expression of the condition of a newborn infant, determined at one minute and at five minutes after birth, being the sum of points gained on an assessment of the heart rate, respiratory effort, muscle tone, reflex irritability, and color.

Brainwaves: A rhythmical fluctuation of electrical potential in the brain.

Classical conditioning: Learning in which a response is elicited by a neutral stimulus made directly effective by its repeated association with a stimulus normally evoking the response.

Concomitant: Existing or occurring together.

Continuum: A coherent whole made up of elements that vary only by minute degrees.

Derivative: A chemical substance obtained from another substance either directly or by modification or partial substitution.

Dizygotic: Derived from two separate fertilized eggs, or zygotes (as fraternal twins).

Dopamine: A neurotransmitter used in the functioning of the sympathetic and central nervous systems.

Epilepsy: A disorder of cerebral function marked by attacks of unconsciousness with or without convulsions.

Etiologic: Pertaining to the causes of diseases.

Etiology: The study or theory of the factors that cause disease and the method of their introduction to the host.

EMG (electromyogram): The record of the intrinsic electrical properties of skeletal muscle.

Functional injury: An injury affecting function, as opposed to structure.

Glucose: A simple sugar containing six carbon atoms. Glucose is an important source of energy in the body and the sole source of energy in the brain.

Hertz (Hz): A unit of frequency equal to one cycle per second.

Hypoglycemia: A deficiency of glucose in the bloodstream, causing muscular weakness and incoordination, mental confusion, and sweating.

In utero: Within the uterus.

Layperson: One without training or skills in a profession or branch of knowledge.

Monozygotic: Pertaining to or derived from one fertilized ovum, as identical twins.

Norepinephrine: A hormone closely related to epinephrine and with similar actions, secreted by the medulla of the adrenal gland and also released as a neurotransmitter by sympathetic nerve endings.

Operant: In psychology, any response that is not elicited by specific external stimuli but that recurs at a given rate in a particular set of circumstances. To condition a response by giving an appropriate reward.

Paradigm: Any pattern or example.

Peripheral: Pertaining to the outer part or surface; away from the center.

Proband: The original person presenting with or likely to be subject to a mental or physical disorder and whose case serves as the stimulus for a hereditary or genetic study.

Psychostimulant: A drug producing an increase in psychomotor activity.

Rhythmic activity: Measured movement; the recurrence of an action or function at regular intervals.

Schizophrenia: Any of a group of emotional disorders characterized by a disintegration of the process of thinking, of contact with reality, and of emotional responsiveness.

Serotonin: A compound widely distributed in the tissues, particularly in the blood platelets, intestinal wall, and central nervous system; acts as a neurotransmitter, especially concerned with the process of sleep.

Tachycardia: An increase in the heart rate above normal.

Tardive dyskinesia: A form of impairment of the power of voluntary movement marked by involuntary repetitive movements, induced by antipsychotic agents, and that may persist after withdrawal of the agent.

Tinnitus: A buzzing or ringing in the ear.

Index

abdominal breathing, 118
Abernathy, Anne, 159
abuse, 155
Academy of Child and Adolescent Psychiatry, 269
acidophilus, 237
activated charcoal, 257
active alert children, 58
Active Alerter (newsletter), 58
The A.D.D. Book (Sears), 89
added fats, 227
Adderall, 174
addictions, 161–163, 280–282
ADHD, adult, 61–73
  alcoholism/drugs and, 71–72
  driving and, 67–68
  employment and, 64–65
  justice system and, 69–71
  marriage and, 66–67
  neurofeedback and, 73
  personal struggles in, 72–73
  public talking and, 65–66
  treatment for, 62–63
ADHD, checklists for, 91–100
  instructions, 94
  repeating, effectiveness of, 94–95
  sample of, 96–98
  scoring methods, 95
  summary chart, analyzing, 99–100
ADHD, childhood, ix, 41–60
  arousal and, 51–55
  diagnosis for, 43–45
  distinguishing between real/false, 58–59
  gender statistics for, 50–51
  identifying signs of, 49–50
  overstimulation/overload and, 47–48
  psychological differences with, 56–58
  sporadic performance involved with, 45–47
ADHD, theories concerning, 75–90
  bad child factor, 75–76
  brain injuries, 81–84
  brainwaves, study of, 86–88
  causes, principle, 88
  environmental influences, 78–79
  family discord model, 76
  genetics, role of, 79–81
  nonexistence, 76–77
  poor parenting, outcome of, 77–78
  practitioners, role of, 88–90
  stress, role of, 84–86
adult sleep deprivation, 131
Advanced Magnetic Research Institute, 159
aerobic exercise, 135
affect regulation, 128
Agency for Toxic Substances and Disease
    Registry, 245
aggression, 268–269
  See also dysregulation

aggressive tendencies, 280
alcoholism, 71–72
allopathic medicine, x–xi
alpha, 168, 197
aluminum, 246
American Academy of Ophthalmology, 37–38
American Academy of Pediatrics, 269
American Medical Association, 268
American Psychiatric Association, 2
American Psychological Association, 269
Amphotericin B, 257
amplitude, 19
anticonvulsants, 177–179
antidepressants, 175–177
antifungals, 257–258
antipsychotics, 177
Antisocial Personality Disorder, 70
anxiety, 110–117, 166
APGAR scores, 83
arousal, 51–55, 167–168
arsenic, 245
artificial colors, 224
artificial flavors, 224
artificial sweeteners, 223
Aspartame, 223
Asperger's disorder, xiv, 1, 2
Association for Applied Psychophysiology and
    Biofeedback (AAPB), 300
attachment disorder, 126–130
attentional disruptions, xiv
attentional problems, 266–267
attention deficit disorder (ADD), xvi
attention-deficit/hyperactivity disorder (ADHD).
    See ADHD
auditory integration training, 38
aura, 144
autism, 1–22
  as biological disorder, 5–9
  causes/triggers of, 11–12
  criteria for, 2–5
  defined, 2
  diagnosis for, 2–5
  genetics in relation to, 12–14
  history of, 5
  interventions for, early, 9–11
  medical understanding of, 4
  regulation training for controlling, 15–19
  treatment for, 14–15, 19–22
Autism: Effective Biomedical Treatments
    (Pangborn), 19
Autism Research Institute, 14, 251
Autistic Spectrum Disorders, 2
autonomic nervous system, 146
Ayers, Margaret, 155

Babesia, 260
bad child factor, 75–76

Baker, Sidney, 19
Barbara Muller-Ackerman, 89
Bartonella, 260
bedwetting, 287
behavioral disruptions, xiv
belt phobia, 111
beneficial bacteria, 238, 258
Berard, Guy, 38
beta, 197
Big Pharma, 173
biofeedback
    changing involuntary processes with, 182–184
    defined, xviii–xix
    EEG, 185
    instrument, 184
    for migraine headaches, 144–145, 148
    temperature, 117
    thermal, 301
    treatment procedures of, 183–184
    Western medicine belief system and, 184
    See also neurofeedback
Biofeedback Certification Institute of America
        (BCIA), 300
biological disorder, 5–9
bipolar disorder, 109–110
birth trauma, 155
Blaylock, Russell, 305
Blum, Kenneth, 72
Bonlie, Dean, 21
boredom, 211
Borrella, 250, 260
bowel dysbiosis, 255–259
brain, importance of developing, 272–274
brain injuries, 81–84
Brain Othmer Foundation, 300
brainwaves, 86–88
    ADHD theories and, 86–88
    balancing, 201–203
    biofeedback and, 138, 148
        (*See also* neurofeedback)
    continuum, 197
    dysregulated, 195–200
        (*See also* dysregulation)
    low-frequency, 199
    patterns of, in closed head injury, 157
    research on, 191–195
brainwave training, 16, 104, 189
breathing bags, 119
brominated flame retardants, 244
Budd, Linda, 58
Burke, Harold, 157
butter, 227–228
butter substitutes, "no trans fat," 225

cadmium, 246
Candida, 255
Cannell, John, 252
canola, 228
carbohydrates, 234–237
case control analytic studies, 14
casein, 12, 258
case series studies, 14
Celexa, 175
cerebral palsy, 155
certification, 226
charcoal, activated, 257
checklists. *See* disorders, checklists for
chelation, 15
childhood obesity, 269
chlorine, 247

chronic low-grade depression, 107
Churchill, Winston, 24
classical conditioning, 200
Claycomb, Suzanne, 288
closed head injury, 155–160
    brainwave patterns with, study of, 157
    forms of, 155
    mild, symptoms of, 156–157
    MME for treatment of, 159–160
    neurofeedback for treatment of, 155–156
    strokes, impact of, 156
    traumatic brain injury and, 157–159
Coben, Rob, 8, 89
coconut oil, 228
cognitive problems, 266–267
Cohen, Michael, 301
Comings, David, 81
commercially processed foods, 223
communication, 208–209
Concerta, 174
concomitant depression, 65, 105
concussion, 155
conduct disorder, 285–286
cones (light receptor), 271
continuous performance testing, 318–319
conventional medicine, 2, 4, 31
cordless phones, 261
costal breathing, 118
Cranton, Elmer, 257
Crawford, Judy, 301

dairy products, 231–232
Daniel, Kaayla, 234
Daytrana, 174
dazed staring, 267
Deaner, 175
Deanol, 175
deBeus, Roger, 89, 110
deep fat fried foods, 224–225
Depakote, 177
depression, 103–109, 166
derivatives, 252
detoxification, 249, 254
Dexedrine, 174
*Diagnostic and Statistical Manual of Mental
        Disorders, Fourth Edition (DSM-IV)*, 2, 44
diaphragmatic breathing, 117–120
die-off reaction, 250
diet, 11–12, 238
digestive enzymes, 239
Dilantin, 177
dimethyl glycine (DMG), 253
DiRicco, Lori, 130
Disney, Walt, 24
disorders, checklists for, 101–142
    anxiety/panic attacks, 110–117
    attachment disorder, 126–130
    bipolar disorder, 109–110
    depression, 103–109
    diaphragmatic breathing, 117–120
    epilepsy, 101–103
    immaturity, 136–139
    self-esteem, 120–126
    sleep disorders, 130–136
    tic disorder/Tourette's syndrome, 139–142
    See also ADHD, checklists for
divorce, 106
dizygotic pairs, 80
dominance, 196
dopamine, 162–163

Down syndrome, 13
driving, 67-68
drug rebound, 279
drugs, 71-72
dyslexia, 33
dysregulated brain waves, 195-200
dysregulation, 275-292
    addiction and, 280-282
    behavioral patterns related to, 287
    conduct disorder, 285-286
    conflicts concerning, 282-284
    eating disorders and, 166
    family relationships, role of, 277-279
    impulsivity/impulse control and, 166, 276, 282
    medication rebound, 279
    neurofeedback for, 203, 279-280
    ODD, 284-285
    summary of, 288-292
    violence associated with, 276-277
dysthymic disorder, 107

E. coli, 229
Edison, Thomas, 24
EEG Institute, 299
EEG Spectrum International, 299
eggs, 231
Einstein, Albert, 24
electroencephalogram (EEG), xiii, xix, 168
    quantitative electroencephalogram (qEEG), 18, 317-318
electromagnetic field (EMF), 12, 260-261
electromyogram (EMG), 146
emotional abandonment, 76
emotional disorders, xiv
emotional stress, 145
emotions, 128
empathy, 128
employment, 64-65
encopresis, 198
Endangered Minds (Healy), 271
endogenous depression, 107
enuresis, 287
Environmental Protection Agency (EPA), 230, 242
Environmental Working Group, 242
enzymes, 238-239
epilepsy, xix, 101-103
epileptiform
    activities, 157
    discharges, 102
    patterns, 157
Equal, 223
Erlichia, 260
Eshleman, Lark, 130
essential fatty acids, 313
etiologic, 82
Evans, James R., 280
evidence-based medicine, 14
Excitotoxins: The Taste That Kills (Blaylock), 305
executive functioning, 136, 163
exogenous depression, 107

Fahrion, Steve, 290
family discord model, 76
family relationships, 277-279
fats, 227-229
fecal incontinence, 198
Federal Trade Commission (FTC), 242
Fehmi, Les, 114
Feingold, Ben, 79
Feingold Association, 79, 224, 307-308

fermentation, 234, 236
fiber, 237-238
Finnick, John, 31, 302
fish, 230
Fisher, Sebern, 130
FitSmart, 238, 258
flavor enhancers, 224
fluoride, 247
flu shot, 255
Focalin, 174
food additives, 307-308
Food and Drug Administration (FDA), 165, 219, 242
fraternal pairs, 80
free-range, 226
frequency band, 187
fructose, 223-224
fruits, 238
functional injury, 81-82

gastrointestinal tract, 253
generally recognized as safe (GRAS), 233
genetically engineered/modified (GM) food, 222-223, 242
genetics, 12-14, 79-81
German measles, 255
global dysregulation, 189-190
glucose, 234-235
glutathione levels, 253
gluten, 12, 258
glycemic index, 315
Gore-Tex, 244, 248
grain finishing, 229
Gray, Stephen, 130
Green, Elmer, 183
Green, Elmer and Alyce, 144
gullibility, 270

Hamlin, Ed, 110
Hardt, Jim, 169
headaches, 143-149
    biofeedback for, 144, 145, 148
    migraine, 143-145
    school absences and, 147-149
    stress, 143
    tension, 145-147
healthy foods, types of, 240
Healy, Jane, 271
heavy metals, 15, 309
Herxheimer reaction, 250
Hill, Robert, 159
Hilsheimer, Von, 89
Hirshberg, Larry, 89
homeopathy, 21
home trainers, 304
homogenization, 232
Hopkins, Mitch, 159
Human Genome Project, 13
hybridization process, 228
hyperactive children, 62
    See also ADHD, childhood
hyperactive syndrome, 51, 175
hyperbaric oxygen treatment (HBOT), 20
hyperkinetic syndrome, 51, 175
hypoxic/anoxic trauma, 82

identical pairs, 80
immaturity, 136-139
immunoglobulins, 233
impulsivity/impulse control, 166, 276, 282
inositol, 176

insoluble fiber, 237
Institute for Responsible Technology, 221
insulin, 222
intake interview, 206
Integrated Visual and Auditory Continuous
      Performance Test (IVA), 319
Interactive Metronome (IM), 36
interesterification, 225
internal body messages, 181–184
International Society for Neurofeedback and
      Research (ISNR), 300
international ten-twenty system, 199
involuntary processes, controlling, 181–184
IQ-Achievement Discrepancy model, 28
Irlen, Helen, 38
irradiation, 230

Jarusiewicz, Betty, 22
Jefferson, Thomas, 241
juice, 236
justice system, 69–71

Kamiya, Joe, xix
Keppra, 177

lactoferrin, 232
Lamictal, 177
Lancet (journal), 75
language problems, 271–272
layperson, 43
lead, 245
leaky gut, 256
learning disabilities (LD), 23–39
   behavioral issues concerning, 29–31
   diagnosis for, 28–29
   indications of, early, 24–28
   neurofeedback and, 31–35
   treatment for, 35–39
lectins, 219
Lemon, Peter W., 312
Lexapro, 175
licorice, 259
lighting, 212
light receptors, 271
live viruses, 255
Lou Gehrig's disease, 260
low arousal hypothesis, 51
low-frequency brainwaves, 199
low frustration tolerance, 280
Lubar, Joel and Judith, xix, 87
Luvox, 175
Lyle, Randy, 89
Lyme disease, 11–12, 250, 259–260

magnetic treatment, 21
manganese toxicity, 234
mania, 177
manic depression, 109–110
margarine, 225
marriage, 66–67
Marx, Karl, 241
McDonald's, 221
McGee, Sherene, 158
measles, mumps, rubella (MMR) vaccine, 256
meat, 230
medication rebound, 279
medications, 171–179
   anticonvulsants, 177–179
   antidepressants, 175–177
   antipsychotics, 177
   for children, benefits of, 171

side effects of, 104, 171
stimulants, 173–175
tranquilizers, xv
Menninger Clinic, 144, 161–162, 183
mercury, 245–246
metabolic enzyme activity, 239
Metadate CD, 174
metals, 11, 244–247
Metamucil, 258
Methylin ER, 174
microwave frequencies, 260
migraine headaches, 143–145
milk, raw, 232–233
Miller, David, 72
minerals, 311–312
minimal brain dysfunction (MBD), xv, 77, 82
molecular magnetic energizing (MME), 20, 159–160
monosodium glutamate (MSG), 222, 305
monounsaturated fat, 227
monozygotic pairs, 80
Monsanto's herbicide, 220
Morrison, J. R., 80
Moss, Vicki, 130
motor delays, 25
motor tics, 140–141
multiple sclerosis (MS), 158

naps, 134–135
National Vaccine Information Center, 255
neural fields, 267
neurofeedback, xvii, xx–xxi, 56
   addictions and, 161–13
   adult ADHD and, 73
   in brain rhythms, 195–203
   in brainwave research, 191–195
   closed head injury and, 155–156
   dysregulation and, 189–190, 279–280
   equipment used in, 187–188
   internal body messages and, identifying, 181–184
   learning disabilities and, 31–35
   learning process and, 188–189
   in operant conditioning, 200–201
   providers of, 299–304
   solutions, 293–297
   technology of, advanced, 184–185
   training/treatment, purpose of, 185–187
   See also neurotherapy sessions
neurological damage, 267–268
Neurontin, 177
neurotherapists, 205–206
neurotherapy room, 209–210
neurotherapy sessions, 205–215
   benefits of, 208
   debriefment period, 214
   goals of, 205–206
   grading system used in, 212–213
   intake interview and, 206
   lighting used in, 212
   neurotherapy room and, 209–210
   results of, 214–215
   sensors, placement of, 210
   symptoms, evaluation of, 206–207
   training report, 208
   treatment protocols, 213
   waiting room, 208–209
neurotoxins, 11
neurotransmitters, 267
non-genetically engineered/modified (GM) food, 223
non-instant powdered skim milk, 233

nonmetals, 246
nonorganic butter, 227
nonpharmaceutical brainwave training program.
    See neurofeedback
Norris, Patricia, 290
NutraSweet, 223
nutrition, healthy, 12, 225–240
    carbohydrates, 234–237
    enzymes, 238–239
    fats, 227–229
    fiber, 237–238
    foods, types of, 240
    nutrient-dense foods, 226–240
    protein, 229–234
    recommendations for, 311–313
nutrition, unhealthy, 217–225
    artificial colors, 224
    artificial flavors, 224
    artificial sweeteners, 223
    butter substitutes, "no trans fat," 225
    commercially processed foods, 223
    deep fat fried foods, 224–225
    flavor enhancers, 224
    GM foods, 222–223
    margarine, 225
    partially hydrogenated fats/oils, 224
    positive role of society on, 219–225
    preservatives, 224
    soft drinks, 224
    sugar, 223–224
    white flour, 224
    white rice, 224
nutritional supplements, 251, 259, 311–312
Nystatin, 257

obesity, 165–166
    childhood, 269
    depression/anxiety related to, 166
    dysregulation disorders related to, 166
    factors related to cause of, 165–166
    impulse control, 166
obsessive-compulsive disorder, 166, 177
ocular lock, 267
olive oil, 229
Open Focus, 114
operant conditioning, 73, 200–201
oppositional defiant disorder (ODD), 207,
    284–285
organic certification, 226
Organic Valley Farms, 227, 233
Othmer, Sue and Siegfried, 17, 89, 299
overload, 47–48
overstimulation, 47–48

Pangborn, Jon, 19
panic attacks, 110–117
parasympathetic nervous system, 146
parenting, poor, 77–78
partially hydrogenated fats/oils, 224
passive-dependent behavior, 270–271
patch, 174
Patricia Norris, 290
Patterson, Bob, 130
Pavlov, Ivan, 200
Paxil, 175
peak performance training, 167–169, 184
    arousal, theories concerning, 167–168
    benefits of, 168–169
    purpose of, 167
peanuts, 235

Pearce, Larry, 20, 159
Pearl, Moshe, 280
Pelvic Muscle Dysfunction Biofeedback, 301
Peniston, Eugene, 71, 166, 290
peripheral, 186
Pervasive Developmental Disorders (PDD), 2
pesticides, 242–243, 247
Petchel, Bob, 35
petrochemicals, 244
Pexeva, 175
physical underdevelopment, 269–270
phytoestrogens, 234
polio, 255
polyunsaturated fats, 228
posttraumatic stress disorder (PTSD), 130, 291
powdered protein, 233
powdered whey, 233
prefluorinated chemicals, 244
premenstrual syndrome (PMS), x
preservatives, 224
protein, 229–234, 312
Prozac, 175
psychological testing, 318
psychoneuroimmunology (PNI), 182
public talking, 65–66
Pusztai, Arpad, 219

qualitative impairment, 3
quantitative electroencephalography (qEEG), 18,
    317–318
Quick Test, 319
Quirk, Douglas A., 89

Rafael, Robert, 130
Rama, Swami, 183
rapeseed plant, 228
raw milk, 232–233
Raynaud's disease, 184
reactive depression, 107
Recommended Daily Allowance (RDA), 311
red meat, 229–230
regulation training, 15–19
regulatory capture, 241
Response to Treatment Intervention (RTI), 28
Rett's syndrome, 2
rhythmic activity, 195–200
Risperdal, 15, 177
Ritalin, xi–xiii, 42–43, 174
rods (light receptor), 271
Rolandic, 101
Roundup, 220
rubella, 255

S. boulardii, 259
Saccharine, 223
S-adenosylmethionine (SAMe), 176
Salk polio vaccine, 255
saturated fat, 227, 228
sauna, 254
schizophrenia, 177
Schoenthaler, Stephen J., 311
Schummer, Gary, 89
Scotchgard, 244
Sears, William, 89
seizures, 102
self-esteem, 120–126
self-healing, 187
self-regulation, 187
sensorimotor cortex, 101
sensorimotor rhythm (SMR), 101, 197
sensors, 210

serotonin, 162
single-field firing, 268, 273
situational depression, 107–108
skeletal muscles, 146
sleep
    apnea, 133
    deprivation, 130–131
    disorders, 130–136
    exercises, 135–136
    snoring and, 134
Smith, Jeffery, 221
snoring, 134
socialization, 272
social problems, 272
soft drinks, 224
soluble fiber, 237
sound therapy, 35–36, 38
soy, 234
    infant formula, 234
    phytoestrogens, 234
    processed, 233
soybeans, 233
spatial problems, 28
Speckhart, Vincent, 21
Splenda, 223
Sterman, Barry, xix, 8, 87
Stewart, M. A., 80
Still, G. F., 75
stimming, 9
stimulants, 173–175
stimulation, 52
Stimulus Condition Autonomic Repression, 89
stress, 84–86, 146
stress headaches, 143
stress injury, 84
stretching, 135
striate muscles, 146
stroke, 155–156
Sucrulose, 223
sugar, 222–224
sulfur-containing nutrients, 253
supplements, 251, 259, 311–312
sweating, 254
Sweet'n Low, 223
SweetSpot Therapy, 158
sympathetic nervous system, 146
Synergistic Trauma and Attachment Therapy
        (STAT), 130
synthetic chemicals, 243–245

tachycardia, 337
Tansy, Michael, 195
tardive dyskinesia, 337
Tattenbaum, Rae, 169
Teflon, 248
Tegretol, 177
television, negative impact of, 263–274
    on brain development, 272–274
    cognitive/attentional problems, 266–267
    gullibility, 270
    neurological damage, 267–268
    passive-dependent behavior, 270–271
    physical underdevelopment, 269–270
    social problems, 272
    violence/aggressiveness, 268–269
    visual/language problems, 271–272
temperature biofeedback, 117
temperature training, 151–153
tension headaches, 145–147
Test of Variables of Attention (TOVA), 319

thalamus, 52
thermal biofeedback, 301
thermometers, 151
Thompson, Lynda, 89
thyroid gland, 245
tic disorder, 139–142
tinnitus, 337
tofu, 234
Tomatis, Alfred, 38
Tourette's syndrome, x, 81, 139–142, 206
Tourette Syndrome and Human Behavior
        (Comings), 81
toxicity, 241–261
    antifungals and, 257–258
    avoiding, 247–249
    beneficial bacteria and, 258
    bowel dysbiosis and, 255–259
    brominated flame retardants and, 244
    of chlorine, 247
    of EMFs, 260–261
    of fluoride, 247
    of GM foods, 242
    Lyme disease and, 259–260
    of metals, 244–247
    of pesticides, 242–243
    of petrochemicals, 244
    removing, 249–254
    of supplements, 259
    of synthetic chemicals, 243–245
    vaccinations and, 254–255
training report, 208
tranquilizers, xv
transcendental meditation, 192
traumatic brain injury, 157–159
trimethyl glycine (TMG), 253
tyramine, 144

unrandomized studies, 14

vaccinations, 11, 254–255
vasoconstriction, 143
vegetables, 238
violence, 268–269, 276–277
vision therapy, 35–36
visual disturbance/problems, 144, 271–272
vitamins, 233, 249, 252, 311–312
VitaMix, 236
vocal tics, 142
Vyvanase, 174

waiting room, 208–209
Walker, Jonathan, 158
Walters, Dale, 71, 162
Western medicine, 21–22, 184
whey, powdered, 233
whiplash, 155
white flour, 224
white rice, 224

xenoestrogen, 244

Yasko, Amy, 21
yeast, 250, 255

Zoloft, 175

About the Authors

Robert W. Hill, PhD, founded The Oaks Psychological Service in Abingdon, Virginia, where he specializes in health psychology and behavioral medicine using hypnosis, behavior modification, and neurofeedback. Dr. Hill was one of the early pioneers to bring neurofeedback to the general public, and for more than twenty years he has used the procedure to treat a wide variety of physical and emotional problems. He trains other practitioners to use neurofeedback and lectures widely on the topic.

Eduardo Castro, MD, is the medical director of Mt. Rogers Clinic in Trout Dale, Virginia, one of the leading alternative and complementary medical clinics in the United States. He also established the Neurofeedback Center in Charlottesville, Virginia.

Drs. Hill and Castro previously published *Getting Rid of Ritalin* (Hampton Roads, 2002).

Hampton Roads Publishing Company

. . . for the evolving human spirit

Hampton Roads Publishing Company
publishes books on a variety of subjects,
including spirituality, health, and other
related topics.

For a copy of our latest trade catalog,
call toll-free, 800-766-8009,
or send your name and address to:

Hampton Roads Publishing Company, Inc.
1125 Stoney Ridge Road
Charlottesville, VA 22902
E-mail: hrpc@hrpub.com
Internet: www.hrpub.com